ALL BUTTONS
GREAT *and* SMALL

Lucy Godoroja has always had an interest
in the creative process, whether through
the handcrafts of sewing and needlework or
jewellery making, to the design of large or small
objects. A serendipitous meeting in Amsterdam
with a button shop owner inspired her to open
her own button shop in Newtown, Australia,
called All Buttons Great and Small. There
followed both a career path and a life of shared
stories and exchanged ideas ... and buttons.

ALL BUTTONS GREAT *and* SMALL

A COMPELLING HISTORY OF THE BUTTON, FROM THE STONE AGE TO TODAY

LUCY GODOROJA

EXISLE
PUBLISHING

First published 2023

Exisle Publishing Pty Ltd
PO Box 864, Chatswood, NSW 2057, Australia
226 High Street, Dunedin, 9016, New Zealand
www.exislepublishing.com

A CiP record for this book is available from the National
Library of Australia.

ISBN 978-1-925820-83-6

Typeset in 10.5 on 15.25pt Abril Text Light
Printed in China

This book uses paper sourced under ISO 14001 guidelines
from well-managed forests and other controlled sources.

10 9 8 7 6 5 4 3 2 1

For Oscar, Zoya and Kira

'It is wonderful, is it not? That on that small pivot turns the fortune of such multitudes of men, women and children, in so many parts of the world; that such industry, and so many faculties, should be brought out and exercised by so small a thing as a button.'
—*Charles Dickens, 1852*

Contents

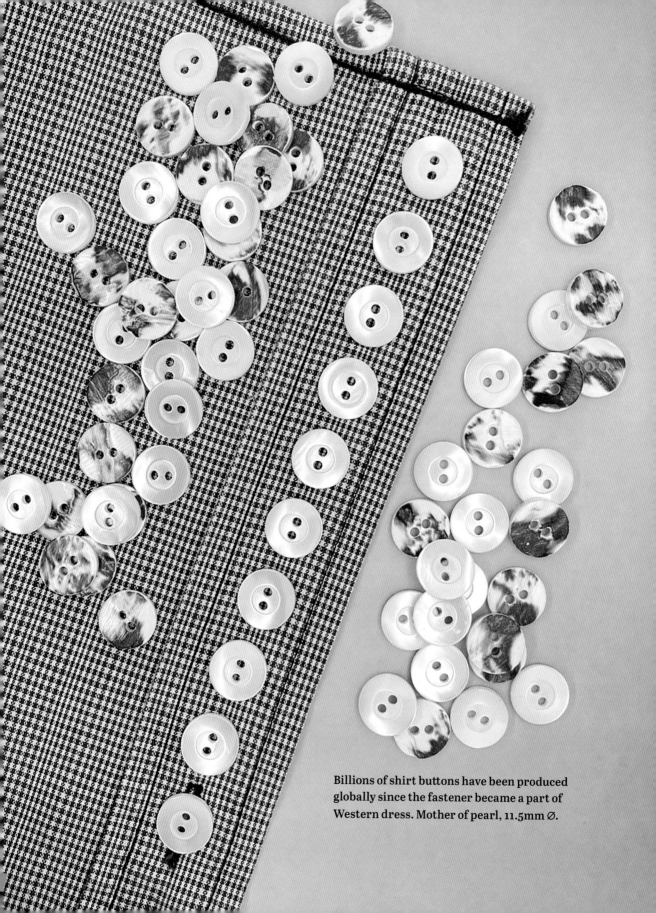

Billions of shirt buttons have been produced globally since the fastener became a part of Western dress. Mother of pearl, 11.5mm Ø.

My life
with buttons

YOU MEAN BUTTONS? LIKE THESE?
DO YOU THINK THAT'S A BUSINESS?
—COMMONWEALTH BANK OF AUSTRALIA BANK MANAGER, TO AUTHOR

Throughout its history, the button has reinvented itself. It has been a simple fastener of basic need; a non-functional decorative expression adding to the design of a garment; a marvel of creative design desired by the elite. It reached a period in history where laws had regulated its use, only to be undone by the Industrial Revolution and its ability to be mass-produced for the greater population. It spurred the imaginations of scientists and engineers as they strove to create new materials and methods of manufacture, materials that could withstand the conditions of use and laundering, and manufacturing that could prove most cost effective. Throughout its journey, one common conclusion remains: it is a small object, often of necessity, that has entranced its makers the world over.

I am not a collector of buttons. I have always, however, been enthralled by them, and over the past 35 years millions of buttons have passed through my hands. Unlike many people, I did not discover them while poring through my grandmother's button box. Both of my grandmothers were refugees who fled their countries of birth,

For many people, myself included, buttons have a way of recollecting past events, sparking memories.

crossing a continent looking for a home. My parents were both born stateless in a country that did not want them, and lived into their adult lives under these conditions, until together they chose to seek a country where they would feel secure. Because of this, there were few items they took with them, and certainly a box of buttons was not among them.

For many people, myself included, buttons have a way of recollecting past events, sparking memories. As I look at contemporary manufactured buttons, they can be reminders of the past. New cloisonné styles remind me of the Fabergé eggs of Imperial Russia, while Soviet era military ones spark my grandmothers' flights. Chinese writing

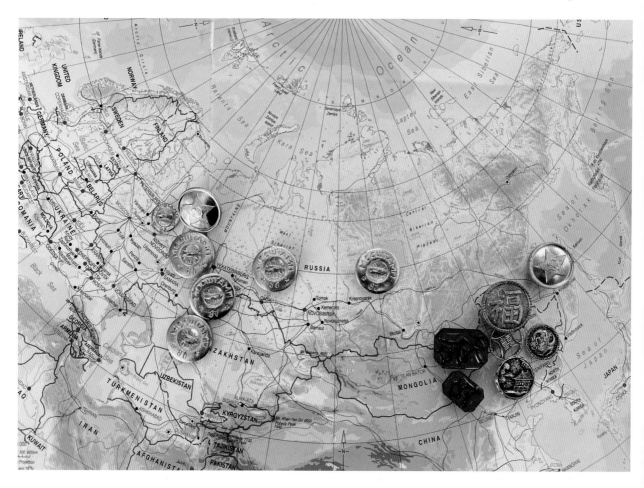

Maple leaves and Dutch clogs. Overdyed and laser etched polyester, round 23mm ⌀; frosted acrylic leaves; olive wood clogs.

depicts the place where my parents were born and spent their youth, with occupation by, and then study in, Japan — represented by the wonderful interpretation of Hokusai's famous woodblock print. Tagua nut and coconut buttons represent the possibility of a home in Brazil, only to find eventual sanctuary in Canada. And my own journey, where buttons established my passion for details.

I was introduced to the fascination of buttons from the age of five during my frequent trips to the fabric store, where my mother would search out fabric for the garments she would make for herself and for us children. While she was busy with her task, I would explore the fascinating 'notions' (or haberdashery) section, captivated by the revolving stands of buttons sewn onto cards in neat rows, ordered by colour, in a multitude of styles. I watched my mother sew, and to my delight she allowed me to use her precious sewing machine. When I was old enough, I would take my own trips to the fabric stores, my favourite being Dressew on the east side of downtown Vancouver, Canada. Here, two floors of wonder stood ready for my project, offering fabrics and patterns on one floor and every embellishment under the sun on the other. I would peruse the pattern books, searching for suitable designs that would hopefully include buttons, and then make my way downstairs to the treasure trove that waited below.

Life has an interesting way of taking you places where you never thought you would go. I was a capable, but self-taught sewer, and tried my hand at a professional career. I lasted three days. I watched with horror and amazement while the couturier tore seams apart from luxurious fabrics in order to re-sew them to a different line, and when I couldn't bring myself to do it as fast as she could (for fear of ruining the fabric), she fired me. My next endeavour was in graphic design. I enjoyed my job, but at the time couldn't find fulfilment. I studied to become an architectural/structural and civil design draftsman, and worked for a utility company drawing hydroelectric dams. I loved it; using my brain and my creativity together was very satisfying. Unfortunately, due to economic circumstances, I lost my job when my department was whittled down from 300 employees to eight. In a state of limbo, I moved continents and continued my drafting career, but a year later followed my heart to another continent where my occupation was put on hold. During this time, I met and started working with a neighbour, Thea de Boer, who started a button shop, the *Knopen Winkel* (Buttons Shop) in Amsterdam, the Netherlands. When the time came to leave Amsterdam, I was convinced to open a similar shop, and upon my return to Australia I did just that. Hence, I found my way back to the world of buttons that had so enthralled me as a child.

Here began my education of the button. Having started in Europe in the mid-1980s, I was surrounded by innovations in colour and design from contemporary manufacturers as well as the vast and varied amounts of vintage buttons then available throughout the flea markets of Europe. When I came to start my own button business, I was lucky enough to travel to Milano, Italy, where I was pointed in the direction of a button merchant. Upon meeting with her, I found only costume jewellery, some made from buttons, some not. I asked her if she had any buttons to sell, at which she replied, 'Oh, only old ones.' I was most

Thea de Boer commissioned giant buttons as door handles for our shop, and since then more than 100 giant buttons have left our premises. Re-purposed Australian timbers, large one shown here 400mm ⌀. Made by Oscar Prieckaerts.

enchanted, and she sent her employee to fetch the sample cards, which, unbeknown to me, were two hours away. We met four hours later, and I purchased a vast quantity of different styles of late nineteenth to early twentieth century Czech glass buttons, as well as the same era in pressed metal with coloured and clear diamantés. This was the collection that I started with when I first opened the doors of All Buttons Great and Small in 1989, incredible works of art in miniature.

In a year's time, I would once again cross the globe to look for more finds. I was to return to Italy to purchase the small remainder of the initial hoard, driving by car from the Netherlands. In the days before GPS, a combination of the map and Italian signage took us on an unplanned side trip, and we found ourselves in the middle of a field in the dead of night. Deciding to sleep in the car, we awoke to the rumblings of the tractor as the farmer started his daily work; we left with a thank you and a wave goodbye. The warehouse was situated in the Riviera town of Savona where the address took us to a palazzo in the piazza of the old town. Being dishevelled and unwashed, we made our way to the beach to rent a cabana and purchase shower tokens, and prepare for our meeting with our lovely proprietress. Unfortunately, a

Some of the original find of buttons from my trip to Italy in 1988. I have sold most, but these few remain, stashed away in my own archives as evidence of the former fashion in buttons as one century turns to another. Early twentieth century Czech glass and pressed and/or cast metal buttons with clear and coloured strass. All brass stampings, some plated, with white and coloured strass; large brass coloured hexagon 31mm ⌀.

burst water main had rendered the showers without water, and we were forced to use the open bottle of drinking water we had on hand to freshen up as best we could.

In 1992, on another such trip, we headed to Prague as a side trip while visiting our usual European haunts. We arrived in the city, as yet to be discovered by the masses that were later to come, and made our way to the main square, finding buildings still riddled with bullet holes, grey and dilapidated from lack of funds to improve them. A small market was underway. Of course, I found some buttons. I pride myself in always attempting to learn a bit of the language of the country I am travelling in, but found myself without any knowledge of, or phrasebook in, Czech. How to ask about these buttons, the maker, the story, and the price? The young man at the stall was also uneasy as to how to proceed, until we started rattling off languages that we both might know. This is how we progressed — with the conversations between he and myself in Russian, the conversations between he and my partner in German, and with the conversations between ourselves in English or Dutch, both languages we had in common. Word soon spread among the other stallholders of this hilarity, and we were soon surrounded by a small mob, encouraging the young man and congratulating us for supporting his endeavour. It turned out the ceramic buttons were made by his two sisters, Magdalena Dyntarova and Štepanka Denkova, who lived not far from Prague near the community of Davle, once a major producer of buttons during World War II. They started their ceramic button-making business in 1990, wanting to reignite the old button-making traditions of the past.

I find it handy to know at least the relevant phrases of various languages when buying buttons (sizes, colours, numbers) and also polite to make the attempt. I am always graciously complimented, regardless of my sometimes poor pronunciation, and especially when it turns out my host speaks my language fluently. A trip to Japan found me poring through the phrasebook; armed and ready, I boldly stepped forward

The remaining stock of the original ceramic buttons purchased in Prague, Czech Republic, in 1992. They are all made from earthenware, dark brown or terracotta in colour. The collection was glazed in a whole spectrum of colours: deep reds, oranges, yellows, greens, blues, violets, browns and black, and all glazes painted by hand using brush and pen. The shapes and sizes were varied; not only rounds, but all manner of symmetrical and asymmetrical styles. They were deliberately produced in small production runs, retaining their uniqueness and originality. Round with yellow glaze, 30mm ∅.

There seems to be a calming element for people in sifting through an accumulation of buttons, carefully scrutinizing each one, looking for a set that may or may not be there, the thrill of the hunt.

and asked the assistant at the counter for the *'Botan, onegai shimasu'* from which she answered, *'Ikutsu?'* — how many. When I again, boldly, answered *'Zenbu'*, she replied *'Zenbu?'* to which I shook my head in agreement. I was to take all of the quantity of the styles I had chosen.

My knowledge continued to grow by visiting factory floors and small workshops, where new creations were made, and by having conversations with sellers whose family businesses were connected with the industry from days gone by. As someone with a curious mind, I strove to continue the conversations with even more makers and sellers, and when that wasn't enough I spent hours in libraries, eventually creating a vast library of my own on the subject. I have learned so much from these books and from the collectors who wrote them, but I am also interested in the materials the buttons are made from and their method of manufacture.

As I visited museum collections and came across smugglers' buttons with secret openings to hide illicit goods, I was reminded of a Mexican silver ring with a hidden compartment under the turquoise stone, given to me by a dear lifelong friend. I read stories of Allied World War II pilots and paratroopers who were equipped with small escape compasses concealed in their uniform buttons — the fancy metal buttons where the top unscrewed (British and Canadian forces) or was hinged (American forces) to reveal a tiny compass. The unexceptional black Bakelite buttons with metal shank and three dots on the back; when hung from a string, two dots side by side pointed north, one dot south. Another using two trouser buttons in combination, so that when placed on top of each other the top would rotate to point the way.

Friends and customers started bringing me their button tins, often inherited from passed loved ones, or from their own collection — items they were loath to throw away yet happy to pass on to someone who appreciated their subtleties. Here, I found an array of styles, sizes, shapes and colours, and from many different eras. My mind would wander as I thought about the life they had lived, adorning adults' clothing, children's clothing, menswear, ladieswear, formal, workaday, uniforms. Some buttons I reminisced about, evoking memories of clothes once made or worn, how my own family had worn similar buttons on a faraway continent across the sea. About how these buttons travelled the world, as export stock, imported by haberdashers everywhere. I am more likely to share these treasures with others, either in the form of collages or other art on display, as historical examples when warranted, or in the community chest 5¢ basket. There seems to be a calming element for people in sifting through an accumulation of buttons, carefully scrutinizing each one, looking for a set that may or may not be there, the thrill of the hunt. This is perhaps how people become button collectors, either seriously committed to finding certain types or just gathering them for future projects, storing them for 'just in case' moments of need. The latter become unwitting collectors, for who in their right mind would throw such a useful object away?

As well as button tins, people often share their own button stories with me. A dear friend related his childhood story of growing up in a Sydney suburb, Naremburn. In about 1965, truckloads of plastic buttons from an insolvent importer/wholesaler were dumped in the nearby Willoughby tip. A neighbour who lived opposite couldn't let them go to waste, and filled buckets to share among the neighbourhood. My friend remembers his mother receiving one such bucket (of which he believes his sister may still have some) and of every home he went into having one as well. As rubbish dumps across Sydney began to fill, they were closed and reclaimed as parkland. Those now enjoying Hallstrom Park and the heritage listed Walter Burley Griffin Incinerator Art Space and studios may be unaware of the hidden layer of button history that lies beneath.

We've all heard stories about expensive jewellery being found in discarded button tins, but another dear friend shares a different story. Growing up in Eastern Europe, as a four-year-old visiting her grandparents she was given the button tin to play with. Hidden deep inside she came across a small revolver, the type found in a ladies' handbag in a James Bond film. Thinking it was a toy, she came into the kitchen pointing it at her grandma, who quickly retrieved it from her and hid it away, warning my friend to never tell anyone about it. Years later, as the country held an amnesty to retrieve illegal handguns, her grandmother called the authorities to collect it. When they asked where it had come from, she pointed to her husband sitting in the corner, at this point incapable of any form of communication, and said, 'Ask my husband, it's his.'

As I stated before, I am not a collector and do not profess to have the knowledge that goes with identifying certain buttons. I do, however, have a deep appreciation of the beauty of buttons — what they are made from, the craftsmanship involved, a curiosity about the people who made them and the hands they have passed through to get to where they are today. This interest in buttons has taken me around the world and introduced me to a raft of fascinating people. I have met and made friendships with people all over the world, as we bump shoulders in markets or back-alley shops in pursuit of a possible treasure trove. While I mostly look at buttons from a practical, utilitarian perspective, I am mesmerized by their decorative beauty, impressive details,

What's in a button box? A seemingly random collection of odds and ends: many including spare buttons that come with purchased clothing, sets of buttons removed from past garments, perhaps waiting for the next or too personal to part with. Buttons found, buttons lost, buttons inherited. In the corner, an arbitrary collection purchased by a couple on their 60th anniversary trip to Rome to remind them of their stay — gifted to me because they knew I would appreciate them. Beutron buttons on cards, 13mm ⌀.

A series of travel inspired buttons.
Amsterdam, Berlin, Paris, Rome, 23mm Ø.

and the social history that they are a part of.

As a part of my business, I encourage others to find the joy in these tiny objects, and each button that is exhibited on the shelves has a story of its own. In this contemporary age, once again buttons are often regarded as small, insignificant items, only fit as a means of keeping one buttoned. While the methods of manufacture of old buttons from centuries past are no longer cost effective, there are still small artisan-based workshops with a large output, creating incredibly wondrous articles, presumably with the same joy as the inventors from the past, utilizing new and creative

Whatever your context, you will meet others who share your enthusiasm for this humble yet incredible fastener. Thus, I hope to also entice you into this miniature world of wonder.

materials and methods of manufacture. Today, it can astound me that new buttons are expected to be beautiful, hardwearing and completely indestructible by carefree laundering, and at the same time inexpensive. Some buttons just have to be specially cared for — you wouldn't remove your jewellery and throw it in the washing machine.

I continue the hunt for the exquisite, the different and the less ordinary. With an eye on quality, I continue to seek out the sources and manufacturers of these fasteners, meeting people who share my passion and share their stories with me. Perhaps you will be inspired to create wondrous garments that highlight and elevate the button to a worthy position, or perhaps it will become your muse in art or jewellery making. Whatever your context, you will meet others who share your enthusiasm for this humble yet incredible fastener. Thus, I hope to also entice you into this miniature world of wonder.

Measuring up

Throughout the book you will see this symbol ⌀. This refers to a button's diameter, given in millimetres. For a full description of the history and application of button measuring, see page 249.

A selection of buttons made from the readily available materials of wood, bone, stone and shell, reminiscent of twigs, teeth and small bones that may have been used by early humans. Twig button, 85mm long. All examples 1990s to 2010s, Europe, Africa, India, Malaysia.

2

Buttons as fastening

While the above statement seems rather inflammatory, the need to adorn appears to be an inherent trait of human nature. I really like clothing that has buttons, and I am personally more inclined to choose buttons that make a statement rather than just serving as a fastening. Like jewellery, they make me feel well dressed, and I appreciate the tiny details that have gone into their making. Garments with hidden button plackets are not for me; they're almost an insult to the button-maker.

The button in prehistory

It is unclear who invented the button by today's definition, but early versions of button-like items have been found in excavations in Egypt, Iran and Greece. Dating from around 6000 BC, toggle-type buttons were found, made from bone, wood or teeth, wrapped in animal tendons to form a loop. Since the garments they may have been attached to have perished, there is little evidence as to their usage. Neolithic finds housed in the Museum of Pre-History in Halle (Germany) also show decorated shell buttons.

Predating the Bronze Age, Early Stone Age buttons have been found dating from about 4500–4000 BC. These include both stone buttons with a self-shank and decorated front, as well as flat, round stones covered in fabric recovered from Coptic graves around the same time. Early buttons found at Mohenjo-daro in the Indus Valley of Ancient India (dated 2800–2600 BC) are made from carved shell. All of these early buttons were more likely used as decorative embellishment rather than for practical purposes.

With the advent of the Bronze Age and metalworking around 2000 BC, Egyptian finds show, for the first time, recognized buttons. They have been identified as such because there is evidence of some sort of loop or shank, or holes, to sew them on with, although they are still thought to have had a decorative purpose.

Among Estonian Bronze Age finds, 'double buttons' occur. Made from local materials amber, antler and bone, as well as bronze, these 'double buttons' resemble a precursor to the cufflink. It is unclear what their function was, but amber (fossilized tree resin) has been used for jewellery items and cult objects since prehistoric times, and was thought to cure various diseases. Germanic tribes (from 1000–500 BC) are thought to have used 'double buttons' to fasten their cloaks. Considering the climate and their eventual movements towards northern Europe, this may have been a necessary invention. Small animal bones were ideal, the heads of which were easily adapted for the purpose; pieces of timber have also been noted.

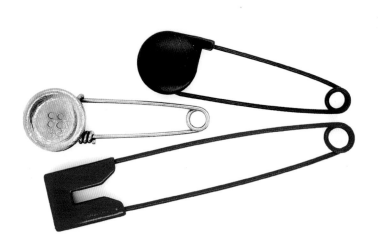

The fibula can be thought of as the precursor to the safety pin and, in turn, the safety pin has reverted to fastener status, on show and holding wraps and shawls in place. Steel, enamelled or plated. Red enamel is 110mm long. 2000s to 2010s, Italian.

Leading up to and including the early medieval period, some buttons were fabricated using metalworking techniques and decorated with simple embellishments, as shown here in these contemporary versions that may have taken their inspiration from long ago. Zamac; rectangle 34mm long. 1990s, Germany.

New materials, new techniques

New materials and metalworking techniques caused a blip in the progression of the button as fastening. With the Iron Age and ancient Roman expansion came the introduction of the fibula, a brooch-type fastening consisting of a body, a pin and a catch. It replaced the long, straight pins previously used on cloaks and became the precursor to the modern safety pin and brooch. Secured at the shoulder of a draped cloth or cloak, fibulae were first found made from bronze (copper alloy) or iron, or both. Continuing into the medieval period, the migration of Germanic tribes brought contact with diverse ethnic groups resulting in the borrowing of materials and techniques, and leading to the finds of these pin clasps made from precious metals, gemstones and techniques such as niello and *cloisonné*. Gemstones were used not only for their colour, but also for what was thought to be their healing properties — for example, amethyst gave the wearer supernatural powers and stability, and guarded against drunkenness.

In spite of the fibula being a common form of garment clasp closure throughout

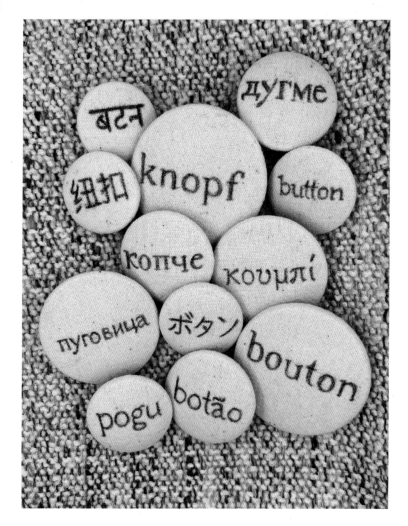

The word 'button' represented in a few languages: Greek *koumpi*, Macedonian *kopče*, Chinese *niŭkòu*, Russian *pugovitsa*, Latvian *pogu*, Serbian *dugme*, Japanese *botan*, Hindi *batan*, Portuguese *botão*. Calico fabric-covered buttons, ball point pen. *'Bouton'* and *'Knopf'*, 44mm Ø. 2021, Australia.

antiquity, there is evidence that the ancient Greeks and Romans had made buttons from various materials including lead, glass and cut agate, as well as toggle buttons from bone and glass. While metals were previously hammered into shape, the discovery of casting technology opened up a new realm of ideas, expanding jewellery techniques, which in turn expanded the design of the button.

In 1849, the French-born British archaeologist A.H. Layard discovered a tomb belonging to the biblical King of Assyria (705–681 BC). 'Scattered in the earth amongst these objects,' Layard wrote, 'were several hundred studs and buttons in mother of pearl and ivory, with many small rosettes in metal.' There is, however, no evidence to suggest that these buttons were used for anything other than decoration or funereal purposes. Buttons unearthed centuries later, in finds further north dating from the ninth century, show similarities to those in wider use from twelfth century continental Europe. The site of Breclav-Pohansko (now Czech Republic) in the Slavic Moravian stronghold has been studied continuously since 1959, where gravesites expose glass buttons with metal wire shanks. They may also have been used as a funerary object, and were found almost exclusively in the graves of children and women.

What's in a name?

While archaeologists have identified items as 'buttons' from ancient sites, the common word was first documented in Europe in written form in the late eleventh/early twelfth century in the French medieval verse, 'Chanson de Roland'. Introduced into European culture as a result of contact with the Middle East during the time of the Crusades, returning soldiers brought back souvenirs (loot!), including closer fitting garments with buttons and buttonholes. With the development of the button, in both form and function, the word, too, has undergone a metamorphosis of its own. From the Proto-Indo-European (PIE) languages, the Proto-Germanic word *buttan* comes from the PIE root *bhau*, meaning to strike, developing into the meaning of something that is pushed up, or thrust out; this definition is shared with the Old French *bouter* or *boter*. Progressing to the French word *boton* for bud, Middle High German used *knospe* for the same meaning. With the introduction of the new garments, and their round, bud-like fastenings, one can see how the modern language words of the French *bouton* and the German *knopf* has penetrated the European languages. A few anomalies exist within the continent: the Serbian word *dugme* is a borrowed word from the Turks of the Ottoman Empire during their advance into the Balkan Peninsula, bringing vocabulary for items of trade otherwise unknown; the Russian word *pugovitsa* comes from Old East Slavic *pugūvī*. Anecdotal conversation links the *pugovitsa* with the word *pugat*, meaning to scare — this could correspond with the superstition that a row of buttons may protect from evil spirits.

Enter the button as fastener

While it's difficult to say for certain how and when ancient cultures used buttons as fastenings, the discovery made an impact in Europe, where previously, garments were generally draped or pulled over the head and secured with belts or lacings. The dress brought back with the Crusaders resulted in new styles of clothing that could be more closely fitted to the body. Some men's garments, especially those worn under armour, were buttoned. The buttons were probably made of cloth — a round of fabric, stitched and stuffed with the remaining material — or leather. These first bud-like buttons were practical in use and construction, and considered by people of the Middle Ages as something small and of little value. The famous medieval verse 'Chanson de Roland' advises, 'the counsels of pride are not worth a button.'

During the thirteenth century, buttons became more and more an important part of daily life, causing new guilds to form in the trade of button-making. King Louis IX of France (1226–70) included the trade of *buttonniers* (button-makers) within the older trade of rosary making. Later, the Registry of Trades in Paris included button-makers further categorized into three groups: *paternotriers* used horn, bone and ivory; *boutonniers* used various metals such as iron and archal (an early form of brass); and *orfèvres* used precious metals and glass. The guild had regulations that completely prohibited the manufacture of *ersioz* or asymmetrical buttons; each half of a button had to equal the other half. Any variations to this rule resulted in fines and led to confiscation of the irregular articles.

Similar associations began in Italy. From the fourteenth century until their eventual demise after the mid-nineteenth century, guilds throughout central and northern Italy covered many aspects of production, with later centuries seeing an overlap of skills. From the mid-sixteenth century, button production in Italy was no longer solely the domain of the goldsmiths and jewellers; innovations in new materials, work techniques and an increasing number of button shapes included craftsmen belonging to different guilds. Embroiderers, tailors, glassworkers, brass-makers, engravers and rosary-makers all had a part to play in the production of buttons. The *coroneri*, who produced beads from wood and bone for rosaries, now included *anemeri*, who produced button moulds from wood or bone. These moulds would move further into other guilds; goldsmiths or brass workers covered them in metal;

During the thirteenth century, buttons became more and more an important part of daily life, causing new guilds to form in the trade of button-making.

Buttons, representative of the early bud-like type that may have been handmade from leather, or wool and linen fabric. 17mm Ø.

embroiderers, tailors or braid producers covered them in threads or fabrics. Glass button production was assigned to *perleri*, representatives of the ancient glassmakers' guild, an offshoot of the *paternostreri* who produced glass rosary beads. The artisans who worked within the guilds laboured hard to innovate with the changing times, especially as the 'fashion' of clothing began to take hold. Eventually, autonomous skilled workers from various disciplines came together to form button-makers' guilds around the eighteenth century.

Around 1330, the greatest change in European clothing occurred. New cutting techniques for clothing, notably the set-in sleeve, allowed new forms of fashion. Dress began to be a signifier of wealth — men's and women's sleeve styles, in particular, became more contoured, with buttons running a length from wrist to elbow, often on both sides. Detachable sleeves had been a part of Florentine dress since the thirteenth century, a practicality that enabled one to wear simple sleeves at home and more elaborate ones for going out. Sleeves were attached at the shoulder with a series of buttons, and as they were the area of a garment most likely to get dirty, could be detached for washing. Detachable sleeves now became an elegant addition to the wardrobe; elaborately embroidered ones

Thirteenth century buttons were at first utilitarian, made from cloth, brass, copper or glass. As their use began to increase, Italian *pomelli* (round apple-shaped buttons) and *peroli* (pear-shaped buttons) were made from coral, amber, ivory and pearls and, increasingly, gold and silver, influencers of these 21st century examples. Large pearl with decorative pin shank, 18mm ⌀, 2000s to 2020s, Europe.

Buttons became more ornamental and made from increasingly more valuable materials as they progressed towards the fourteenth century and beyond. Fourteenth and fifteenth century inventories show vast numbers of gold and silver buttons, sometimes totalling more than 100 on one garment. Buttonholes were also sometimes made from precious metals, with the fasteners being hooks and eyes purchased from goldsmiths. Cast buttonholes; buttons, stamped brass, hand assembled, gilt plated; 18mm Ø; 1980s–1990s, European.

could be purchased ready-made, and were part of the export market. Men's garments embraced the use of buttons, allowing for a more contoured, tighter fit on the body, but women's dress, apart from sleeve treatment, had few buttons if any at all. Buttons were almost exclusively the domain of men.

As the Renaissance movement spread from Italy towards the West, it brought a curiosity of new arts and ways of learning, sparking many changes in dress and fashion, among others. As an era of discovery and invention, and with changes in thinking towards the self-worth of human beings, dress and the beautification and display of the human figure increased. More and better-quality fabrics from Italy and further east spread across Europe, enhancing the limited selection of linen and wool previously available. As clothing became more expressive, so too did the embellishments. Buttons became more decorative and made from more precious materials; they were often regarded as ornaments, made and sold by jewellers. While the nobility always had the means to accent their garments with the best quality finishes, the rest of the social hierarchy soon followed. The newly rich merchant class, along with hardworking members of the middle class, now had the resources to copy their wealthier peers. Innovations in increasing a material's value came in the form of weaving a gold or silver thread through a fabric, or developing glass that mimicked crystals and gemstones.

With the increase in button ornamentation came rules regulating their use. In Italy, wasteful spending on luxury items was frowned upon, and in Florence, Venice and other mercantile centres, sumptuary laws were enacted, aimed at limiting extravagance of non-noble classes and preventing too much capital from being tied up unproductively. It covered all luxury goods, and in particular regulated styles and ornament of dress — the structure, use, materials, and often colour of, among others, garments, ribbons, laces, braids, embroideries, and of course buttons. The governments of the day set the bar quite high, however, as they understood the need to stimulate the market with new products and innovations, meaning that most people would not reach the limits. They were, however, aware that the merchant class could now blur the lines of social status and disrupt the established guidelines that clothing and fashions exhibited. In spite of this, the laws were not very well respected and loopholes were explored as to how to embellish without penalty. There is evidence that the noblemen, merchants and shopkeepers were sometimes penalized for non-compliance — this was in the form of a cash payment as well as having a small stamp put on the objectionable garment indicating payment of fine, the mark in itself becoming a status symbol.

Despite the regulations facing the Venetians, their commitment to fashion and crafts made the city an early fashion capital, along with Paris. During these centuries, there was an abundance of skills and frequent use of expensive handmade materials.

The next centuries continued the trend for buttons, but in many cases they moved from utility to luxury — often the use of precious materials was reserved for the wealthy and ruling class, with lower classes restricted to cloth and thread-covered buttons. Court jewellers were common among the noble class, where buttons were commissioned by and for the rulers of the day, becoming pieces of gold and silver jewellery. These precious buttons were associated with the person, not the clothing, and were listed as inheritance, passed down through the generations.

Francis I of France (1494–1547) owned and wore the first *parures,* the buttons of which increasingly used precious gemstones; a portrait of Louis XIV (1638–1715) shows a coat with at least 100 diamond buttons.

While the British fourteenth century upper classes were adorned with ornamental buttons, much like their continental peers, the craft of metal button-making was not important in Britain until the reigns of Henry VIII (1491–1547) and Elizabeth I (1533–

Passementerie buttons, replicas of the era. The black buttons are from 1930s Paris, all of which are set in resin, one a with a winding black cord and a hematite-like stone in the centre, the other with glittering ribbon, while the third has French jet beads around the outer frame, pushed into the still malleable resin and left to harden. All others are from 1990s India, and more accurately depict the buttons of the eighteenth century, made from: velvet embroidered with metallic threads and glass beads; metal fabric with cord, metallic embroidery and glass beads. Largest button shown, 40mm ⌀.

1603). Soon, however, sumptuary laws were enacted to particularly make clear the differences between the levels in society.

Perhaps the biggest trend in the wide use of buttons came towards the end of the seventeenth century and into the next, when buttons and buttonholes again came together for fastening clothes, losing their mainly ornamental role. In the domain of fashion, the French led the way: men's breeches evolved from baggy pantaloons with drawstring to a form-fitting style with buttons at the knee; men's *surtout* was a longer style of overcoat (knee length, from previous shorter variations) with a single line of buttons from neck to knee, large buttoned cuffs, and buttons on and around the pocket flaps. Buttons were often larger and mostly made from cloth, and later metal, and each garment required a substantial amount of buttons. *Passementerie* buttons, hugely popular in the fourteenth century, were reintroduced in the eighteenth century, with silver and gold threads intertwined with sparkling paste, sequins, pearls, etc. *Passementerie* buttons were often used on the new *l'habit à la française*, a longer line overcoat adopted everywhere by the military, and which led to the British frock or riding coat at the turn of the eighteenth century. These coats had extensive numbers of buttons, all of which had a purpose as opposed to their ornamental forebears. Stamped metal imitations of these *passementerie* buttons were also in vogue, being more durable than their cloth counterparts. A new social order based on wealth, rather than birth right, became the norm; hallmarking, a measure introduced in the thirteenth century to protect against sales of inferior silver, remained an indicator of quality as precious metal buttons were still favoured by the wealthy and indicated social standing. The gentleman wore hallmarked buttons, while the working class was imitating in silver plate and other white metals, and pewter, steel and brass.

The eighteenth century is considered the period when men's clothing reached its ultimate opulence. It seems as though clothing, and the wearing of it, was meant to create a sense of awe, with buttons being more lavish and larger than they had been before. Jewels and all things sparkly were in favour — the nobility and wealthiest class used gemstones such as rubies, sapphires, emeralds and chalcedonies, among others, with diamonds especially favoured. After the invention of the brilliant cut in 1700 by Venetian gem cutter Vincenzo Peruzzi, the craze for diamonds escalated.

Georges Fréderic Strass, an Alsatian jeweller, is credited for developing the industry of paste stones, producing imitation diamonds for use in both jewellery and fashion. His name is synonymous with these gems, and many Europeans still refer to imitation cut stones as strass. By using different metal oxides in glass, he was able to create various colours and an imitation jewellery craft sprang up and spread from there. While angering the long-established fine jewellers, it allowed the less wealthy to imitate more affluent citizens.

Another important innovation in the sparkly realm of adornment was the brilliantly polished steel buttons made by the industrialist Matthew Boulton from Birmingham, in the West Midlands of England. Consisting of polished steel facets riveted into place on a solid button mount, they were initially made only by request. However, they were quickly adopted by continental Europe — goldsmiths became button-makers using these steel 'diamonds' in their creations, refining the process using delicate filigree patterns.

The century was the culmination, or the beginning, of several important periods in history. The Enlightenment (1650s–1780s), born out of the Scientific Revolution (1640s–1700s), was an intellectual movement with three central concepts: reason over superstition; science over blind faith; the belief that progress could create better societies and people. The Scientific Revolution fast-tracked new ideas and discoveries, forcing people to think differently about the world around them. Before the eighteenth century, clothing indicated one's station in life; your social class predetermined your choices in styles, fabrics and embellishments. The introduction of 'fashion' as a passing fancy saw the beginning of the end of the class system based on birth. Perhaps this is why the eighteenth century is known as the heyday in buttons — there was no material or design technique that evaded the button-makers. The wealthy began to order buttons with themes; these 'miniatures' recreated landscapes and scenes from paintings, and used an assortment of methods to fabricate them. Sometimes a storyline or related designs could be told in sets, some consisting of five to 35 items.

In Venice sumptuary laws were decaying, and by the end of the Venetian Republic

The artisan craft of button-making in Europe during the eighteenth century produced buttons that were miniature works of art. With the Enlightenment came the idea of leisure time spent in nature, with themes of nature and the outdoors depicted on pendants, pins and buttons. Modern leisure-themed buttons, various metals and methods of decoration, fabrication, 1970s to 2010s; large gold enamelled tennis button, 23mm Ø.

A selection of buttons that may have been found on the waistcoat of the 'dandy'. Metals, gilt; floral button 15mm ⌀. Late twentieth century.

(in 1797) they were abolished. Throughout Europe, the French Revolution (1789–99) and its consequences spread. An independent and self-governing form of labour management replaced the guild systems, abolishing the rules that had previously bound them. In spite of this, the European craft economy continued, producing some of the most exquisite examples of buttons known. France allowed free competition among its button-makers and favoured fine workmanship using any material, with other European countries following. The sixteenth century art of enamelling was perfected and used for fine buttons; painting and drawing on paper, ivory, porcelain and silk was another skill used by button-makers; reverse painting on glass, set against various grounds, created a perception of depth and was immensely popular. European production of buttons reached a proto-industrial stage, with large-scale production.

In Britain, however, English law encouraged the important metalworking industry, and prohibited the production of cloth buttons in favour of the professional button-

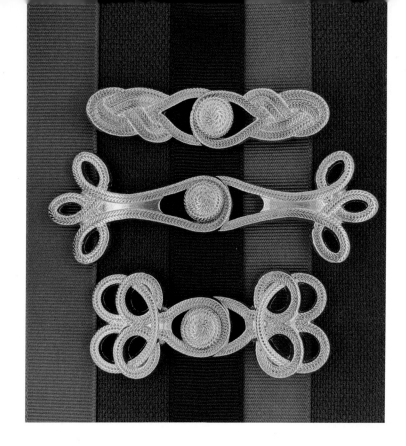

Silk brandenburgs replicated in metal. Zamac, gold plated, longest measures 100mm long, 2010s, Italian.

maker's trade. Birmingham, especially, became the British centre for the metal button-making industry, and from 1750 to about 1825 it dominated world production. Originally made from sheet copper, buttons were decorated and shaped. Each loop shank was placed by hand and soldered to the back. Some 200 million buttons were made this way until the development of machinery to take over the task. Cloth buttons did not disappear, however; because of their lower cost and popularity, most ignored the law until it was eventually dismissed.

By the late eighteenth century men's clothing became excessively elaborate with the introduction of the dandy. The waistcoat became a must-have item of dress and the true dandy needed several, made from colourful, fine fabrics, embroidered with popular scenes. Valuable, decorative metal buttons, always fastened, were the focal point. Waistcoats were an independent article of clothing and while worn together with a topcoat did not necessarily match.

Most buttons produced in Britain were functional and utilitarian compared to their European counterparts. With a changing social structure and the discovery of new materials and methods of manufacture, Britain was heading for the gradual mechanisation of its industry and dominating the export market with its metal utilitarian buttons.

Men's clothing has buttons attached on the right side; women's clothing has buttons attached on the left side.

The eighteenth century was also a heyday for European silk cord trimmings. The military uniforms of the Hussars, with their brass buttons and rows of braid across their chest, transformed the dress uniforms of other military across Europe. The Brandenburg militia had a similar form of dress. What we know today as froggings, first appeared at the end of the seventeenth century on their uniforms and were originally known as brandenburgs — silk cord trimmings that joined to similar corded buttons. The British metal button-making trade, well on its way towards industrial production, was poised to capture the market for uniforms, and many of the military buttons used throughout Europe and abroad were of British origin. Towards the end of the century, military dress uniforms became fashionable for aristocratic men and women outside of the militia, with elaborate froggings and gilt buttons. Women's garments may have been in support of their husbands and brothers, but they were also very flattering to the figure, as were the riding coats of the time.

Right or left?

The increase in women wearing more garments resembling those of men may have coincided with the difference in buttoning between the sexes. Men's clothing has buttons attached on the right side; women's clothing has buttons attached on the left side. There are numerous theories on this subject as to why, with no definitive absolutes, but let's explore some here.

One reading states that all buttons, going back to medieval times, were originally sewn on the left-hand side, buttoning from right to left. This is supported by the fact that most people are right-handed; women, while nursing a baby under their left arm, had their right arm free to do chores, fasten and unfasten their garments, etc.; similarly, men had their right hand free to perform a variety of duties. However, this doesn't quite measure up, as early on women's clothing had few, if any buttons. Enter the theory of how men dressed for war. The change, if in fact there was one, may have come about with the use of armour, when the left side, with shield in tow, was presented to the enemy and the sword or lance was held in the right hand. The armour plates were overlapped left to right, to avoid the enemy's lance point slipping between the plates, thus setting a new precedent in fastening. This theory coincides with evolving soldiers' uniforms, allowing soldiers to draw their weapons with their right hand, and allowing their free hand to adjust or unbutton.

A popular theory in women's right-to-left buttoning has to do with the complexity of the clothing women wore during the Renaissance and into the Victorian period, with petticoats, corsets, bustles, etc. Middle- and upper-class European women needed help getting dressed, and servants were most likely engaged to help. The premise is that it is easier for the servant to button up right to left. I have tested this theory, and my conclusion is that it is just as easy to button on either side — how many of us have helped a child (of either sex) to get dressed? I think it shall remain a mystery as to why the difference. One fact is certain: with the advent of buttons becoming a visible and functional part of women's clothing, by the end of the nineteenth century there was a marked difference made between which side the buttons on male and female clothing were attached.

The origin of men's buttoning left to right is attributed to the wearing of wartime armour. Large size button, 20mm ∅; knight on horseback.

The military button is said to be the precursor of most of the metal blazer buttons we use today. Contemporary styles reminiscent of past examples. Metals, 20mm Ø and 15mm Ø; 1990s to 2020s, Europe, United States.

The many and varied types of metal buttons from across the globe. Large gold sun, 50mm Ø; 1990s, remake of Todd Oldham design, Switzerland.

3

Metal as button

BUTTONS ARE THE FOSSILS OF THE SARTORIAL WORLD, ENDURING LONG PAST THE GARMENTS THEY WERE DESIGNED TO HOLD.
—MARTHA STEWART, AMERICAN BUSINESSWOMAN AND FOUNDER OF MARTHA STEWART LIVING OMNIMEDIA

My appreciation for metal button design began with my initial purchases for the shop, among them wonderful variations using the same brass stampings, folded differently to create distinct sizes and shapes. This was a recurring theme that I noticed with the construction of some of the buttons I've purchased over the years, especially ones that have been manipulated by hand in the final production.

Metal is perhaps the most important material used for button-making owing to its flexibility, strength and longevity. It can be cast, rolled, stamped, engraved, tooled into a variety of shapes and uses. It can be made liquid to form a permanent and lasting solid. Its ability to be alloyed with other metals can create even stronger and more stable versions of itself. It can be gilded or plated with a variety of finishes to increase its value or permanence. All of these qualities allow the button designer to create a vast array of styles, using various methods of production, with the constraint of being mindful of the ultimate weight of the object.

These early twentieth century buttons are formed from a single metal stamping with either four or six projecting parts, to allow for a variety of models. Claw or bezel set central stones, glued-in side stones. Brass stampings, some plated; large silver coloured button, 28mm ⌀, European.

As discussed previously, buttons began their journey in metal as far back as the Bronze Age, with buttons in use in ancient Egypt. The Egyptians wore all forms of jewellery, including buttons, believing it made them more appealing to the gods and attracting good fortune. The wealthy had these items made from gold and precious gemstones, these being an additional adornment and not a functioning button.

With the Bronze Age came the knowledge of new metals, through alloying, which allowed for further exploration of stronger materials with which to produce items. Casting technology was another innovation that helped the button, although it would be centuries before it was used in the production of the article and was an extremely slow advance to its fastener status.

While the trend of rulers adorning themselves with finery continued for many centuries, in thirteenth century Europe the arrival of buttons and new styles of clothing spurred craftsmen to experiment further. This led to spectacular buttons made from precious metals of either gold or silver, with precious or semi-precious gemstones and pearls, which can be seen in painted portraits of the nobility. Button sizes, and the number required for a garment, altered depending on the style of clothing or the whim of the ruler. One-upmanship was common.

As the button found its way into daily life, over the next centuries regulations attempted to control their growing use by the lower classes with the use of sumptuary laws in many countries. As precious metal buttons always indicated wealth and social status, it appears from the outside that these laws were mostly enacted to make distinctions between the levels of society.

In thirteenth century France, nobles were the only people allowed to wear metal buttons, with lower classes relegated to wearing cloth and thread-covered buttons. As the fourteenth century approached and the guilds were formed, the rules relaxed somewhat; nobles wore buttons of precious metals and gemstones, while the middle and lower classes were now able to wear buttons of the new, less precious metal alloys if they could afford or chose to. Buttons were still part of the craft economy in Europe, with workshops producing various designs by bespoke order. During the next centuries, European metal buttons evolved in their style, but continued to be made by the craftsmen and artisans of the day, following a path of quality over quantity. Precious metal buttons now represented an investment, carried around in case of emergency. These were not sewn on with thread, but rather pushed through the fabric and secured with a metal strip, probably something similar to the contemporary

The nobility had the means to commission buttons made from noble metals and precious gemstones, creating elaborate, jewelled pieces as adornment. This selection created from brass stampings, or cast mounts, with stones glued in place. European made, large button with red cabochon, 32mm ⌀.

'R' clip, used later by professions such as nursing and still used in formal attire by the military. Buttons now made the rich man — it was considered that a man whose clothes carried twenty gold and sixty silver buttons could never become bankrupt.

Charters, patents and competition

After more than 100 years of pewter making in Britain, and with some less than desirable qualities among what was available, the Pewterers' Company was organized. The company was first granted a charter by King Edward IV in 1473/4 to form a guild, setting guidelines for the grade of pewter, procuring raw materials, quality of pewterware and trading, among other related concerns. A finer grade of pewter was used for buttons, called trifle pewter, which was able to take larger stresses.

In 1683 a patent was granted that led to an improved, simple method of casting hollow pewter buttons. The low melting point of pewter made it easy for a home craftsman or small shop to produce their own buttons, as long as they had a mould. Brass (alloy of copper and zinc) was the usual material that moulds were made from, with the moulds mostly purchased from professional mould makers.

Much pewterware was exported to the colonies. As household items became unusable due to excessive wear and tear, and as the United States did not have the same

Finely crafted, or simply made, precious metal buttons were a form of portable wealth. Large, solid-looking round (military) button; 20mm Ø, brass two-part, stamped Gaunt, London.

Modern style buttons
in pewter colour. Large
buttons 28mm ⌀,
2000s, Italian.

**London-based manufacturers of buttons, from L to R:
Firmin & Sons Ltd./A S N Co.; J.R. Gaunt & Son Ltd./
New Zealand Forces; three from Gaunt/Royal Air
Force/Plain high dome/Full ball.**

regulations regarding pewter quality as in Britain, it was easily melted down to make buttons worn by all levels of society. After the American Revolution, all imports from Britain were cut off, leading American factories to start their own button industry.

With the interest in military uniforms and organized armies during the late seventeenth century, there appeared another, separate, demand for metal buttons. While their individual value was not high, being made from iron, brass, copper, tin and pewter the numbers required were great enough to be important. Birmingham, the largest centre for the production of small items in metal, had a healthy competition among the various firms, owing to the prohibited production of cloth buttons. The button-makers, especially, were able to pioneer methods of manufacture, processes that were later taken on by the wider metal producers throughout Britain.

The fashion of military dress was not confined to the armies and navies of a nation, but was adopted by many varying organized groups. Besides the wearing of military regalia by aristocratic men and women, French and English pirates also took up the outfits of the day, with real gold buttons adorning their garments, an investment carried around in case of emergency. Their value was real and portable.

Birmingham button manufacturers, L to R: Sword Make/Plain top with rim; Buttons Ltd/New South Wales Railway; G. Preston Ltd/English Coat of Arms; Player Bros./English Coat of Arms; Sydney Griffith/English Coat of Arms; and the competition from across the Channel, La Belle Jardinière (Paris)/Plain top.

Copper, brass, gilt

In eighteenth century Britain, several patents were issued to Birmingham men, all of which applied an increasing amount of mechanisation and contributed to the Industrial Revolution in that country. Copper (a native metal) and brass (an alloy) were extremely popular for several reasons. Copper, a ductile metal, resists rust and its strength allows it to wear well; brass, being an alloy, can be easily cast and has working properties similar to copper. Both could be stamped, engraved, plated, decorated. Gilding became extremely popular — buttons were enhanced with a thick gilt coating, a mixture of 24-carat (Au) gold added to a mercury bath, painted on, fired in a furnace and polished back. The initial, quality, recipe was 5gm of Au to mercury mix to 1 gross of buttons. These gold-coloured buttons could be polished to a mirror finish.

With metal buttons gaining more importance and value, the regulations pertaining to cloth buttons were largely ignored. This led to initially successful lobbying of politicians in favour of the metal buttons, but with makers now using a cheaper method of gilding that allowed increased profits, the wearability decreased, with buttons tarnishing after only a few weeks. A second attempt of lobbying was unsuccessful and

Engraved, stamped, enamelled, and with inlays of mother of pearl and bone. Top: Victorian vest button with red and green enamel, mother of pearl inlay, brass wire decoration; stamped GILT on shank, 14mm ⌀, England.

led to the downfall of the gilt button by the 1840s. Birmingham companies did, however, survive several decades by manufacturing parts, mostly metal backs and shanks, for use in the other button-making industries of cloth, glass, and Jasperware buttons.

The first three quarters of the eighteenth century in general saw buttons increase in both size and ornate decoration; they were engraved or chased, combined with mother of pearl shell, enamels, and inlays of other materials. They were made from silver, copper, brass, and pinchbeck (in Britain) and tombak (in Europe), these last two being alloys of copper and zinc. Pinchbeck, developed by watchmaker Christopher Pinchbeck (1670–1732) was a durable, warm golden-coloured metal alloy that retained its colour and could be worked in the same manner as, and was more affordable than, gold. Its formula was a closely guarded secret but was thought to be four parts copper and three parts zinc. Pinchbeck usage declined in the mid-nineteenth century, due to 9-carat gold entering the market in legal form, allowing for a less expensive version of the precious metal. The electro-gilding plating process, invented about the same time, also contributed to pinchbeck's decline. However, collectors of Victorian jewellery and buttons still value the original

The rivalry between Britain and France was often fierce when it came to buttons.

Modern gilded buttons, 1990s, Italy, France. Knot button, 28mm ⌀.

pinchbeck versions, as they were made with greater care than the latter, cruder, stamped 9-carat versions. Tombak was a metal alloy, resembling pinchbeck, introduced on the continent in the seventeenth century from Siam (known as Thailand today). It was an alloy of 82–98 per cent copper and 2–18 per cent zinc (called tombac and similor in France, Mannheim gold in Germany), durable and easily given to high polish, with a reddish yellow colour.

The British domination of the production of buttons, due to its early industrialization of the industry, led the Europeans to invent new ways of recapturing their share of the button market. The rivalry between Britain and France was often fierce when it came to buttons. The British were considered good businessmen and were renowned and respected for their approach to improving metal alloys and forms of gilding. The French, on the other hand, were considered the artisans, masters of taste, known for their creativity and design. They were, however, behind in the technique of gilding. Their technique with the polishing and burnishing of tombac was highly successful, but their gilding methods were not considered satisfactory until, with continuing experimentation with gold (either in leaf form or ground) and mercury, they were able to achieve similar results in the eighteenth century. This became known as 'ormolu', from the French *or moulu*.

France, Germany, Italy

One leader in button production in France was the company of *Albert Parent et Cie*. Founded in 1825, they combined their artistry with industrialized methods; as well as a wide variety of metal buttons, including enamelling, they produced a diversity of cloth, papier mâché and pearl ones. Another competitor to the British domination was French company Trelon Weldon & Weil (1845), who specialized in military buttons and supplied both the Confederate and Union armies of the American Civil War.

In Germany, the town of Lüdenscheid had been the centre for ore mining of the surrounding areas since the Middle Ages. With the arrival of the Industrial Revolution, the production of buttons and buckles played an important role. Founded in 1780, the Lüdenscheider button industry kept abreast of the changes in fabrication, becoming the centre for the production of metal buttons in Germany. This was due in no small part to watchmaker and mechanic, Caspar Dietrich Wigginghaus. In striving to produce elegant and shiny buttons available at an affordable price for all, his experiments with composition metal (an alloy resembling brass, usually containing 80 per cent pure copper) proved fruitful. By adding the metals of lead and tin, and the metalloid antimony, he achieved the desired results — a metal alloy that was easy to melt and

Some stamped buttons can be lightweight, as in these European brass examples from the 1990s. Large button with rope surround, 31mm Ø, France.

Buttons and buckle of cut steel faceted pieces, mimicking gemstones, were riveted onto a steel base that could be engraved, stamped or pierced for a more decorative look. Button, 25mm ⌀; eighteenth century, England.

pour, and showed no signs of warping when solidified. Because of its hardness, it did not bend and scratch, and when polished in the 'Paris method' it remained shiny. Wigginghaus kept the recipe of his alloy a secret but did deliver to every Lüdenscheider button manufacturer their sought-after amount, ensuring that they could collectively compete with the English and the French. The supporting industries that produced forms (blanks) for stamping, pressing and casting then emerged, and played an important role, as they still do today.

Predominant in the northern territories, Italian button production between the Middle Ages and the Renaissance was monopolized by the strict guidelines of the guild of goldsmiths and jewellers. These worked in precious materials such as gold, silver, precious gemstones, crystal and other metal mixtures, and they held the exclusive production of small objects. When Italy began seeing an influx of imported metal buttons in their markets, authorities there were keen to start their own manufacturing. From the second half of the sixteenth century, button production was less in the hands of the goldsmiths and jewellers guild, and increasingly shared among the various orders; tasks were given to craftsmen based on their skills and their likelihood of having the correct tools, these being apportioned by the guild system. This interdisciplinary

A sample card showing plating colours, this one from Italian firm Lotti's 1995/95 autumn–winter collection.

LOTTI
SIGNA FIRENZE
COLOR CARD
AUTUMN-WINTER 95/96

ORO
OPACO
LINO

ARGENTO
VECCHIO

NIKEL
OPACO

OTTONE
VECCHIO

RAME
VECCHIO

NERO
CERA

method of button production eventually led, around the eighteenth century, to autonomous guilds of Italian button-makers. Local governments were interested in competing in the burgeoning button businesses seen elsewhere, providing grants to attract foreign artisans, particularly the French, to share their expertise and techniques. Their aim was to eventually use the British techniques, together with the French elegance in design, to compete both locally and globally.

Evolving techniques

When, in the 1720s, Birmingham's Matthew Boulton invented cut steel, he was attempting to recreate the more expensive marcasite. Marcasite was in itself a substitute for diamonds, and buttons made from this pyrite mineral were fashionable at the time. Mr Boulton's method of manufacturing cut steel buttons had disadvantages, rusting when repeatedly exposed to water and tarnishing with wear, making them only popular in court apparel or for special occasions and not for everyday use. Nevertheless, they were an important evolution in button manufacturing. Europe found itself in a position of catch-up with regard to the vast quantities of metal buttons coming from across the Channel. Techniques were borrowed and often refined, as in the French versions of cut steel buttons, finetuning and simplifying the process, creating a more delicate version than the British originals. Later versions were tinted by a use of metal oxides, or gilded or plated, not only adding colour but also protection against decay.

Damascene became popular. This labour-intensive technique of ornamenting on metal, used in ancient Damascus (Syria) on weapons and battle accessories, shows no evidence of being used on buttons then, but the

A mass-produced
modern take on
damascening.
28mm Ø, 1990s, Italy.

Marcasite was in itself a substitute for
diamonds, and buttons made from this
pyrite mineral were fashionable at the time.

process of damascening had been used in Europe since the mid-eighteenth century.
One technique was to engrave fine lines on a base of steel, iron or bronze, which
was filled with gold or silver threads, hammered into place, then surface smoothed
and polished. Niello, another form of decorating metal, used by the ancient Greeks,
is a process whereby the niello — a black material mixture of copper, silver, lead
and sulphur — was coated onto an engraved metal surface, then heated until the
composition, when liquefied, penetrated the engraved area. The excess black niello was
removed and a final polish revealed the original base material. With their fine, two-tone
ornamentation, damascening and niello work, both similar art forms in that they are
engraved on a metal surface, became popular on jewellery and buttons.

   A less expensive method of producing metal-type buttons was the wood and bone
backed versions, made from the late seventeenth century, through the eighteenth
century and into the next. Thin metal caps were stamped out of silver, brass, silver or
gilt-plated copper, or cast from lead or pewter. They were produced for both military
and non-military use; military buttons carried the emblems associated with militia
and corresponding groups, while the civilian versions mimicked the popular thread-

Twentieth century examples of metal buttons depicting their woven cloth, thread and knotted counterparts. Large gold knot, 30mm Ø, 1990s, European.

woven or embroidered buttons of the time. Geometric patterns were also popular, and more fancy versions incorporated pierced-out patterns with coloured foil backing, multiple plated colours in metal, or mimicked decoration of glass stones or metal purl. The metal caps were bonded with resin cement to a wood or bone button blank, then crimped over the sides of the mould. Initially, a shank of catgut was created by weaving threads through the four holes of the button moulds, but disintegration of the shank eventually led to the catgut being replaced with metal shanks embedded into the button blanks. A common form of metal button in the eighteenth century, this type was not as popular in the nineteenth century but continued to be worn by some French military officers until 1820.

Continuing change

As the end of the eighteenth century loomed and revolution was in the air (whether Industrial or French), changes were in store for the button. In Britain, metal buttons became smaller and were made from different material; the demise of the larger sized gilt/copper in 1790 led to the smaller sized gilt/brass version that became the norm on all types of men's coats by 1810. Birmingham was now definitively the world leader in industrial metal button production.

Now that Napoleon was firmly ensconced in France as leader, he set his eyes further

As well as patterned metal buttons, insignia, clubs and associations, and company logos remain popular, particularly due to the longevity of the material. Olympic rings, 23mm Ø, 1972 Munich Olympic Games, Germany. All others twentieth and 21st centuries.

Aluminium buttons have ¼ the weight of silver. Die-stamped, machined. Dragon, 23mm Ø.

afield. He amassed a considerable army, complete with a variety of uniforms for all his various regiments and, as history has shown, with buttons made from different materials depending on the level of command. Metal buttons were made from silver, gilt brass, brass and pewter. There is a popular story that identifies the 'tin' buttons of Napoleon's army as the deciding factor in the dismal retreat from his invasion of Russia. This urban legend suggests that tin disease, and the subsequent decay of the French army's buttons (leading to the uniforms falling apart), was the source of Napoleon's failure. While it's a good story, it is doubtful things happened that way. Tin was used as an alloy to make bronze, not usually as the sole metal in the making of buttons, and while shiny metallic tin starts to change into a crumbly non-metallic powder due to extreme temperature drops (as in the sub-zero temperatures of the Russian landscape), this structural change takes a very long time to happen — very much longer than Napoleon's invasion. The tale, however, led contemporary scientists to use the story as a way of referring to chemical structures and historical events, and shows how society's development hinges on the chemistry of certain compounds. Thus it became known as 'Napoleon's button factor, the neglect of a known molecular property being responsible for a major tragic event'.

Buttons made in the Antipodes and beyond, from L to R: three variations on the two-part button from Stokes & Sons, Melbourne/Plain dome with rim/Victorian Railway/New South Wales Tramways; A. Levy, Wellington, New Zealand Railway; Waterbury Co's Inc./United States LSS.

Nineteenth century gilt metal buttons, often shiny with a mirror-like finish, began to have more decorated faces. The buttons were hand engraved or engine-turned to form fine patterns (reminiscent of Spirograph patterns). Nickel silver, a white metal alloy first discovered in Germany in 1770 and perfected in 1823, was introduced for button-making. Insignia became popular, as did buttons with coats of arms, monograms, emblems of associations, etc., especially in the military or livery service. Buttons, which were at first flat, became convex. Metal buttons could be produced in two parts, and sometimes three.

Leading up to the year 1815, more than 1000 people were employed by the Birmingham button trade. Unfortunately for them, the closely guarded secrets of gilding, and industrialized techniques of decoration, were appropriated by the French, and later by the Americans. The French now dominated the European market; *Albert Parent et Cie* revolutionized the button industry by using both the British industrialization process combined with the hand-finishing techniques of French artisan craftsmen. Meanwhile, the Americans began their own button industry.

In 1824, Danish physicist and chemist, Hans Christian Oerstad, produced (impure) aluminium for the first time. The most abundant metal on Earth, it is not found in mines, lodes or ore, so to be able to extract it into its metal form was a huge achievement. German chemist Friedrich Wöhler continued Oerstad's experiments and was able to prepare aluminium in its pure form. This important discovery led Henri Saint-Claire Deville to work on a commercial process, and bars of aluminium were exhibited at the Paris Exhibition in 1855 under the name of bauxite, in honour of the sedimentary rock the mineral was found in near Les Baux-de-Provence, in southern France. From the 1890s, it was often combined with other materials such as mother of pearl, wood and cut steel, among others. Aluminium is similar to brass in that it is easily worked; it can be die-stamped, hand chased, lathe turned. It is also a useful alloy in other metals due to its positive attributes.

Considering the overtly ornamental aspects of button decoration, it is worth mentioning that until the mid-nineteenth century two-thirds of button consumers were men.

Peasant-style buttons

With industrial methods of manufacturing in both textiles and buttons, European rural folk, who previously had a self-imposed style of dress with visible buttons both

Some examples of peasant-style buttons, one type showing toggle attachment for easy transfer from garment to garment. Filigree button, 18mm ⌀, silver (quality content unknown).

925 sterling silver buttons from the Navajo Nation, 1999. Style with turquoise cabochon in centre, 19mm ∅.

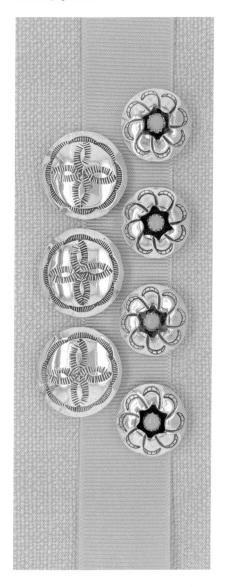

as adornment and fastener, took up the new form of workwear and now wore their traditional costumes only when gathering for occasions. But in earlier times, silver peasant buttons (as they are known by collectors) were an important part of embellishment, sometimes the owner's most valuable possessions and passed on through the generations. They always had a shank, often with a T-bar or toggle attached, allowing for easy removal when clothing needed cleaning or for use on another garment. Early buttons were large in size and worn on the upper body so they could be clearly seen, with their decorative aspect and their function both equally important.

While it's difficult to say when they originated, the popularity of silver peasant buttons was documented from the seventeenth century when jewellers, specializing in the making of these buttons, left identifiable makers' marks on the underside. The established silversmiths, who had expertise in making these items, made the buttons in the correct design according to region and different purposes, and knowledge of the jewellery techniques and patterns was handed down through the generations. While they are all silver, at the time they were not made from the 925 sterling silver we associate with contemporary jewellery; but they were an investment nonetheless. The silver content varied from country to country, with ranges in the nineteenth century from 625 to 875 silver parts per thousand depending on the country of origin.

Local populations wore local dress to demonstrate local identity. Their jewellery, with

Peasant-style buttons from Peru; flower, swan, sun. Flower 26mm Ø, 1990s, silver (content quality unknown).

Considering the overtly ornamental aspects of button decoration, it is worth mentioning that until the mid-nineteenth century two-thirds of button consumers were men.

buttons included, showed their wealth. These buttons were unique in that they were the only type of adornment worn by both men and women alike. They were a valuable asset, bought with care, cherished and repaired when damaged. They were created in sets and were proudly worn, not collected. In the provinces, to show unity both farmers and townspeople wore them, whoever could afford to, and it was common for the aristocracy and their children to wear dress based on the local costume (although made from more sumptuous fabrics and with buttons made from gold and often set with precious gems).

Generally, the wearing of peasant buttons in continental Europe mostly came to a sudden end when traditional forms of dress were no longer worn at the end of the nineteenth century; in some areas, such as southern Germany and Austria, remote parts of Scandinavia and the Netherlands, and rural south and east Europe, the customs remained in daily use until World War II. While they were originally confined to the European continent, their use spread throughout the world in places where

Some examples of actual coins made into buttons, and imitations that were popular in the last quarter of the twentieth century. Constantinos, 24mm Ø, silver.

there was a European influence. This influence was probably responsible for the Asian adoption of flat and domed buttons in the nineteenth century; it is thought that the semi-official silver buttons of Sri Lanka are modelled on British military buttons, and the manufacture and wearing of silver buttons, worn on traditional dress, continued in south and East Asia until the 1960s.

Similarly, what was considered authentic and traditional patterns continued in south-west North America and Mexico. Nowadays, replicas of the traditional peasant buttons are made for the tourist market, produced using the same designs and techniques as in previous centuries. While others are still made in European areas where the traditional dress was once worn, many are made in India and further east, and in the United States, the Navajo Nation creates sterling silver (925) versions with engraved or punched designs.

A button's worth

It's interesting to note how, with the onset of metal buttons, an associated value was placed on these small accessories. In earlier common vernacular, things that were considered of no consequence or value were met with the phrase, 'Not worth a button'. Fast forward to the nineteenth century in northern Greece where, according to Jane Perry in *A Collector's Guide to Peasant Silver Buttons*, 'to buy even one button may mean doing without your next meal'.

Silver coins became a popular source material for making buttons, instantly indicating wealth and especially fashionable in German-speaking Europe, where the practice seems to have started as far back as the seventeenth century. Prior to World War I, the amount of silver used in coins directly represented their monetary value; thus, it became a simple way of showing your affluence and position in society. While laws existed then, as they do today, regarding the defacement of currency, some coins used were no longer valid in the country of issue. In other cases, people used currency from other nations, by-passing the defacement legislation in their own land.

The late nineteenth century and early twentieth century saw an increase in silver buttons, particularly in women's fashion. Foreign coins particularly appealed to the Victorian enthusiasm for anything quaint or unfamiliar, leading to large numbers being sacrificed for new fashions and jewellery. On the continent, the Dutch used a wide range of coins, eventually creating imitation coins in various sizes, more so than other countries. The Austrian ¼ Fl (florin) was imitated to create buttons, and we were still able to purchase these imitations up until the late twentieth century. In the faraway Antipodes of Australia, due to the fortunes made in the pearling industry, there were, as noted in Dorothy Chamberlain's book *Button Up Australia*, 'so many gold sovereigns lying about that blokes used them as coat buttons.'

The industrial production of buttons allowed for excellent items to be made quickly and cheaply, creating a new wealthy class of people (the nouveau riches) who had money to spend on fashions previously denied them. Ladies' clothing became more elaborate, with multiple buttons as fastening adorning coats and cloaks, with buttons on dresses remaining decorative. With the fashion for more fitted clothing in the mid-nineteenth century, quality buttons were considered a treasured item, clipped on with pins or split rings for easy removal for washing of, or transfer to other, garments. They were considered a decent and acceptable gift, and by the end of the century a customary ladies' gift for a 21st birthday could be a set of six silver buttons complete with a leather, velvet-lined display box. However, with the death of Britain's Prince Albert in 1861 and the deep mourning of Queen Victoria, black garments and black buttons became the norm, leading to a temporary stalling in metal button usage, especially among women's fashion. The so-called 'Golden Age' of buttons disappeared.

Moving with the times

By the end of the nineteenth century, women preferred versatile clothing to suit their newfound careers or sporting and leisure activities. They favoured a masculine inspired style of clothing with front fastenings, and independent dressing. New materials in button production came on the market, and Birmingham could not hold its place as the world's metal button producer.

In the mid-twentieth century, there was a resurgence of metal button use. With so many coloured fabrics on the market, it was easier for garment manufacturers to resort to a single metal style, rather than having to acquire various shades of coloured buttons. They were also considered high tech, in line with the futuristic fashion that was inspired by space travel. Garment designers were distinguishing their buttons with logos and company emblems particular to their clothing, a popular practice that continues today.

Today's metal button industrial manufacturing utilizes many of the same metals used in the eighteenth century, tried and tested and proven to last. Historically, the art is in the making of the tools, while the craft is in the application. The same applies

'Twinkles' are a three-part construction, made using intricate cut-out stampings, a highly polished steel reflective insert and a closed back with self-shank. They were relatively simple to produce; English versions were mostly made from brass stampings, but these European versions are made entirely from steel, with various plating. One is stamped TCHECOSLOVAQUIE, suggesting it was made in Czechoslovakia for the French market. Largest button, 32mm Ø.

Today's designers take advantage of the versatility, quality and longevity of metal buttons. Armani Collezioni, 28mm Ø, with enamel.

Author's small-scale studio buttons; prototypes for commission, here showing two examples in sterling silver, and two wax models yet to be cast, 1990s, Australia.

today. For punched metal buttons, brass, iron, copper, stainless steel and aluminium is used in high-speed mechanical presses. These buttons are characterized by their versatility, durability and lightness of weight. An alloy that is widely used for die-casting and rubber mould centrifugal casting is called zamak, composed of zinc, aluminium, copper and in some cases magnesium. Zamak exists in ingots; for centrifugal casting, the addition of magnesium (the lightest structural metal) allows for a specific liquidity to enable the metal to flow evenly within the rubber mould due to the centrifugal force. The ingots are smelted in furnaces before pouring into the button moulds. The rubber mould method of manufacture allows a versatility of shapes, with fine details and a handmade look and feel. In the die-casting method of manufacture, the zamak alloy contains no magnesium and is melted in a special oven (at a slightly lower temperature than required for centrifugal casting) before being injected and pressed into the die. Once removed from the moulds, in either method, the buttons are trimmed and polished in large tumblers. They are submerged into electroplating baths for both addition of colour (gilding, silver, nickel, copper, etc.) with the added benefits of corrosion and anti-abrasion protection, wear resistance and aesthetic qualities. After this process, they can be enamelled and/or embellished with the addition of gemstones (usually crystals or glass).

An artisan method of mass production still exists within the contemporary metal button industry. Components are made using the methods described above, and then handcrafted to produce spectacular results. As well, new technologies of 3D printing can be used to create innovation designs and shapes; wax prototypes can be further cast in metal and finished in the usual metal procedures.

A selection of moulded black glass buttons with various plating styles, twentieth century, Europe.

4

Glimmer glamour: Glass, enamelling and ceramics

I HAVE A WEAKNESS FOR BUTTONS.
I'M ALWAYS COLLECTING ORNATE AND
NICELY DECORATED ONES.
—RILA FUKUSHIMA, JAPANESE MODEL

Ceramics, glassmaking, glazes and enamels were all known to the ancient civilizations as far back as the Bronze Age. While ceramics and glass can be dated back to ancient Egypt, experts consider that the birthplace of true enamelling is centralized around the Mycenaean empire, an area we now know as mainland Greece. Yet the knowledge of the techniques of production of these materials has not always been continuous, with techniques lost then rediscovered, sometimes centuries later, and also applied to the production of buttons.

Glass

Glass has fascinated me ever since I first experienced seeing a glassblower at work. In the early 1970s my father took us to Seattle, Washington, to visit the glass studios of the burgeoning Pacific Northwest glass movement. I watched the masters at work, and was even allowed to help; a slight exaggeration — I got to help the assistant turn the steel rod while the artists were at the hot end. The studio also made lamps in the style of Louis Comfort Tiffany. Observing the makers cut the pieces of coloured glass to shape, mould them into the lead edging and solder them together was something I longed to do one day. While that dream remains unfulfilled, it's definitely on my bucket list. The visit to the studio gave me a new perspective on the everyday glass objects I had previously taken for granted, and made me look closer at them. I thought about the glass fishing floats wrapped in rope that sometimes washed up on the wild coast of Vancouver Island from Japan, and how someone, somewhere in Japan, was in a workshop like the one I had been to, handcrafting these beautiful objects for a practical, commercial use.

Decades later, when I purchased what would be the first stock for my new button shop venture, I again marvelled in the ability of glass to transform into tiny, intricate objects. The patterns on the faces of the buttons were as varied as an imagination can wonder. Most of these buttons were press-moulded with intricate, fine patterns imitating woven and/or beaded fabrics or cut glass. Later, I was to purchase another hoard of Czech glass buttons, this time via New Zealand. In 1960, the owners of a haberdashery shop closed their doors and, after they passed away, they left their niece the leftover stock. She contacted me and I gained another collection of glass buttons (just in time, as the stock I had opened the shop with had all but sold out), these ones from a later era of Czech glassmaking than my initial stock. The difference in these buttons led me to research more and more about their manufacture. There were 'moonglows' galore, in varying shapes and sizes, and bright iridescent designs that I had not had before. All this from the simple ingredients that come together to form

Some of the original purchase of glass buttons for the shop: early to mid-twentieth century, press moulded, some with brass four-way shank, some with brass loop shank, some with moulded self-shank. Large black with gilded winged horse, 40mm Ø.

glass, in collaboration with inventive, scientific minds and creative thinkers that foresee designs and attempt to produce them.

Glass has seen significant developments throughout history, but the main ingredients of sand, soda and lime are still in use from its early origins. While primitive glass is a naturally occurring formation, either due to volcanic activity (as in obsidian) or the product of lightning strikes or meteorites, the first evidence of human-made glass is located in archaeological finds in Egypt and Mesopotamia, dating from 3500 BC. It may have been a serendipitous discovery — according to the ancient natural historian, Pliny the Elder, legendary ancient traders of natural soda made an unanticipated discovery when they used soda ash in a sand firepit, which when heated and fused together created a strange liquid that eventually hardened, the origin of glass. The first objects that can be traced from this period are mostly non-transparent beads, showing that early glassmaking methods were fairly limited; the raw materials were, however, used as glazes on ceramic wares. Phoenician and other merchants and sailors spread this new art form along the coasts of the Mediterranean.

By 2500 BC, finds in Mesopotamia show the first transparent true glass, with beads, seals and architectural decoration among the objects discovered. It would

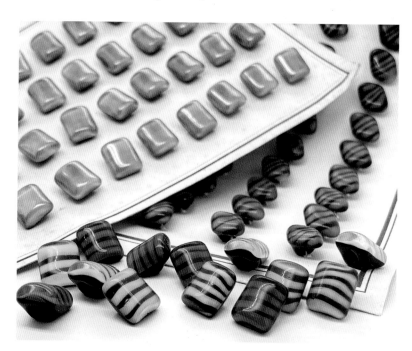

Moonglows, all on black glass base with characteristic clear glass top. 11mm length; mid-twentieth century, Czechoslovakia.

Glass buttons with brass rosette shanks, in ball shape, slightly domed, and flat profiles (L to R). Grey glass with black and gold stripes, 14mm ⌀; early twentieth century, Europe.

be another 1000 years before vessels would be produced, coinciding with the area becoming a primary producer — ancient Egyptians advanced their glassmaking technologies, where glass factories produced materials for further use by others. Crushed quartz was melted to make semi-finished glass, then re-melted and coloured, and formed into glass ingots. Imitations of precious stones such as lapis lazuli and turquoise were popular, and glass was considered such a prized commodity it was frequently interchanged with gemstones.

Further discoveries in glassmaking, for example the invention of glassblowing by the Syrians in 62 BC, meant that by the late first century BC principal glassmaking centres were in Syro-Palestine and Alexandria, Egypt. Ancient Rome's later dominance of these territories and its expansive trade networks saw the techniques of glassmaking brought into European areas where they were previously unknown. Glass use in Europe continued for several centuries, mostly for architectural purposes, but the production of luxury glass items comes to the fore from the thirteenth century in both Venice and the northern European area of Bohemia.

The origins of Venetian glassmaking have their roots in the Roman Empire, with expertise in the art form obtained from the Byzantine, or East Roman, Empire. Due to its geographical location, being at the crossroads of trading between the East and the West, Venice emerged as an important glass-manufacturing centre as early the eighth century, and glassmaking was the major industry of the city by the late 1200s when the Glassmakers Guild was formed. The main purpose of the guild was to keep safe the secrets of the glass profession and ensure profitability of the industry. Laws were passed in 1271 forbidding foreign glass imports, or employment of foreign workers, in the city.

With the burgeoning trade in Venice, in 1291 the government of the day made the decision to relocate the glass industry to the island of Murano, for fear of fires from the furnaces breaking out and spreading to the city centre, but particularly, with the added benefit of being able to shield industrial secrets from prying eyes. A few years later, laws were passed that forbade glassmakers from leaving the city. In exchange for their work and loyalty, the glass artisans were given a privileged social status; they could marry their daughters into the wealthiest and noblest Venetian families, and thus bring their offspring into the glassmaking craft, ensuring that trade secrets were kept within the family.

The fourteenth century was generally a period of unrest across Europe, but the next two centuries saw Venetian glass in all its splendour and at the peak of its popularity. By the fifteenth century, experimentation brought about new innovations in both colour and techniques: in 1450, glassmaker Angelo Barovier invented *cristallo*, a very clear soda glass; glass colours of green, azure, blue and amethyst were produced; techniques of gilding and enamelling were used on glass; white glass, *lattimo*, mimicking the porcelain craze, was invented. Mosaic glass, using *murrine* and *millefiori* rods (canes), was reintroduced in the early sixteenth century, after a long period of absence. Other glass techniques created were *filigrana*, in the form of glass canes

Simple glass ball-type buttons, with brass loop shank and foil inserts, 11mm Ø; early twentieth century, Europe.

Lampworked buttons from
Murano, Italy. Large blue with
gold and multicolours, 25mm Ø.

twisted with differing colours, ice glass, with a characteristic fine cracking throughout, and *aventurina*, where metal flakes were embedded into the glass mixture to create a shimmering effect.

While the large furnaces had moved to Murano, production of small-scale objects remained in the city and the Venetian mainland. The Muranese furnaces fed the small producers by providing a variety of thicknesses of glass canes from which to work from. Artificial gemstones were made by cutting and shaping the 'stones' from cut pieces of glass, and further developments in a method of working glass rods (canes) in front of a heat source (oil lamp), known as lampwork, produced beads and artificial pearls.

By the sixteenth century, Murano glass was very sought after throughout Europe, and many Italian glassmakers were encouraged to leave their country and settle elsewhere. Venetians had rare, in-depth knowledge of glassmaking, and when European royal leaders invited these craftsmen to their countries, some took up the challenge, taking up residence near Paris under the patronage of King Henry II and his wife Catherine de Medici, and in London under the patronage of King Henry VI. The glassmakers were very well respected and in France could gain the social status of 'glass gentleman'.

As button production in Italy moved increasingly away from precious materials and more towards bijouterie-like objects, which used metal alloys and imitated gems, vitreous pastes were at the forefront. Glass, in the form of enamels and crystal stones, was an important extension of the new non-precious metal buttons, but during the seventeenth and eighteenth centuries glass buttons came into their own. The glass guild was further categorized into two branches. The *smalteri* (enamel makers) produced semi-finished products of vitreous paste in the furnaces of Murano. The *perleri*, who produced artificial pearls and beads by lampwork, had increased their

Another Italian specialty is the 'paperweight' button, the height of artistic creativity in glass button production. These truly wonderful works of art are made with the same care as large paperweights, just in a teeny-tiny size and proportion.

range of accessories to include hair and shawl pins, and now buttons. Raised decorations on glass created some interesting three-dimensional accents. By the eighteenth century, the colour range of vitreous pastes was so great that it motivated the imitation of minerals and precious stones, *calcedonio*, named after the originals they resembled in both colour and characteristics, for example, cornelian, agate, lapis lazuli, ruby, mother of pearl.

A popular technique of button manufacture was the so-called 'winding button'. A wire pin is inserted into a mass of glass using a winding motion, then pushed into a metal shape. Italian glassblowers were, and still are, renowned for their creative use of colour, producing wonderful combinations of glass by adding different colours during the winding process. Another Italian specialty is the 'paperweight' button, the height of artistic creativity in glass button production. These truly wonderful works of art are made with the same care as large paperweights, just in a teeny-tiny size and proportion. They are typically made using a three-stage process: the internal design first, followed by the surrounding glass layers of the base, and then a clear, crystal glass encases the whole, fusing all parts of the glass together. The glass artist uses a variety of methods to produce designs — small slivers of coloured glass or *murrine* canes produce flowers or scenes, or the use of winding colours for effect. A wire pin, later bent into a shank, is inserted into the base while the glass is semi-molten or, less frequently, a glued shank may be used. They are assembled glass, elaborately lampworked through each of the stages. These labour-intensive treasures continue to be made by studio artists from around the world. They rose to popularity in the 1920s and remain a favourite among lovers of buttons.

Murano glass was almost exclusively used in the European bijouterie industry until the seventeenth century, because of the Muranese glassmakers' extensive trade network, fine workmanship and knowledge of creating beautifully coloured glass. The Venetian quality of production was linked to their distinctive, closely guarded formulas

A selection of classic paperweight-style buttons with characteristic clear glass top, sizes 9mm Ø to 13mm Ø, 1990s, Italy.

for their semi-finished products, the basis for their final creations. Murano was an important and thriving commercial enterprise, and the dominant European centre for glassmaking until the late eighteenth century.

From Italy, glassmaking knowledge spread east to Istria, west along the Mediterranean and north to Germany, Czechoslovakia and further to Belgium and Holland. Itinerant craftsmen may have been the reason for created production centres, as they took their skills wherever they were needed. Competition from Bohemia, France and Britain started in earnest during the seventeenth century although France's glass production was not as advanced as other European countries. In 1760, the Académie des Sciences instigated further research into glassmaking by offering a prize for the best new innovations, but the most important rival to the Venetian industry lay in Bohemia, with the main trade taking place in the village of Gablonz.

Bohemia

Located in the heart of Europe, the Bohemian glass industry was spread throughout a series of villages, with a cultural mix of both Czech and German Bohemians. Glassmakers were encouraged to come from Silesia (now Poland), and Saxonia and Bavaria (Germany) to join

An important glassmaking innovation was the invention of faceted stones, used in bijouterie items and buttons, as in these contemporary, hollow, claw-set examples. Large size, 31mm ∅, 2010s.

Faceted glass to imitate gemstones glued into a metal button mount, 35mm ∅, mid-twentieth century.

with other craftsmen and merchants; while they kept to themselves socially, they worked together amicably and created a thriving economy. Both the Hussite Wars (1419–36) and the 30 Years' War (1618–48) devastated the communities, each time leaving them to rebuild and repopulate, but Bohemia began a prosperous trajectory, experiencing a rapid growth, particularly after the second half of the seventeenth century. Its central position within Europe, however, led to further periods of political unrest, with competing monarchies vying for control.

The early domination of the Muranese glassmakers' artificial gemstones in the bijouterie industry led the Bohemians on a quest to replicate the mysteries of this highly reflective glass, which differed from the glass used in glassblowing by having a high lead content. It wasn't until after the 1611 publication of *De Arte Vitraria* by Italian, Antoni Neri, and its subsequent translations, that other European craftsmen began their own experiments in this, and all areas, of glassmaking. Indeed, this experimentation may have led to further developments in the French industry when around 1730 Georges Fréderic Strass invented his famous artificial diamonds, later known as strass, used in the metal buttons of the time.

In Bohemia, it led to what became known as 'composition glass' and initially proved a source of tension between the stonecutters guild and the glasscutters guild. A conflict regarding the cutting of this new material eventually led to a peaceable agreement — the stonecutters were able to use the larger capacity equipment of the glasscutters, and

A selection of faceted glass gemstones in various metal button mounts, both claw-set and glued in place, from the 1950s to 2000s. Square button, 25mm x 25mm, Europe.

the glasscutters were given the right to cut the composition glass.

This spirit of cooperation was evident throughout the villages of the Gablonz area, and there are some key factors for Bohemian glassmakers' success and eventual domination of the 'small glass' industry. The many small producers eventually grew into innovative dynasties, embracing foreigners to join their workforce, with skills passed down through the generations. They had a steady working relationship with the various metalworkers in the area, who were able to provide tools to improve their glassmaking techniques. This included the *Gürtlers*, metalworking craftsmen who would later provide metal mounts for bijouterie items. A major technological breakthrough from Bohemia was the introduction of press-moulded glass. The cooperation of glass engravers and metalworkers led to an exchange of knowledge, with metalworkers developing tools, in the form of tongs, that could hold the moulds for the various beads, gems and buttons that fine metal engravers would fashion. Many glass engravers converted their skills to work in metal, specializing in mould engraving for buttons with increasingly intricate details.

Cut and faceted clear glass and crystal buttons, early twentieth century to 2000s. Large faceted ball button with metal loop shank, 15mm Ø, Austria.

Prior to the Industrial Revolution, decorative glass buttons were mostly purchased by the wealthy; the time and skill required to produce them was beyond the price of the ordinary citizen. Many of the buttons produced during this time were made in England and France, but with the development of the first button moulds, the Bohemian glassworks soon eclipsed the rest of Europe.

Within the European glass button industry, the Venetians perfected their

Press-moulded blue glass buttons with
gilded decoration, self-shank or brass
loop shank, early to mid-twentieth
century. Diminutive buttons, 9mm ∅;
early twentieth century, Europe.

A selection of green glass buttons
from the mid-twentieth century,
all press moulded with self-shank.
Large flower, 32mm ∅, Europe.

lampworking skills with metal wires embedded in the glass, afterwards shaped into a
loop. Bohemian-made glass buttons began towards the end of the eighteenth century,
initially as glass blanks mounted on metal backs much like the French, and during the
beginning of the nineteenth century were made *à la façon de Venise*, in the Venetian
style, using the techniques of lampworking. It wasn't until the 1830s that buttons
could be produced in greater quantities — a decade earlier, new composition glass was
developed that was able to accept an embedded metal shank without damaging the
glass while it cooled.

The Bohemian press-moulded method of production, and the cooperation between
the skilled metal engravers and the inventive glass artists, allowed the Bohemians

to expand into a unique method of glass design, being able to stamp out intricately detailed patterns, especially on their buttons. Like lampworking, the press-moulding workshops were small cottage industries. The raw glass material, made by the large glasswork furnaces, was delivered in the form of canes to the smaller workshops.

The Bohemian press-moulder was a skilled craftsman. Working in front of a heat source, the glass must be heated to the correct temperature before being pressed into the tong mould. If the glass is too soft, it may shrink in the mould; if it is not hot enough, it cannot be compressed enough to accept the shape. Similarly, the die temperature is important. If the metal temperature is too cold, the glass will emerge with minute cracks on the surface; if it is too hot, the glass will stick to the metal and make it impossible to remove. The early tools for press-moulded items at the beginning of the nineteenth century were a little primitive, with further cutting and polishing of the glass required. But by the second half of the century, with improved dies of more complex design, glass could be finished with a single fire-polishing.

The Bohemian button industry began a period of expansion due to the great demands of fashion. During the Victorian era, and especially after the death of Queen Victoria's husband Prince Albert in 1861, the public demand for formal mourning attire increased. Strict mourning periods were put in place and all mourners, including children and servants, were expected to follow the rules by wearing black silk crepe clothing; women were further expected to have all of their accessories in black, including jewellery and buttons. For the British queen and her court, jewellery and buttons were made from jet, a form of fossilized driftwood found near the fishing

Black glass buttons, press-moulded, engraved, hand-cut; late nineteenth to mid-twentieth century. Large oval button has brass loop and plate shank, 42mm long, Europe.

A selection of contemporary Swarovski crystal buttons, sew-through or tunnel shank, foil backed in clear or various coloured finishes. Large rectangle has black base with Tabac finish, 22mm x 11mm, 2000s, Austria.

OPPOSITE: Victorian-style ornate black glass buttons, press-moulded with brass or self-shank. Large button with tassel design and brass four-way box shank, 30mm ⌀; late nineteenth century, Europe.

village of Whitby on the Yorkshire coast. With the entire country following their queen into public mourning, this material was soon copied in the form of black glass, a less expensive alternative.

The Bohemians were well placed to provide such items, with their production of press-moulded black artificial gems and their black glass buttons. Black had long been a colour of nobility throughout Europe, gradually developing into a mourning colour. Until the 1870s most Bohemian glass buttons were made in the colour black, some with metallic plated or painted finishes to add interest. The increasing demand for their buttons gave way to further technological changes in the form of an improved loop shank with a metal back plate, and an enhanced colour palette to satisfy new markets in fashion. Eventually, from the 1920s onwards, modifications to the dies saw the shanks of buttons included in the press-moulds, creating a completely glass button with self-shank.

Due to the geographical isolation of this skilled workforce, and the great distance of their eventual market, dynasties of merchants operated

Contemporary haute couture bijouterie buttons using Swarovski crystals. Large blue square, 45mm x 45mm, 2010s, Italy.

Of the Bohemian producers to break out and market their own products, and still internationally prominent today, is the Swarovski company.

harmoniously alongside, and sometimes within, the makers' dynasties. By the mid-eighteenth century, newly formed organizations of import/export companies were founded, with affiliates in Europe, the United States and the Middle East. Large production in glass components for, and finished items of, bijouterie meant items were exported to countries all over Europe. Gablonz was the central trading area; buyers came from outside of Bohemia to purchase articles that would be on-sold to various manufacturers of fashion accessories. Unlike Venetian glassmakers, the individual Bohemian manufacturers were not known outside the region; products were not marketed under the local makers' names, but rather

Contemporary Czech glass buttons in a variety of finishes. Large iris blue flower with white wash, 29mm ⌀, 2020s.

under the collective of Bohemia. Black glass became known outside Bohemia as French jet, exported from Gablonz in great quantities and probably then exported to Britain via France. Bohemian finished costume jewellery, or components thereof, sold in the United States through manufacturers such as Coro, Trifari and Miriam Haskell.

Of the Bohemian producers to break out and market their own products, and still internationally prominent today, is the Swarovski company. Daniel Swarovski was born in 1862 in the village of Georgenthal bei Gablonz. His father was a glass-cutter who worked within their small, family-owned workshop, producing hand-cut stones for various bijouterie items. Instead of following his father into the glass-cutting profession, Daniel chose an apprenticeship to learn the *Gürtler* craft, afterwards returning to the family glass-cutting business. When in 1883 he was given the opportunity to visit the first electricity exhibition in Vienna, the interaction with modern technology sparked his imagination and led him on a path to seek out new methods of production.

Daniel Swarovski made continuous improvements on cutting machines for crystal glass stones, as well as innovations in composition glass, enabling an even colour match across all sizes of stones, something not previously attainable. He further developed the process of electroplating the backs of the stones and buttons with foils, to create a more sophisticated reflective front. In partnership with Franz Weis, he started his own company of bijouterie items, marketing directly to Paris without the traditional Bohemian brokers. In 1895, the company moved its operations to Wattens, in Tyrol, where a good water supply ensured a hydroelectric energy source to power the cutting machines, and kept things away from the prying eyes of his competition.

The company celebrated its 125th birthday in 2020, marking five generations of the family business. While crystal button manufacturing is only a small part of the Swarosvki empire, their crystal stone elements are frequently used within the products created by button, jewellery and interior designers and manufacturers. While they are not the only company to

Transparent coloured glass buttons from the early twentieth century to contemporary times. Large blue faceted button, 35mm ⌀, Argentina.

produce quality crystal stones and buttons, they are by far the most well-known, and remain the market leader.

After World War I, Bohemia was incorporated into the new nation of Czechoslovakia, a move that left the majority Sudeten Germans at a disadvantage. They successfully lobbied the Czechoslovakian government to accede Sudetenland to Germany in the late 1930s, but at the end of World War II the areas were returned to Czechoslovakia — the lands were seized and all Germans expelled — and an era of Bohemian cooperative glassmaking ended. Many German glassmakers relocated to Bavaria, to a district in Kaufbeuren created to provide for the displaced population, calling it Neugablonz. Gablonz reverted to its Czech name of Jablonec. Both areas continue with a glassmaking industry today.

The time-honoured methods of glass button production have, for the most part, not altered since the 1700s. While the labour-intensive faceting of glass by hand has given way to a mechanized system of cutting, the mechanical processes of moulding or pressing buttons into a shape remain in place, a laborious craft that produces an eclectic range of variables.

Glass colour and opacity

While manufactured glass is considered clear, adding chemical elements and/or minerals (such as gold, copper, tin, iron, lead, among others) to the basic formula can change the colour and opacity. Glass buttons may have an opaque, clear transparent, translucent or partially transparent, or satin or 'silk glass' body colour. Transparent glass buttons that are clear and have not been tinted are called crystal, but this is in reference to the lack of colour rather than the lead content — lead crystal glass buttons reflect a slight bluish tinge, while glass buttons without lead reflect a slight yellowish tinge. Colours may be solid in form, as in opaque glass buttons, or slightly tinted as in transparent and translucent glass buttons. Satin glass may be opaque, or sometimes translucent, and has an even, soft pearly lustre; a favoured body glass for the

Uranium glass buttons with varying degrees of uranium additive, producing a milky, pale yellow colour or a milky, pale green colour. Shown under standard fluorescent vs ultraviolet light, 18mm Ø; 1930s, Europe.

formation of 'moonglows', it is what creates the distinctive depth characteristic of these buttons. Glass may be intermixed, as in the Venetian *filigrana* style, using any and all combinations of coloured or clear glasses, where the colours are seen throughout from front to back. An unusual addition to make coloured glass was the element uranium; it was found associated with silver mines in Bohemian glassmaking as well as other areas, and uranium glass, recognized as 'depression glass', in the form of buttons remain a curiosity.

Multicoloured glass buttons can be achieved by a variety of methods, one of which consists of intermixing various colours, whether they are opaque, transparent, translucent or any combination of these. They may be striped in a few colours, creating a wide stripe, or in many, creating narrow or threadlike veins. They may be marbled in contrasting or monotone colours, creating attractive displays or imitating natural products such as tortoiseshell. To be considered 'intermixed' glass, the colours should be seen on the front and the back of the buttons. If the colours are only seen on the front, they are known as 'overlay'. This method of decoration consists of adhering amounts of glass to the surface, whether by random 'spatter' of small amounts, controlled lines or swirls either whole or twisted, or sheets of contrasting colours, among others. Moonglows could be mistaken as a type of overlay, but they differ in that they are either solid or striped glass, often with a satin finish, with a cover of clear glass fused on top. They are easily identified when looked at sideways, with a clearly defined transparent top, the clear glass cover giving them a wonderful, focused depth of field when viewed from the front, a little like paperweight buttons. These attractive glass buttons were first made in Czechoslovakia in the 1950s, and in West Germany in the 1960s.

Besides colouring the glass base, further additions to the surface give added decoration to the buttons. The finish of press-moulded glass is not as shiny as blown glass, so to create the high lustre most press-moulded buttons are finished with a fire-polish, a process by which the buttons are reheated just enough to produce a smooth glossy surface. Satin glass, on the other hand, is polished in a tumbler. Frosted or matte finishes and details may be achieved either by using hydrofluoric or other abrasive acid (known as acid etching) or through a process of sand blasting. Lustres on the surface of glass buttons enhance details or patterns — gold, silver, copper and gunmetal gildings were popular finishes on black glass buttons, as were iridescent lustres, especially during the Victorian era. Either adding metallic salts to heated glass or making a paste of metallic salts and painting on to the surface of cold glass achieves iridescent lustres,

ABOVE: Intermixed and moonglow glass buttons, press-moulded with self-shank. Large blue/pink cushion square sew-through buttons, 32mm ∅; Europe.

ABOVE RIGHT: Dichroic, aurora and iridescent glass finishes on this selection of Czech glass buttons from the mid-twentieth century to contemporary times. Dragonfly buttons of dichroic glass both shine purple when a light source is used from behind, large size 42mm ∅; 2020s.

RIGHT: Early strass buttons with a central pearl; the external coating of the pearl finish shows signs of bubbling and will most likely chip or peel. 20mm ∅; Europe.

with their multiple rainbow colours that change when moved from side to side.

The discovery of iridescent and dichroic glass can be traced back to ancient Rome in the fourth century AD, when glassmakers discovered that adding precious metals — such as gold and silver — during the production of molten glass resulted in finished articles that changed colour depending on the light. In the case of dichroic glass, looking through the glass (the transmitted colour) differs from the reflected colour. Iridescent pastes were re-introduced by the Venetians during the Renaissance, and by the Bohemians in the nineteenth century. Throughout the twentieth century, iridescent lustres were widely embraced and transformed not only black, but also other base colours of glass; the introduction of an improved formula in the mid-century, called aurora borealis, was especially vibrant. Besides on glass buttons, its inclusion in the Swarovski crystal range meant it was seen on many fashion accessories, from buttons to bijouterie items. Czechoslovakian buttons from the 1950s made use of this effect in their glass buttons; it could be slightly translucent and lightly cover the button to allow the colour of the base glass to show through (for example, as used on the black glass buttons from the Victorian era and onwards), or a heavier layer could cover the base glass completely. A Czech Republic 1990s revival of these finishes in their glass button range showed new, more vibrant iridescent aurora finishes, as well as a wonderfully brilliant dichroic glass range where the aurora finish adhered to the back and created the same colour play as their ancient counterparts.

Pearls have long been favoured among the elite class, and due to their rarity, scarcity, and high costs, the replication of natural pearls has been pursued since the first century BC. The secret of the rich lustre of pearls, the shimmering nacre, had been sought for centuries, with limited success. Attempts at reproduction, especially in Venice, included metals under glass (silver, mercury, lead, among others), the use of ground mica or ground shell nacre under glass, or opal glass with its milky iridescence. But it wasn't until 1656 in Paris when Frenchman, François Jaquin, finally unlocked the truest form of imitation still in use today. By extracting the crystalline guanine from the fish scales of the bleak (*Alburnus alburnus*) and suspending them in liquid, he captured the lustrous material, calling it *essence d'orient* or pearl essence. Initially used to internally coat clear glass beads to replicate pearls, it later progressed as an external coating, being used also on glass buttons throughout the twentieth century. Unlike the multicoloured iridescent finishes, the pearl finish mostly reflects a silvery white colour, emulating the inner glow of natural pearl nacre. These earlier, external pearl lustres had a tendency to chip, flake or peel, but towards the end of the century and into the next, pearl finishes reached a higher standard.

Embellishments and decorative techniques

Embellishments to glass buttons may take other forms, such as inlay or painting. Inlays into glass buttons, using other materials such as mother of pearl carvings or metal stampings, produced a great decorative effect when they were first introduced in the late nineteenth century, as did the later 'glass-on-glass' inlays. Inlay buttons are produced in two parts and then cemented together; the glass-on-glass inlays often have a smooth, ground flat face whereby the surface feels as one to the touch.

Painted buttons known as 'miniatures', produced in France between around 1770 until the end of the eighteenth century, were introduced in the new fashion journals and became popular items on clothing. Often between 35mm and 40mm in diameter, they were not miniature in size but rather in scale. While miniatures were made using a variety of methods, many of them incorporated a glass face. Well-known artists sometimes painted them as a means of income, commissioned by wealthy patrons. Paintings on paper, bone or ivory were inserted between a glass face and steel backing, with a copper or brass wire shank. A copper or brass collet held all the components in place. While watercolours and etchings on paper were popular, so too were scenes created using dried foliage and other matter, artistically arranged and inspired by the naturalist, Georges-Louis Leclerc. Reverse painting on the underside of the glass was perhaps the oldest

Press-moulded Czech glass buttons showing various techniques: painting, foil backing, gilding. Large brown flower is a two-part button with separate faceted centre, matte finish petals and self-shank, 33mm ⌀; mid-twentieth century.

form of these miniatures. A reflective or mirrored backing, brought about by either a tinned steel base, a tinned steel sheet or silver-plated brass foil insert, while not always used, could enhance the painted colours. Inserted embellished backings on paper, mica or ivory and combined with reverse paintings made for an enhanced decorative effect.

Painting on glass was a simple decorative technique employed in the mass production of glass buttons. Powdered glass enamels could be painted onto glass buttons, which were then fired a second time to create a long-lasting effect. Painting could also be done using cold pigments; originally, oil paints were thinned with linseed oil or other resin varnish. These cold pigments were not long-lasting, and chips in the paintwork frequently occurred. In an effort to create a more robust cold painted button, glass buttons could be incised on the face, then the paint rubbed in and

Press-moulded glass buttons with self-shank in intaglio style, painted and rubbed back. Large oval storytelling buttons, 27mm long; mid-twentieth century, Europe.

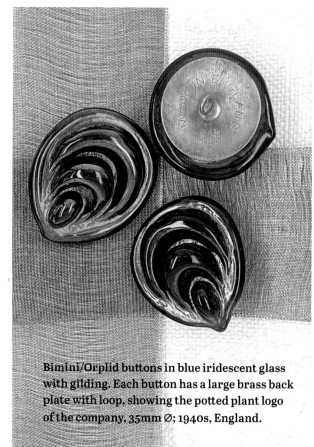

Bimini/Orplid buttons in blue iridescent glass with gilding. Each button has a large brass back plate with loop, showing the potted plant logo of the company, 35mm Ø; 1940s, England.

smoothed off, leaving the painted finish in the shallow grooves; or a deeper *intaglio* design could be created on the reverse side of transparent glass and painted from below. Czechoslovakian buttons in the mid-twentieth century attempted to imitate the Venetian paperweight style using the intaglio technique in a two-part button; the carved design was hand-painted from the back of a domed top, and a glass bottom with shank was cemented to it. This style was very labour intensive, without the dramatic effects of the artistic Italian versions, and its production has not continued.

Considering the strength of the Bohemian industry, the French also had a considerable glass button industry, as well as art glassmakers who, from the end of the nineteenth century and into the twentieth century made smaller objects as an adjunct to their practice. Most well-known are Émile Gallé and, later, René Lalique, both of whom perfected the *pâte de verre* technique of glass art. Details of organic, botanical concepts, especially popular during the emerging Art Nouveau period of the 1900s and continuing through the Art Deco period that followed, were also achieved through press moulding or acid etching of glass elements. These small discs were often set in a precious metal surround with shank, to create wondrous, exceptional accessories. The use of precious metals attests to their artistic value and worth.

The war years and beyond

While glass button production slowed during the years of World War II and immediately after, one producer who continued during the war years, and further, must be mentioned for their quality lampworked and pressed-glass buttons: Fritz Lampl from Bimini (later Orplid) glass studio in London.

Austrian-born Lampl grew up to become a poet and glass artist, starting Bimini glass studio in Vienna in 1923 with a flowerpot logo as trademark. Due to political unrest, Lampl moved to England in 1938 where he re-started his glass company in London. The main production of the workshop was decorative objects, but from the 1940s they also produced wonderful glass buttons. The buttons are very distinctive objects of art in themselves, each one individually crafted — a pattern is deeply impressed into a semi-molten blob of glass, leaving bulging edges and slight variations in size. A common decorative effect was the use of gold lustre. A large brass plate with a shank and the company name and logo were cemented to the back.

Due to difficulties with registering the name 'Bimini' in England, the name of the company was changed to Orplid. Lampl employed many friends and fellow émigrés

Australian studio glass buttons, some identified as Darian/G.F.D. glass buttons. Large clear glass with gilding (waratah, waves), 48mm Ø; small blue with silver, 20mm Ø; mid-twentieth century.

in his workshop in London, especially during the years of button-making. One such employee was Lucie Rie, employed first as a designer of glass buttons and later as a maker of ceramic buttons under the Orplid name.

There were others that followed in the Bimini/Orplid style of glass button-making: Glass Developments Ltd and English Glass Co. were among the followers, but without a stamped back plate it is difficult to identify other makers. One maker of this style who can be identified is Grant Featherston from Australia. Featherston was a self-taught designer working in lighting and glass, before being sent off to World War II between 1940 and 1944. Upon his return, together with his first wife, Claire, he designed glass buttons under his company name of Darian, using brass back plates with shank. Initially, the back plates were not engraved, but later they were stamped with G.F.D. and Darian. Like Lampl, buttons were not his main business but rather filled a need. The buttons were made from clear glass; some had solid colours applied to the backs, some

Contemporary studio buttons from Murano (Italy), New Zealand and Canada. Large ladybeetle, 35mm Ø; 2010s, New Zealand.

Mass production of glass buttons started in the
1860s and over the following 100 years enjoyed
a flurry of design and scientific developments
to produce items for all facets of society.

had metallic lustre finishes, and others had both. Grant Featherston went on to become one of Australia's foremost designers, especially noted for his shell plywood chairs, but during the years of 1946 to 1954, he produced some 40 designs of glass buttons.

Mass production of glass buttons started in the 1860s and over the following 100 years enjoyed a flurry of design and scientific developments to produce items for all facets of society. Sadly, by the 1950s the push towards plastic buttons saw their eventual decline in the 1960s. With the dissolution of the Soviet Union in 1991, however, Czech producers once again started producing a limited number of glass buttons using the original moulds from the glass factories of Bohemia. Besides these, contemporary glass button production is mostly as an accompaniment to the lucrative glass bead production, as in Murano, for example, or in small glass studios. Still, they remain outstanding works of sculptural art.

Something to look forward to is new innovations in 3D printing, namely printed glass. Bastian Rapp, a researcher at Karlsruhe Institute of Technology, has been experimenting with new techniques using an inexpensive unmodified 3D printer to produce intricate glass objects, which only require being placed in a high-temperature oven to fuse the glass particles. In cases where, previously, acid etching was used as a form of decoration, this new technology does away with the use of chemicals to achieve similar results. As the 3D printer is a familiar technological tool, the glass polymer being developed is an exciting possible future method of intricate button- and jewellery-making for the small art glass studio.

Enamelling

I first discovered the joy of enamelling as a six-year-old. My father enrolled us children into an all-ages short course in arts and crafts at the University of British Columbia. I was the youngest; the oldest was 70 years. The things I remember most were sand casting of wax candles, metal casting of wax carvings, and enamelling on copper —

Contemporary enamelled buttons. Yin yang cats, 34mm ∅; 2010s, Italy.

sawing the copper sheet to size, preparing the surface, and then gently sifting the powdered enamel colours into a freeform design. Later, my father bought us a tiny kiln and we spent a lot of time experimenting/making colourful pendants — hey, it was the 1960s and all the rage.

Many years later, I embarked on a course of jewellery study, intent on bringing back the style of precious buttons from previous centuries. Customers had been asking me for 'more expensive buttons' for a few years, so I began my studies applying the skills learned towards making buttons. It must be mentioned here that I had the honour of having two amazing jewellers as my mentors, Craig Hill and Marcus Avery, both of whom I learned so much from and who gave me more than just their time and expertise. Halfway through my four years of study, I travelled overseas on a buying trip and found a family business that was making the most exquisite enamelled buttons — beautiful, intricate, affordable, and made with artisanal pride and passion for their craft. Needless to say, upon my return I refocused my study on jewellery making, but while I haven't made any more buttons in the noble metals, I have the skill to do so if I choose.

Enamel is a glassy medium that is applied to the surface of metals, glass and

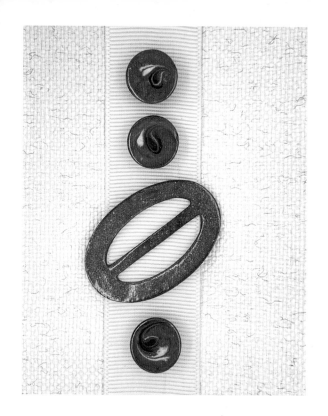

Enamel on copper button and buckle set. Buttons, 14mm ∅; 1970s, Australia.

Early nineteenth century enamel button in oval, 18mm long. Round memento mori button, hand painted, centre with woven hair. Back marked GESCHUTZT — protected by law, 22mm ∅; Germany/Austria.

ceramics (as in glazes) as a form of decoration or as a protective layer, like a varnish made of glass, but the term enamelling is most often used in regard to the adornment of metal. While vitreous enamel is a form of glass, it differs in that it is a finer compound of ingredients creating a relatively softer type of glass. The ingredients of flint or sand (both forms of silica), with red lead, and soda or potash, are melted together to produce an almost clear glass with a slightly blue or green tinge. This is known as flux, frit or fondant in French. The proportions of the components determine whether the enamel is considered hard or soft, the former firing at a higher temperature creating a longer lasting surface. Softer enamels fire at a lower temperature, making them easier to use, but do not wear as well and may crack or chip under friction.

Clear frit is the base from which all coloured and opaque enamels are made. After the addition of metallic oxides to create colours or to render the glass opaque, the liquefied ingredients are poured into a slab and allowed to cool into small cakes. Glassmaking centres such as Murano produced many of these enamel cakes for their own use, and for export. In order to use the enamel, it must be ground to a fine powder in a mortar and pestle, and cleaned thoroughly in distilled water until the water runs clear. The surface of the metal must be dry and free from contaminants before the addition of the enamel, and enamel pastes must be dried before being placed in the kiln. Through the firing process, the powders melt and fuse to the metal surface.

The earliest known enamelwork pieces, vitreous pastes fused on to gold rings, are dated to the thirteenth century BC Mycenaean empire. The Ancient Greeks were fond of enamelling, using the technique of *cloisonné* since the sixth century BC; the techniques of both *cloisonné* and *champlevé* were widely used by the Byzantine Empire from the fourth to twelfth centuries AD. *Cloisonné* uses fine, flat wires to create the design and designate the areas of colour, while *champlevé* uses the techniques of intaglio engraving, chasing and/or repoussé tools for the same intention. It is considered that the art form originated in Europe and spread further west, and east from Constantinople and to Asia via the Silk Road.

Cloisonné style contemporary enamelled buttons. Large size, 21mm; 2010s, Italy.

Hand-constructed metal buttons with faceted glass stones and enamel centre. Large size, 43mm ⌀, Italy.

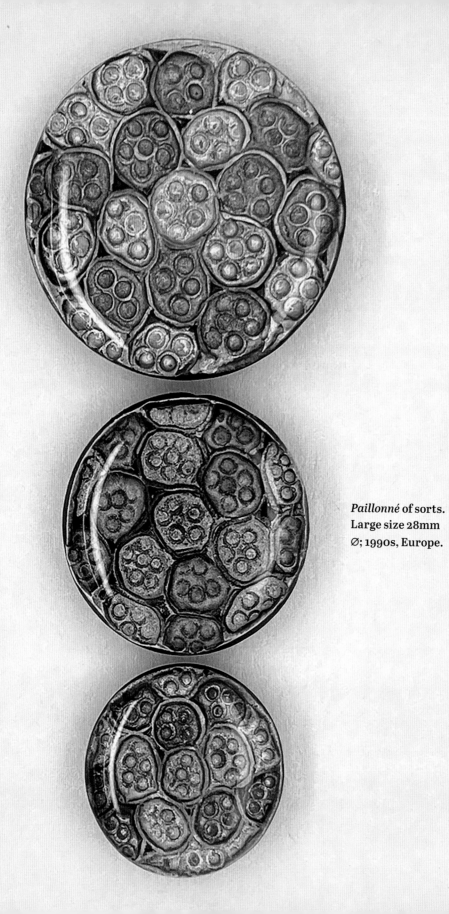

Paillonné of sorts.
Large size 28mm
Ø; 1990s, Europe.

Large square button with grapes and grapevine,
using the techniques of *baisse-taille* and *cloisonné*.
40mm x 40mm; late twentieth century.

While the use of enamelling as an art form
spread throughout Europe, the first enamelled
insets into buttons were thought to be those worn
in the sixteenth century by Francis I of France, an
avid patron of the arts. These were probably made
in Limoges, being the first place to embrace this
style, with the enamel on gold set in a gold bezel.
Few if any of these buttons remain, and due to their
precious metal base they were likely melted down and remade into something else.

The technique of *émaux peints*, or painted enamels, emerged during the
Renaissance. It is thought that Flemish artisans working in the fifteenth century
Burgundian territories of the Low Countries (what is now the Netherlands, Belgium
and Luxembourg) brought the skill to Burgundy; the art form then expanded in France,
and through to Northern Italy. The town of Limoges, already known for its enamelware
since the thirteenth century, and with this newfound knowledge, became the centre for
painted enamels by the late fifteenth century and over the next 100 years made further
developments in their miniature portrait range. While interest waned in Italy, Limoges
became synonymous with the technique of painting in multiple colours without the use
of separating metals, such as cloisonné or *champlevé*. In the first half of the sixteenth
century the Limoges' enamellers developed two new enamel painting approaches,
grisaille and *paillonné*, techniques that spread across Europe. *Grisaille* was a form of
two-tone painting; a black ground was enhanced with a design in white enamel, built up
layer by layer and in varying opacity. *Paillonné* made use of *paillons* (ultra-thin sheets of
metal) to create a lustrous background, or add details, for the painted design.

The court of Francis I of France (1515–47) had introduced the French to the beauty
and richness of the Renaissance. But Francis' grandson, Charles IX (1560–74), who
ascended the throne thirteen years later, was a killjoy when it came to fashion, issuing
decrees regarding the manufacturing of these enamel buttons, among others. Despite
the influence of fashion coming from the Italian homeland of his mother, Catherine de'
Medici, Charles IX showed a great disdain for fashion and attempted to curb the trends

While not technically enamel painting, these contemporary buttons nonetheless depict classical paintings. Large size 29mm Ø; 2000s, Italy.

The *guilloché* technique depicted on contemporary buttons. Large size 29mm Ø; 1990s, Italy.

of the day with sumptuary laws prohibiting certain fabrics, colours and trimmings. Followed by Henry III (1574–89), by 1583 the production of all enamel, glass and crystal buttons was controlled by the court. Enamel button-making came under the guild of goldsmiths and metalworkers, and followed jewellery-making techniques.

The technique of *basse-taille* enamel had its origins in thirteenth century Italy, where precious metals such as gold or silver were manipulated into a low-relief pattern using engraving, chasing and/or repoussé tools, then covered with translucent enamels. The designs were clearly seen from below the enamel layer, and the various levels of the design created the differences in colour. This method of working produced some stunning 'paintings' in enamel, decorating the rooms of palaces with its brilliant, never fading colours and detailed luminescence. Nearing the end of the Renaissance, a seventeenth century revival of the *basse-taille* and all other enamel techniques could be found on trinkets for the wealthy. Artisans from across Europe were engaged in creating jewellery, watches, snuffboxes and buttons.

From the mid-seventeenth century, Geneva (Switzerland) took over as the centre for painted enamels, improving on the techniques they had been using since the fifteenth century. While it is not certain that they produced any buttons, they created exquisite articles of jewellery and watches using painted enamel techniques into the nineteenth century. They are, however, given credit for instigating the use of enamel techniques onto copper (as opposed to gold or silver), allowing for a less costly product.

In mid-eighteenth century England, the technique of painted enamels on copper was further developed at Battersea Enamels (London) with the introduction of transfer printing from paper onto a fired enamel base. This furthered the opportunities for a less expensive product, and the Birmingham area (including the firm of Matthew Boulton) continued production, with its peak in the last 30 years of the century. These buttons were unmounted with a rolled over rim, made from thin copper with a wire shank, and enamelled on both sides to prevent warping during the firing process. This is known as counter enamelling, without which the enamel surface would crack and chip away. Multicoloured floral and Rococo styles with gilding were the latest style, as were landscapes. While production was mostly geared towards men's clothing, buttons were also created in novelty themes aimed towards women of society. With French enamel buttons returning to fashion by the end of the century and Napoleon's ban on English imports, the production of enamelled buttons dwindled substantially in England but did not disappear altogether. France again became the centre for this enamelled accessory. Into the nineteenth century enamel buttons were made not only in France, but also in England and by craftspeople and the button industries in Russia and Germany, an art form of decoration rediscovered and enhanced with innovative techniques.

Some of the most exquisite enamelled buttons were produced at the end of the nineteenth century and into the twentieth century during the resurgence of the art form in this accessory. *Basse-taille* enamel examples used more opaque enamels, and a new extension of the technique called *guilloché*, which first appeared in the eighteenth century, surpassed *basse-taille* and was used extensively by jewellers and button-makers. Jewellers such as Peter Carl Fabergé embraced this technique in his famous Fabergé eggs, as did the Parisian jewellery company of Cartier, both creating, among other items, exquisitely elegant buttons and cufflinks. The *guilloché* technique differs slightly from *basse-taille*; while both have a pattern cut in low relief below an enamelled surface, *guilloché* is always covered by a clear or translucent enamel and the term is used exclusively for patterns that are cut using a *'tour de guillocher'* or rose engine lathe, creating patterns reminiscent of the Spirograph, a geometric drawing tool.

During the 1850s, the opportunities afforded by the new opening of trade with Japan exposed the Europeans to the Japanese sensibility of art and design and their depictions of nature. This was to have a great influence on the later styles of Art

Nouveau in continental Europe and enamelling was the perfect medium. Coveted by collectors, exquisite nineteenth century Japanese buttons using the methods of *champlevé* and *cloisonné* with a crackle glaze are a rare treat. The ensuing trade between East and West continued a design exchange throughout the world, and buttons were among the items that benefitted from this input.

Notably, French Art Nouveau artist René Lalique, synonymous with fine craftsmanship, created beautiful silver and gold enamelled buttons and cufflinks in his inimitable style, incorporating *plique à jour* enamelling techniques alongside others, and bringing an ethereal beauty to his works. In Britain, Liberty of London commissioned a range of silver pieces, including buttons, designed by Archibald Knox. The series, trademarked 'Cymric', was created in the Art Nouveau/Arts and Crafts style, melding nature themes with Celtic design influences in phosphorescent greens and blues, examples of which can be found in the Victoria and Albert Museum collection. The range was manufactured by W.H. Haseler of Birmingham and used factory production methods, much to the disappointment of proponents of the Arts and Crafts movement, but because of its low cost it was popular among Liberty's clientele.

Up until World War I the production of buttons remained whimsically elegant. An ever-increasing amount of smaller sized buttons adorned both men's and women's clothing, but the world events that followed saw a sharp decrease in metal button production. The era of handmade, fine art enamelled buttons had come to a close.

Between the wars, Paris remained the dominant centre for haute couture, and all capitals from across Europe and beyond looked to French fashion designers for their

Between the wars, Paris remained the dominant centre for haute couture, and all capitals from across Europe and beyond looked to French fashion designers for their inspiration. Many designers collaborated with artists and jewellery designers for both their fabric motifs and their fastenings, including buttons.

inspiration. Many designers collaborated with artists and jewellery designers for both their fabric motifs and their fastenings, including buttons. The new materials that were being developed (particularly plastics) came to the fore and competed in the space usually left for high-end enamel creations. The 1925 International World Fair in Paris, *Salon des Arts Decoratifs et Industriels Modernes*, from which the term 'Art Deco' was born, included a vast increase in fashion designers.

Designer influence

Fashion had finally become recognized as an artistic pursuit, and buttons were re-evaluated as an artistic expression. By the 1930s, buttons were again featured widely on clothing; although now fewer in number, they were larger and increasingly imaginative in design. Clothing designers collaborated with others to produce unique buttons and fastenings (as well as bijouterie items) and many of the enamelled buckles, clasps and buttons that were offered bore the new Art Deco style. Metals were white (base metal, silver or platinum for those who could afford it) and black enamel was often used with red, white, blue or a combination of these colours.

Fashion designers Coco Chanel and Elsa Schiaparelli both had a keen eye for detail, down to the accessories used on their garments. The Chanel style was chic and simple; some gilded buttons used minimal enamel filler, often in white or black, or in combination. Elsa Schiaparelli, on the other hand, was influenced by the Cubism and Surrealism art styles, and had a more fanciful vision for her clothing and accessories. While both designers collaborated with jewellery designers, Schiaparelli's whimsical

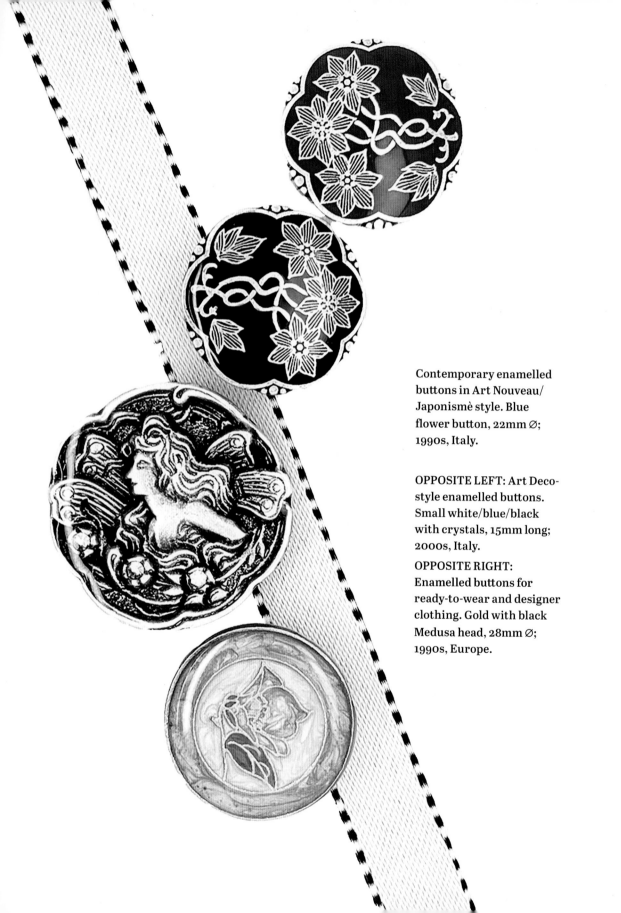

Contemporary enamelled buttons in Art Nouveau/Japonismè style. Blue flower button, 22mm ∅; 1990s, Italy.

OPPOSITE LEFT: Art Deco-style enamelled buttons. Small white/blue/black with crystals, 15mm long; 2000s, Italy.

OPPOSITE RIGHT: Enamelled buttons for ready-to-wear and designer clothing. Gold with black Medusa head, 28mm ∅; 1990s, Europe.

buttons were colourful and knew no bounds. Some of the cast metal buttons, including miniature acrobats in extended pose, circus horses and grand pianos, did not use vitreous enamels but rather enamel paint as decoration, a finish that did not stand the test of longevity, with paint chipping on these wonderful creations.

Once again, geopolitical events would put a halt to fashion during World War II, but afterwards, an energy for rebirth followed, and Paris-based French haute couture was a major world influence. Tickets sold to attend the Paris dress shows meant buyers could purchase the original garments, the patterns for them, or the right to copy them — including all information about fabrics and decorations, including fastenings and buttons. Many Italian buyers took advantage of this arrangement and were able to reignite their industry with the 'Made In Italy' brand. Button producers could bring their artisanal skills to an industrialized method of production, and metalworkers refined their enamelling techniques to suit the new processes. Enamelling onto cast bronze required lower temperature, high expansion enamels, decorated on accurately engraved *champlevé* style bases. Some base metals were coloured with enamel paint, but this form of varnish is not permanent and can wear away or chip over time, and was

not very popular. By the 1960s, synthetic enamels had replaced vitreous enamels on most mass-produced buttons.

Resurgence in the use of enamelled accessories and buttons came after 1969, when couture designers used enamelling as a decoration on their products. It was a new era in branding, with companies such as Gucci, Ken Scott, Dior, Yves St Laurent and many others now using signature buttons in bright colour combinations on men's and women's clothing. Such was the popularity of the decorative technique that it still continues today, as both a recognised trademark of a couture house, or on blazers for sporting and other associations where formerly plain metal buttons may have been used.

On a button-hunting trip, I had the privilege of visiting the workshop of one of my Italian suppliers of enamelled buttons. The family business produces new and past reproductions of designs in enamelled buttons with exquisite detail. The metal bases with shank are mass-produced with intricate engraved designs in *champlevé* style, and then each colour is painstakingly inserted into the designated area. Some may argue that these are not 'collectable' and do not compare with vitreous enamelled buttons, but they are beautiful and affordable examples of a designer's dream, and coveted by our many customers who purchase them for their beloved garments.

Specialty buttons, using mass production or small studio techniques. Small sized red and blue enamel on pewter base, 15mm long; 1990s, New Zealand.

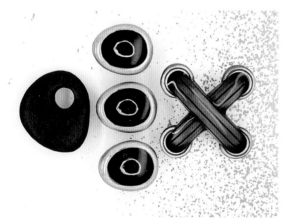

Studio buttons made by jewellers using enamelling techniques are an investment in the accessory, made using the same jewellery techniques from past centuries and sought after by the button collector. One such maker is Karen L. Cohen, a master enameller creating an array of articles including buttons, in silver and copper. Based in New York, she uses a variety of enamelling techniques, with particularly wonderful *cloisonné* examples. Christina Gore is an artist/ jeweller based in Melbourne, who I have the pleasure of knowing. Besides spending time behind the counter in 'buttonland', she dabbled in the fine art of enamelling when she was a Jewellery and Object

Plique à jour technique on these 29mm ⌀ Italian buttons from the 1990s.

Design student in Sydney. As with all makers, she is driven by the need to create, and hers is a pursuit that calms and nurtures the soul. These pieces are influenced by her love of flora and display the passion and skill with which she approaches her practice.

Ceramics

Ceramics and pottery are synonymous with each other, and both are terms that describe fired clay products. The differences in product lie with the differing amounts of metal oxides and organic matter (the chemical composition) within the clay itself, creating different qualities in the clay material. All clays have plasticity when wet (i.e. they can be moulded or shaped), and when fired at high temperatures the clay partially melts, the result being a hard, rock-like mass.

Earthenware, the earliest known clay material and one that can be fired at a lower temperature, contains iron and other mineral impurities that determine the colour of the fired end-product. The most popular colour today is terracotta, but it can also be brown, red, buff, mid grey and even white. The colour of stoneware clay, which fires at a higher temperature than earthenware, is affected by the type and temperature of firing — fired colours range from light grey and buff, to medium grey and brown. Both earthenware and stoneware remain porous after firing. These are often sealed with a glaze or slip, and fired again at a lower temperature to fuse the coating to the surface. Glazes can be powdered glass mixed with water (possibly coloured with metallic oxides), or clay mixed with water to form a slip. If these ceramics remain unglazed, the porous material can have the characteristic of being brittle and easily broken. To make the clay material more durable, the firing temperatures need to be about 1600°C

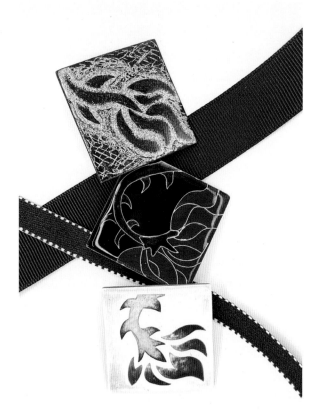

Enamel works on sterling silver by
Christina Gore, Melbourne, Australia.
From top to bottom, enamel styles: a
form of *grisaille; cloisonné; plique à jour.*

(2900°F) to convert it into a glass-like substance. This vitrification also creates a non-porous material.

Ancient ceramics have been found mostly as vessels and homewares, but decoration and adornment in jewellery and button-making does exist. Ceramic pieces, for example, were worn by the non-ruling classes in ancient Egypt, imitating the precious metal and gemstone jewellery and buttons worn by those in a higher social standing and for the same reasons of attracting good fortune. Ceramics had a lesser material cost and could be just as beautifully decorated with the use of coloured glazes.

Kaolin in its natural form consists principally of the mineral kaolinite, with varying amounts of the minerals feldspar, quartz, muscovite and anatase. As opposed to earthenware and stoneware, when fired it is a non-porous, translucent type of clay, varying in colour from very light grey to white. Brought to continental Europe and Britain by Dutch, Portuguese and other East India trading companies since the beginning of the sixteenth century, it was originally known as china or chinaware after the country where it was first discovered — research shows the first source of kaolin clay was mined in Kao-ling in the Kiangsi Province of China as early as the eleventh century. It became known as porcelain after the French word *porcelaine*, which came from the Italian *porcellana* or 'cowrie shell' because of its resemblance to the dense, polished shells.

Clay is the basic material of all types of pottery, but while porcelain is a type of pottery, not all pottery is porcelain. True porcelain is known as 'hard paste' as it requires hard firing at very high temperatures, after which it becomes extraordinarily dense. The secret of this hard paste product was closely guarded by the Chinese, who

True porcelain is known as 'hard paste' as it requires hard firing at very high temperatures, after which it becomes extraordinarily dense.

were willing to sell their products but not the knowledge of its making. Porcelain was tremendously popular in Europe, but the hazards and costs of transportation led many local potters to experiment with glazes and clays in an attempt to reproduce it, with partial success.

Fired earthenware, which became known as faience, majolica and delft, was successful in reproducing the look, with its white background. Introduced through Moorish Spain, it was produced in Italy, Spain and the Netherlands respectively in the sixteenth and seventeenth centuries. This art of 'tin-glazing' produced a decorated, opaque white background — the fired earthenware is first coated with a raw (unfired) glaze, then decorated with high-temperature colours and then fired a second time, fusing the pigments and glaze.

Venetian potters and glassmakers collaborated in the development of a new ware that became known as Medici porcelain, and were the first in Europe to produce a look-a-like product to the Chinese one. By the end of the sixteenth century, most European

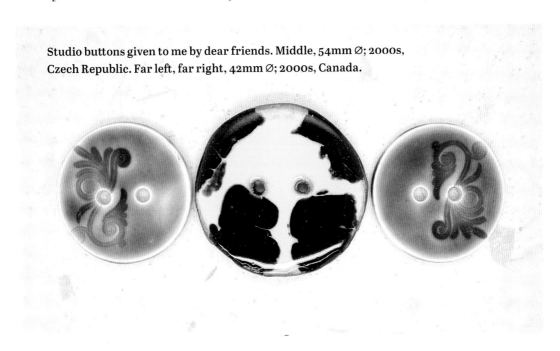

Studio buttons given to me by dear friends. Middle, 54mm Ø; 2000s, Czech Republic. Far left, far right, 42mm Ø; 2000s, Canada.

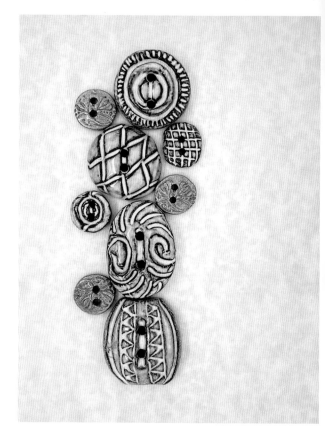

ABOVE: A series of buttons made by a village in Peru, depicting landscapes, harvest, sun and fauna, white clay and glazed. Terracotta owl deity, 28mm long; 1990s.

BELOW: Naïve two-hole sew-through buttons in coloured oxides, small studio production. Large blue button, 30mm ∅; 1990s, Australia.

ABOVE: Earthenware buttons with a semi-transparent glaze. Large oval, 30mm long; 1990s, Europe.

BELOW: Faience, of sorts. Large oval button, 40mm long; 1990s, Europe.

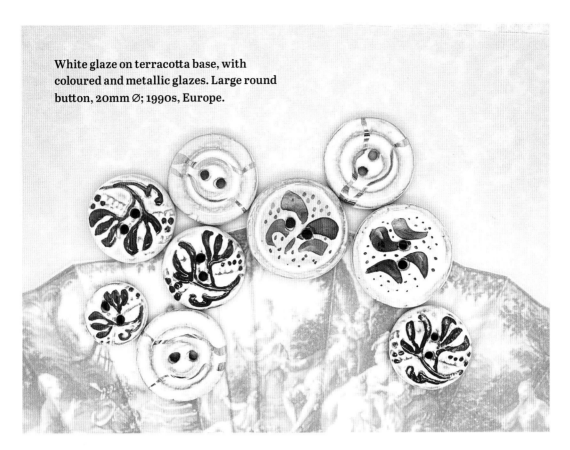

White glaze on terracotta base, with coloured and metallic glazes. Large round button, 20mm Ø; 1990s, Europe.

countries were making such products, with glass powder being the vitrifying additive. While a similar look was produced, the clay fired at a lower temperature — this became known as 'soft paste' porcelain as it was not as dense as true porcelain. In spite of this, by the mid-eighteenth century the French pottery Sèvres became famous for their delicate soft paste wares including teeth, thimbles and a limited production of buttons.

The invention of true porcelain in Europe is credited to two Germans, Ehrenfried Walter von Tschirnhaus and his charge, Johann Friedrich Böttger, resulting in the establishment of the royal factory, Meissen, in 1710. The Meissen factory took great pains to protect their secret, but by the mid-eighteenth century the rest of Europe was producing hard paste porcelains — soft paste porcelain was no longer required and none was made past 1800. By the end of the eighteenth century, the Royal Porcelain Factory of Copenhagen was producing more buttons of hard paste porcelain than any other European factory.

From the middle of the eighteenth century, the British were conducting their own experiments to find a replacement for Chinese porcelain. From the 1750s, Staffordshire potters made headway with fine white earthenware, called creamware due to its rich creamy glaze; Josiah Wedgewood had great commercial success with this clay, but continued his investigations in pursuit of porcelain. During this experimental phase,

Mass produced porcelain buttons from 1990s (goose, round) and small studio production (polka dotted) from 2020s. Large round blue with brass bezel, 28mm ∅; 1990s, China.

Ceramic buttons with oxide glazes. Large spiral button, 29mm ∅; 1990s, Europe.

he pioneered jasperware, a type of fine-grained earthenware that parallels the natural stone jasper in its hardness, but is white in colour and left in its bisque form.

Meanwhile, the British carried on with their examination of soft paste porcelains, using bone ash in an attempt to improve hardness. By 1800, Josiah Spode II introduced a formula of hard paste porcelain using finely ground calcined animal bone, the formula of which is still in use in today's fine bone china. In contrast to the bluish white porcelains from China and now Europe, bone china has a creamy white colour while maintaining its translucence.

Decoration of ceramic buttons

There are a few varying methods of decoration that can be used in the production of ceramic buttons. Processes better suited to studio ceramics involve carving or incising, the technique of *sgraffito* (scratching the surface to reveal another contrasting one below), the use of coloured clay slips, and coloured metallic oxides. Coloured glazes, whether transparent or opaque, can be used for interesting results. The method of tin-

Transfer printed decals on white ceramic buttons. 22mm Ø; 2000s.

Imitation Wedgewood oval button (plastic), and porcelain button with stamped pattern. Round, 36mm Ø, 2010s, Australia.

glazing was rarely used for buttons; instead, colours were hand-painted over the pre-glazed items, and fired lightly to adhere them to the surface.

The method of transfer printing was developed in Britain in the mid-eighteenth century, first used commercially by John Sadler and Guy Green to decorate pottery made by several factories, notably that of Josiah Wedgewood. The designs were printed onto tissue paper, then transferred to the glazed surface and fired again. Small details could be added by hand if desired, and this method largely replaced designs painted solely by hand except in special circumstances.

A decorative technique introduced by Wedgewood was his use of jasperware in two colours: the natural colour white was used in relief decoration applied to a body of coloured jasperware, originally stained throughout with metallic oxide colours, and then fired together. The most popular colour, pale blue, became known as Wedgewood blue; other colours included black, dark blue, lilac, sage and sea green, and especially rare buff and yellow. These original cameo style medallions caught the eye of industrialist Matthew Boulton, who ordered them as inlays for his cut steel buttons in

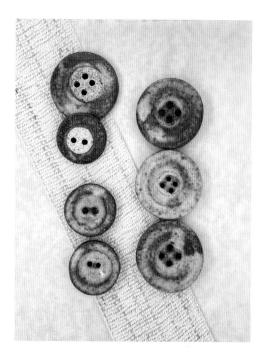

Ceramic buttons, moulded by hand, large size, 27mm ⌀.

1773. Others would set these in gold or silver frames (real or plated), or crystal and mother of pearl surrounds. Later, Wedgewood would produce frameless buttons complete with self-shank. They were commercially desirable, and although imitated by others they were referred to after their inventor as the Wedgewood button, remaining popular from their outset near the late eighteenth century until around 1820.

With the industrial age well and truly entrenched in society, processes were sought to mass-produce ceramic buttons. Previously, clay had been shaped by hand and put in moulds, but by 1840, Birmingham man Richard Prosser patented a new dry process: materials including fine clay and/or ceramic waste, quartz, feldspar, flint, were ground to a powder with a small amount of moisture, pressed into two halves of a cast iron mould and forced together at a pressure of 200 pounds per square inch, then placed into a muffle furnace (a kiln with an outside heat source). These were fired at high enough temperatures to vitrify the clay ingredients into buttons that performed much like the hardwearing Chinese porcelain and became known by collectors as 'chinas' or 'small chinas'. The buttons are glass-like in their appearance and often mistakenly identified as such, with smooth topside, a rougher underside described as 'orange peel', and noticeable side seams where the two parts have come together in the mould. They are, however, neither porcelain nor glass and are referred to by archaeologists as Prosser buttons to avoid confusion. While Prosser buttons have, under microscopic investigation, the same chemical composition as glass, their crystalline structure (not found in glass) places them in the ceramics category. Because of their smooth edges around the holes, they were preferable to glass sew-through buttons, which had sharper edges on the holes and a tendency to cut the thread they were sewn on with.

The advantages of this new machinery allowed for the mass production of small two, three, and four-hole sew-through buttons, as well as spherical gaiter and shoe buttons, whereby a hole was moulded at the back for the insertion of a metal shank. The manufacture was taken up by Minton potteries at Stoke-on-Trent, followed by other British potteries, from 1840. In the following year of 1841, in Patterson, New Jersey, Thomas Prosser (brother of Richard) took out a patent for 'improvements to manufacturing of buttons', with buttons manufactured by the Prosser method by Charles Cartlidge & Co in 1844. In 1843, a Frenchman, Jean-Felix Bapterosses, travelled to Britain and worked in the Minton pottery, learning the Prosser technique. He returned to France after gaining sufficient understanding of the procedure, and in 1844 he developed and patented a machine and process that could exceed the output of the British makes, setting up a factory in 1845, which would eventually settle in Briare in 1851. Bapterosses' method included the addition of milk, in the form of casein, as a wet binder and to improve the plasticity of the clay.

Plain colour buttons made in the Prosser method were mostly manufactured with white bodies, but colours of pink, ochre, green, blue and black were introduced in France from 1848/49, the high firing attaining a glassy self-glaze appearance. Decorated buttons were fired at a lower temperature to protect the decoration, requiring a second glazing and final firing. Transfer printing was used to create tiny

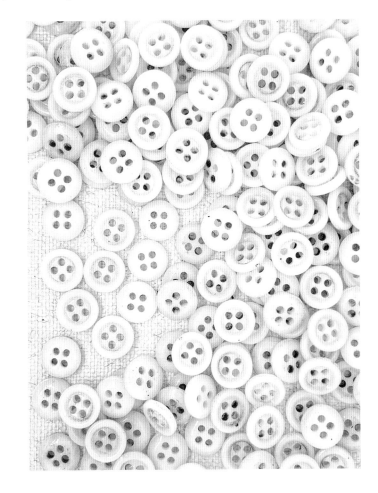

Prosser buttons are often mistaken for glass, but the edge and thread holes are smooth. 11mm Ø; nineteenth century, Europe.

Shiro-Satsuma buttons from
the 1950s, 16mm Ø; Japan.

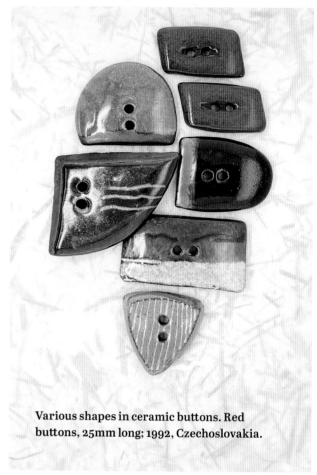

Various shapes in ceramic buttons. Red
buttons, 25mm long; 1992, Czechoslovakia.

repetitive patterns similar to the calico fabrics popular at the time, known by collectors as 'calicoes'. Other finishes include pearl and lustre colour, hand-painted rings and brushstrokes, stencil use applied by spray, fine splatter or stiff brush process, among others. The more complex gingham (known in France as *écossals*) were more labour intensive — crossbars and plaid patterns were spread over the body in a sticky medium, with enamels sponged, sprinkled or sifted over the top and the excess removed.

At its peak, the Minton factory produced 720,000 buttons per week, not enough to supply demand for these popular buttons. Bapterosses' equipment could produce 500 buttons at a single pressing; with new coal burning furnaces, improvements to the shank button process, and running 30 kilns per day, French production exceeded 1 million buttons per week. British production could not compete with the low-cost French imports, and as a consequence Minton pottery wound up button production in 1846 and all other factories ceased production by 1850. Bapterosses continued successfully until the introduction of plastic buttons took over the mass market in the 1950s and 1960s and halted the manufacture of the Prosser buttons.

Satsuma ware, *Satsuma yaki* in Japanese, has a history going back to the late sixteenth century. Pottery played an important role in Japanese tradition, especially among the elite, who coveted pieces of immense beauty to use during rituals such as the tea ceremony. When Japanese ruler, Toyotomi Hideyoshi, invaded the Korean peninsula, his representatives from the Satsuma region brought back 80 Korean potters. These artisans worked continually throughout the Edo period (1603–1868), creating the white *shiromon*, or *Shiro-Satsuma* exclusively for the noble class, and the black *kuromon*, or *Kuro-Satsuma* for the commoners.

It wasn't until after US Naval Commodore Matthew Perry entered present-day Tokyo in 1852 that the Western world was exposed to this art form. With huge interest in their handcrafts, including ceramics, the Japanese ramped up production especially for the export market, sending pieces for inclusion to the Paris *Exposition Universelle* in 1867. They became immensely popular, sparking the movement of *Japonisme*, a French term referring to the influence of Japanese art and design on western Europe in the nineteenth century. The origin of the Satsuma button can be linked to this event, a fusion between East and West. Buttons of old Satsuma were not well known by the Japanese, but rather produced as a means of trade with the Western world.

The original and most desired buttons were produced during the Meiji period (1868–1912), made in Kyoto and decorated in Tokyo. A mixture of clays, kneaded, dissolved in water and the sediment left to dry, produced the fine grains from which the smooth surfaces could be achieved. Their features are a cream-coloured body with an ivory white, deliberately crackled glaze face, made by allowing the clay mass to cool faster than the glaze. They are decorated in multicoloured enamels, and earlier specimens have a characteristic fine gold dot pattern in the background and/or heavy gold ornamentation. Common themes of decoration were flowers, people, dragons, birds, insects and Japanese scenes. Unfortunately, their success led to a decrease in quality through mass production; shortcuts with decoration, including lack of gold

Pottery played an important role in Japanese tradition, especially among the elite, who coveted pieces of immense beauty to use during rituals such as the tea ceremony.

dotted background and/or gold encrustation, led consumers to lose interest by the 1930s. In the 1950s and 1960s, Satsuma buttons were custom-made for collectors, with some Western-inspired designs alongside the traditional, after which the number of artisans of this fine craft dwindled and eventually all producers disappeared.

In 2005, Japanese artist Shiho Murota revived the craft of ceramic Satsuma buttons. After working as a ceramic painter in a *Shiro-Satsuma* teaware specialist pottery for ten years, by chance she saw some antique Satsuma buttons in a magazine article that led her to explore further at a museum in Tokyo. She left her work to set up her own studio, practising her craft for three years before becoming confident enough to work on this miniature canvas. Her first solo exhibition in 2007 in Japan drew much critical acclaim among art enthusiasts, prompting her to continue with further exhibitions. In 2015, Murota participated in the annual convention of the National Button Society in America. The care and attention she brings to her craft means she produces a mere 30 to 50 buttons per month. Customers often wait a year for their order, with some purchasing in the expectation that they are acquiring a valuable collectible.

Studio buttons from the 1950s. Large button, self-shank with blue and silver glaze, 45mm ∅.

Studio potteries have often made buttons, either as their only product or as a sideline to their other wares. Lucie Rie was one of the most well-known of the studio potters to have produced buttons as a means of income for a short period after World War II. Her buttons adorned many designers' collections due to her ability to match the glazes to the fabrics that were brought to her. Rie's buttons were so popular that demand exceeded supply; together with her assistant, Rudolf Neufeld, a fellow refugee, they developed a series of plaster moulds to escalate their fabrication. Her button creations were highly sought after during World War II, selling in stores such as Harrods and Liberty — at the height of production her team of now eighteen émigrés produced 6000 buttons per month. Although she denigrated the worth of her buttons, many credit her experience during this time with honing her skills in developing the original glazes that covered her later, distinctive pottery work. In 1980, Japanese fashion designer Issey Miyake befriended Lucie Rie and was inspired to make clothing for her; in return, she gifted him a collection of her ceramic buttons from the 1950s. These inspired his 1989 autumn/winter collection, with Lucie Rie buttons featuring on his oversized collars. Miyake and Rie's friendship survived until her death at the age of 93, and she bequeathed many of the original moulds for her button-making to her friend.

I came across a supply of buttons that were made in Australia during the early 1940s. During the years of World War II, many materials were requisitioned for the war effort. With its close British ties, Australia was no exception. I can only offer the oral history that was passed on to me by

Aristocrat buttons,
Australia. Square button,
35mm x 35mm.

Large manufacturers and small studios create ceramic buttons of all shapes and sizes, around the globe. Multicoloured stripe button in porcelain, 29mm ⌀; 1990s.

the seller: an enterprising mother and daughter, who owned a dressmaking business in Sydney's eastern suburb of Rose Bay, started making their own ceramic buttons from white earthenware clay, glazed in various colours, with gilded accents. Unfortunately, the cards marked 'The "Aristocrat" Finest Quality' had not been stored well, and all have mildew on the paper, but the buttons themselves, press moulded and hand painted, have survived intact.

Ceramic buttons made a commercial resurgence in the late twentieth century. In the 1980s, Jennifer Pascall started making ceramic buttons at her home in Johannesburg, South Africa. Under the name of Incomparable handmade buttons, the designs centre around African animals and abstract shapes and are sold worldwide. The technique of firing multiple times at very high temperatures allows for machine washing and dry cleaning. In the United States, the descendant of the Coors brewery founder, Joe Coors Jr., instructed the ceramics unit of the Adolph Coors Company to create some indestructible buttons specifically for men's shirts. The idea came after Coors read an article in 1989 about the number of disgruntled customers whose buttons had broken under the conditions of commercial laundering. Coors Ceramicon Designs Ltd (which makes components for cars, computers, bullet-proof vests, among others)

Contemporary studio pottery buttons remain a popular item, especially among the artisan community. They have a wonderful way of enhancing a handcrafted project, especially handknits or items using handwoven fabrics — the two seem made for each other.

came up with a ceramic button made from zirconium oxide, fired at a temperature of 1760°C (3200°F). They were available in a limited colour range and sold to high-end shirtmakers in the United States. However, their higher price range (fifteen times the cost of a regular shirt button) was their downfall and they were only produced between 1993 and 1999.

Contemporary studio pottery buttons remain a popular item, especially among the artisan community. They have a wonderful way of enhancing a handcrafted project, especially handknits or items using handwoven fabrics — the two seem made for each other.

Buttons made from cloth and fibres were, and still are, an important area of button manufacturing. Various styles from around the world: large black button, 44mm Ø, 1960s, Europe.

5

Cloth and fibre buttons

I CAN'T CUT OUT A PIECE OF CLOTH AND MAKE A LOVELY DRESS, BUT I CAN MEND TEARS IN SHIRTS AND SEW ON BUTTONS.

—JOANNA LUMLEY, BRITISH ACTOR

When I was five, I discovered needlework and knitting when my maternal grandmother came to visit. It was the one and only opportunity I had to spend time with her. She brought with her a wondrous array of lingerie items from her factory in Brazil, where she owned a manufacturing business and exported goods throughout South America. She taught me to crochet and to knit. I loved casting on; it was magical to watch her hands as she effortlessly moved them in a rhythmic dance, and I soon followed suit. While I never actually made anything, it was surprising to discover that a sequence of movements produced the cardigans that I wore. I did take to crochet, however — it was faster and could produce quicker results.

Not long after, I was introduced to embroidery, this time by my neighbours, an endearing elderly couple whose home I frequented. One day, as I was busy discharging snails from his prize-winning chrysanthemums, she called me inside and revealed a trunk full of embroidery patterns and wool. I started one under her instruction, and

Embroidered embellishments on cloth-covered buttons are always delightful. The embroidery may be done beforehand and then covered, or they may be embellished after covering — necessary if any beads or protuberances are to be added. Large grey button with bullion roses, 31mm Ø, 2011.

afterwards she allowed me to take more, one at a time. I was prolific — I managed to get through many in her trunk of wonders, and it is something I enjoy to this day. In the following years, I also dabbled in beadwork, macramé, needlepoint, spinning and weaving, and was a proficient sewer, so I felt well informed in the processes of the various cloth-based buttons I encountered as an adult.

Historical evidence of ancient cultures using cloth buttons has not been found, possibly because of the degradation of the fibres, or because they did not exist. However, when the garments worn as everyday clothing by men of the Ottoman Empire found their way to Europe (through returning Crusaders), the fascination with their long rows of buttons was a turning point in the evolution of fashion. Laces, strings, ropes and knots previously used to keep European clothing in place now remained in the realm of the underprivileged and women, while more affluent men in society preferred the button.

Twelfth-century buttons could be easily made by shaping small pieces of cloth or leather into a ball. The nature of humans, and the need for adornment, led to other materials being used to create what were firstly necessary items, but soon became more frivolous and ornamental. Ornamentation soon began to transcend the limits of social class systems, and laws were put in place to make sure no one breached their social standing or caused offence with overtly ostentatious clothing and embellishments. Both governments and the church regulated the colours of fabrics for use; religious orders were confined to more muted colours, with buttons made only from regulated colours of cloth. The less affluent were also confined to buttons made only of cloth. Cloth and fibres nevertheless became materials with which to create stunning buttons in later centuries — linen, cotton, wool and silk were among the fabrics used.

Linen, cotton, wool and silk

Linen is one of the oldest textiles in the world. Derived from the fibres of the flax plant, woven linen fibres from wild flax and dating from 34,000 BC have been found at Dzudzuana Cave in Georgia, as well as in lake dwellings of prehistoric Switzerland dated to around 8000 BC. Known to the ancient cultures of Mesopotamia and Egypt, linen was a high-cost fabric reserved for the higher classes. Ancient Egyptians also used it for mummification and burial shrouds. To procure the fibre, the stalks of the plant undergo a series of processes: a wet fermentation process releases the fibre from the stem, followed by drying, crushing and beating. The resulting woven fabric is stronger and dries more quickly than cotton, is less affected by sunlight exposure, and gets softer with repeated laundering. The Phoenician merchant fleet brought the knowledge of flax growing, and the making of linen, to Ireland, which subsequently became the most

Before the advent of covered button equipment, cloth bud and flat buttons were made by hand. These hand-worked cloth buttons show two styles, one bud-type button, and one flatter style. Bud-style button: Step 1: cut a large round of fabric and make a wide basting stitch around the circumference. Step 2: pull the stitching to gather, flatten and secure in place with a few stiches; use a wide basting stitch to again gather the remaining fabric, tucking the fabric in to create a ball. Step 3: sew the bud closed, in an opposing clockface sequence to make a good shape — 6 (o'clock) and 12 position, 3 and 9 position, and so on. Flat-covered button: Step 1: as for bud-style button, but using a slightly smaller round of fabric. Step 2: insert any flat object, gather the stitches together and secure. Step 3: as above.

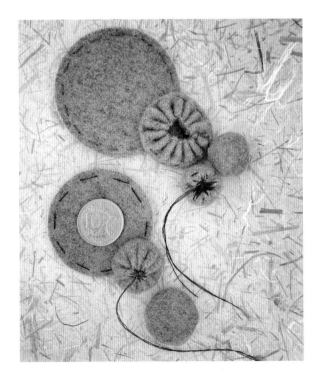

famous linen-producing centre in history — during the Victorian era, they produced the majority of the world's linen.

Cotton is a soft and fluffy, almost pure cellulose, staple fibre that grows around the seeds of the cotton plant. Cotton fibre was used in fabrics by several civilizations, concurrently and independently, in both the Old and New Worlds — from at least 5000 BC in Pakistan, and from 4500 BC in Peru and 3600 BC in Mexico. The Muslim conquest of Spain in the eighth century brought cotton to the European countries, and during the Middle Ages hand-woven cotton fabric was commonly used. During the Renaissance, imported Indian cotton reached Europe — new trading routes by sea, first discovered by Vasco da Gama (Portugal) in 1497, allowed for larger shipments than could previously be made by land. Over the centuries, the concern for cleanliness and fashion, especially among the middle class, gave rise to the popularity of colourful cotton fabrics that were easily washable. The secrets of the Indian craftsmen were eventually revealed to European industry, and together with new inventions and the Industrial Revolution, they rivalled the Indian textiles. By the 1830s, the United States manufactured most of the world's cotton.

Wool is a fibre derived from sheep. Some other animals also produce wool: from goats it is known as cashmere or mohair; from musk oxen, known as qiviut; from rabbits, known as angora. As a fabric, wool's bulky nature causes it to retain air, and as a consequence it is an insulator from the cold, and from the heat. It is easy to spin — the independent fibres attach to each other and stay together. Early domesticated sheep (9000–7000 BC) were more hairy than woolly, and wool breeding by selection began around 6000 BC. At about the same time as the first garments were woven (around

Modern felted wool buttons, handcrafted. Wool felt is very sturdy and can be made into various shapes and decoration — such as these flower, heart, oval and round examples — and can be sewn through, or at the bottom quarter as a self-shank. Round button, 20mm Ø; 2000s.

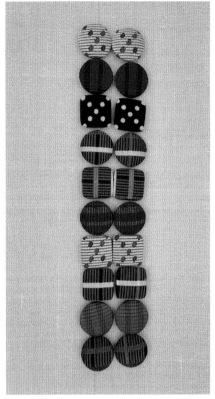

ABOVE: Silk corded button in Death's Head formation. Large button, 38mm ∅; nineteenth century, Europe.

RIGHT: Italian silks remain a sought-after textile, with luxurious textures and an explosion of colours. Men's ties were the source material for these covered buttons, commissioned as an insert into matching cufflinks. Silk tie fabrics, 15mm ∅.

4000–3000 BC), woolly sheep were introduced to Europe from the Near East. In Roman times, the finest wool came from the south of Italy, and by the medieval period wool was a serious business. Major players in the wool trade were England, Castile (Spain) and the city of Florence (Italy). Royal permission was granted for the export of Spain's merino sheep during the sixteenth century, and after the mid-seventeenth century fine English wool competed with silk on the international market. In time, Germany overtook the English market, and in 1797 merino sheep were first introduced to Australia, whose market eventually overtook that of Germany.

Silk is a natural protein filament fibre derived from the mulberry silkworm. Silk fabric has been dated from 4000 BC to 3000 BC in Egypt, but the history of silk textile manufacturing began in China in the second millennium BC. With the opening of the Silk Route around 130 BC, silk began its spread throughout the world; cultivation started in Japan in 300 AD, and eventually began in Korea and India. When the Byzantines obtained silkworm eggs and began silkworm cultivation in 522 AD, the silk industry in the Eastern Roman empire emerged, spreading across Western Europe with the returning Crusaders. In the modern age, Italian silk manufacture was concentrated in the north of the country, which became the early leader in European production through innovations in silk processing; by the late fifteenth century, 15,000 people were employed in the industry in Milan. Italian silk cloth was luxurious and expensive, and production could not keep up with the demands of French fashion, which sought lighter-weight, less expensive fabrics. In 1466 King Louis XI chose the city of Lyon in which to develop France's silk industry, but it was under King Francis I that production really took off. A royal charter was granted to two Italian merchants to develop silk production, and by 1540 Lyon was granted the monopoly of silk manufacture in France, making it the capital of the European silk trade.

The dawning of the Renaissance era

The Renaissance brought many changes to medieval Europe. The concepts spread further west from Italy, where they were adopted particularly in France, Flanders (now known as Belgium and the Netherlands), England and Spain. Merchant sailors from Spain, Portugal and especially Italy explored both east and west, bringing back new textiles and precious metals; this new wealth brought new fashions.

Until 1501, Italy was the centre for fashion. The country's craftsmen had a vast knowledge of the manufacture of rich textiles, including brocades; together with embroidery and needlework skills, citizens of the capital cities in particular were very well dressed. Late fifteenth century fashion for men, which continued into the sixteenth century, consisted of a white silk shirt which was richly embroidered around the neck and wrists, close-fitted hose to show off masculine legs, and a figure-hugging, hip length tunic (later known as doublet) with a central row of several buttons to the waist. During the next two decades, this Italian style spread throughout the rest of Europe, changing and adapting to different cultures and climates. The rich array of fabrics and colours from Italy were translated in northern Europe to more sombre, darker colours in heavier fabrics, as other European countries began to take the lead in the style of dress. Despite the changes, garments from the mid-sixteenth and into the early seventeenth century were some of the richest ever seen in European dress — extensively patterned clothing was embellished with embroidery, lace, pearls and jewels.

By 1620, styles had changed significantly. Previously, the Europeans had adopted the elegant and formal, yet restrictive, clothing of the Spanish, whose conquests of the New World had brought newfound wealth. Men's doublets had made the change to end at the waist, the skirt of which was replaced by loose, mid-thigh length hose, often padded (bombasted) to add bulk and create the fashionable silhouette of the time.

Bombast was made from various materials, and no doubt was uncomfortable. While the Spanish maintained a restrained, dignified, mostly black palette, the European countries that embraced their style did so with the gusto of excess. It's no wonder that after so many years, the new century eventually brought a trend for softer, more comfortable clothing. Rich fabrics and intricate design were still valued, but over-embellishment was limited. Loose-fitting, yet elegant clothing was the new normal.

With sumptuary laws in some form or another being imposed across Europe and England, ingenuity in button design came about with the use of threads from all types of fibre. Covering buttons in the same rich fabric as the garment was an easy way for the rising middle class to adorn their clothing. Common people wore buttons made from wood or bone, and these materials eventually became the foundations for thread-wrapped buttons and embellished *passementerie* buttons. The bone inserts were used for smaller sized buttons, and wood used for larger sizes; the moulds were shaped and a hole cut through the middle. For thread-wrought buttons, a threaded needle was put

Handwoven buttons using silk thread or fine cord, with which various shaped inserts and weaving techniques produce different designs. All have a collection of knotted threads from which to sew through for attachment. Large black square, 66mm ⌀; twentieth and 21st centuries, various countries.

With sumptuary laws in some form or another being imposed across Europe and England, ingenuity in button design came about with the use of threads from all types of fibre.

through the hole from below, and the thread was progressively wrapped around the core until covered. Different patterns and/or colours could be used for effect. In England from the early 1600s, a considerable number of people were engaged in the making of these buttons. Birmingham produced the horn and bone inserts as well as thread-wrought buttons; Leek produced buttons using various fibres, and thread-wrought buttons were the primary product coming from the developing silk industry in Leek from the end of the seventeenth century until the late eighteenth century. In England, it was the beginning of a button industry.

France becomes the fashion leader

France now took over as the fashion leader, especially after Louis XIV took the throne; he was a man who favoured the arts, style and elegance in all aspects of life. The country became the leader in the production of luxury goods in Europe, its cities producing silk, lace and brocades, all of which were extensively sold to other countries. At the same time, they exported their clothing designs through newly established fashion publications.

It was an era when all and any type of material was used in the making of buttons, and the beginning of the button as a fashion accessory; buttons that were previously intended for a person were increasingly made for a garment. Before, precious buttons were easily removed and transferred from garment to garment; now they were firmly attached. Buttons were covered in lavish fabrics or further embellished with embroidery, and *passementerie* and embroidered buttons either matched the clothing, or enhanced it. *Passementerie* is a French word for a decorative trimming made from cord,

Handcrafted *passementerie* buttons produced in the mid to late twentieth century, and modern interpretations from the 2000s. All are made using silk threads, cord and/or ribbon. Large brown, 34mm ∅; Spain, 2000s.

Cloth buttons were very popular, less expensive, and the quality of English metal buttons declined during the time of imposed monopoly in the field.

braid, beads, etc. in any and various forms. While English speakers do not commonly know the word, it is still in use today and, in the case of buttons, refers to any buttons trimmed with cord, braid, gimp, beads, embroidery, among others, although it does not refer to ordinary fabric-covered buttons.

Substantial amounts of French *passementerie* buttons were exported to other countries, including England. During the reign of William III and Mary II (1689–1702), English metal button-makers petitioned the parliament, who duly prohibited the import of all foreign buttons made with fibre. In 1721, Leek and other Cheshire towns successfully petitioned parliament on behalf of their needle-wrought button-makers, this time asking for a ban on cloth buttons and buttonholes. Fines were imposed on imported covered buttons sold in sets or fixed on garments. This was intended to save the work of thousands of men, women and children involved in their manufacture, including the associated work of producing raw materials for the said button trade. It's interesting to note that decades later, during the reign of George III (1727–60), it was the Birmingham metal button-makers who petitioned against their own cloth button-makers; while laws were applied in favour of the metalworkers, they were difficult to impose since most of the public ignored the regulations. Cloth buttons were very popular, less expensive, and the quality of English metal buttons declined during the time of imposed monopoly in the field. English producers of gilded buttons, now having exclusive right of manufacture, made adjustments to their gold content with disastrous results. This contributed to the rise in popularity of fibre and cloth-covered buttons.

Fashion and innovation

A cottage industry of common thread buttons arose in mid-eighteenth century England, centred on the county of Dorset. Predominantly crafted by lacemakers, these handmade buttons consisted of a wire ring wrapped with thread; the outer ring was completely covered, after which a 'cartwheel' pattern of spokes was created. The

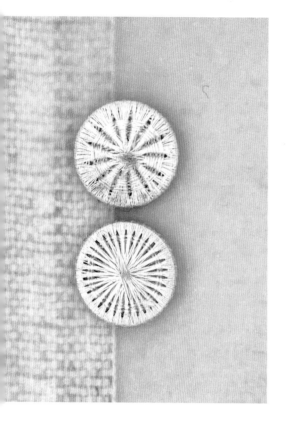

LEFT: Dorset-style button, now often referred to as Heirloom buttons, shown here front and back. 15mm ∅; twentieth century, Europe.

OPPOSITE: Covered button in silk jacquard, hidden on the jacquard fabric. Silk thread-wrought buttons on wooden base, 33mm ∅, nineteenth century, Europe.

simplest versions were gathered in the centre to create a thread shank; more elaborate weaving could embellish these buttons further. These were mainly used for the evolving underwear fashions, or for household linen.

Meanwhile, on continental Europe, French fashion remained the model to aspire to, and was a major influence on fabric-covered and *passementerie* buttons. Garments had increasing numbers of buttons, enhancing sleeve and pocket decoration as well as the full extent of the now longer, knee-length dress coats of the day. In Italy, many buttons made use of the techniques of the embroiderers and braid producers: threads of gold, silver, silk and other fibres were worked over a bone or wooden mould displaying the imagination and hand skills of the artisans involved. Tailors were given the task of producing covered buttons made from the exquisite cloths of the garments they were to enhance, making the ordinary extraordinary. European cloth and fibre buttons could rival their more precious counterparts, and steadily more button-makers took over from the jewellers and goldsmiths in the production of fine adornment for clothing. After the fall of the Venetian Empire, many Italian artisans moved to France, bringing with them their skills in all aspects of button-making. As the eighteenth century progressed and the 'fashion' of clothing permeated society, garments, and buttons, no longer marked the social standing of an individual, but rather one's ability to pay for such luxuries.

The Industrial Revolution led to huge advances in the textile industry with innovations in preparation and spinning, but in regard to silk, a naturally

occurring thread, progress was made in other ways, namely the simplification and standardization of silk manufacture, and the invention of the Jacquard loom. Joseph-Marie Jacquard, a French weaver and merchant, perfected a revolutionary machine that could mass-produce the elegant, sought after patterned silk cloth and ribbons favoured by the fashionable, making them affordable to a wider section of society. The introduction of the Jacquard loom was an important influence in textile history and, as a consequence, on the production of covered buttons. A series of punch cards with varying hole patterns was fitted to the top of the loom, and pins attached to the warp threads were lifted when they passed through a hole. This was a revolution in pattern programming, where the only limitation was the pattern designer's imagination. In the case of buttons, intricate patterns could be woven in detail, over and over again, and used for making elegant covered buttons. The technology spread across Europe, and by 1820 had reached Britain, boosting the rapidly growing cotton textile industry.

The increasing application of science to industry sought increased production with smaller

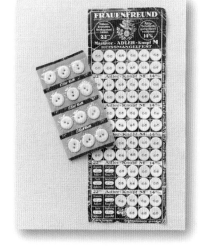

LEFT: Mass-produced buttons for underwear and household linen were affordable, readily available and considered women's friend — '*Frauenfreund*'. We were still able to purchase these Elite Prym buttons in the 1980s. Both German-made, 14mm Ø and 15mm Ø.

The fine fibre of raffia may be dyed in colours and used to wrap moulds, as in this exquisite example. Rattan is a much coarser fibre, eventuating in a more basket-type weave. Rattan button, 23mm Ø; 1990s, Germany.

In 1825, Benjamin Sanders Jr patented the process of using a flexible linen shank in place of the rusty steel, or decaying catgut, shanks. These were very successful and mechanised the industry of cloth-covered buttons.

expenditure of human energy, bringing further changes to the cloth button industry. In Birmingham, the evolution of covered buttons began during the nineteenth century, when in 1813 businessman, Benjamin Sanders, patented a system of manufacture in covering buttons using a two-part metal mould with steel shank, produced mechanically. He later moved his firm to nearby Bromsgrove, and together with his son continued their improvements. In 1825, Benjamin Sanders Jr patented the process of using a flexible linen shank in place of the rusty steel, or decaying catgut, shanks. These were very successful and mechanised the industry of cloth-covered buttons. Another innovation came about in 1841, when a patent by Birmingham's Humphrey Jeffries improved on the covered button, allowing for the cloth to cover the sides and face as well as introducing a completely cloth-covered sew-through button, what is now known as the 'threefold linen button'. This button replaced the hand-worked Dorset button, and millions were produced particularly for underwear and household linens.

The Victorian era and beyond

The changing dress of men and women from the latter half of the nineteenth century saw a big decline in thread-wrought buttons in Britain, with the buttons from Leek and surrounding areas now in decline. The death of Prince Albert saw Queen Victoria and the entire country descend into mourning; black silk taffeta-covered buttons were worn at the very least, but jet and black glass dominated the clothing of most, and eventually cloth-covered buttons declined in England.

However, the *passementerie* tradition remained strong in continental Europe and fabric buttons became more generally available. While Europe lagged behind Britain in embracing industrialized methods of production, companies in France, Belgium, Italy and Germany made innovations in their production to include more modern methods of manufacture. The mid-century advent of French haute couture saw women's buttons

Home button-covering kits are still readily available for consumer use, while varying sizes of button press are available on a more commercial level, from small hand-operated presses to larger pneumatic presses. Shown here are some of the button styles available for a hand press. Large blue button, 28mm Ø; 2022, Germany.

become ornamental, and *passementerie* and covered buttons, in the same colour or fabric as the dress, were popular — *Albert Parent et Cie* was well placed to produce these luxury buttons.

Germany not only experimented with methods of *passementerie* buttons, but also with the fibres used to cover them. Raffia fibre began being used in their button-making some time in the nineteenth century, and continued into the twentieth century until just after World War II. The strong, white raffia (or raphia) fibre comes from a species of palm trees from the family *Arecaceae*. They are huge in size and have some of the longest leaves in the world; the membrane on the underside of each frond leaf is removed, creating irregular widths of fibres up to 1.5 metres (just under 5 feet) long. The resulting strong, white fibre can be dyed and woven and, in the case of the German buttons, wrapped or stretched over a metal button mount. In the 1990s, I purchased some rattan buttons in a circular wicker pattern, from Germany. Although belonging to the same family (*Aracaceae*) with roughly 600 different species, rattan differs from raffia; while the latter is a fibre produced from the leaves, rattan is a type of climbing palm with a pliable woody stem. The outer skin of a strand of rattan is used for weaving, while the core is kept for furniture or construction.

By the early twentieth century, hand operated button-covering machines were manufactured by several companies, both in Britain and overseas, allowing for tailors and dressmakers to easily create perfectly formed, professional covered buttons without the need of hand sewing over a horn or wooden mould. Among, but not limited to, the companies successfully selling the machine presses, as well as manufacturing the dies and moulds, were the American Defiance Button Machine Company (established in 1886), the Handy Button Machine Company (established in 1898) and CC Metal Products Corporation (established in 1914), and in Germany, Astor-Berning GmbH & Co. (established 1919). Many of these companies now specialize their button covering mainly for the upholstery industry, but Astor-Berning covers the entire range — fashion and upholstery items. In 1960, American company Maxant Corporation patented home button-making kits as 'Miracle Buttons — Buttons to Cover by Maxant'; a set of moulds and small tools, which did not use a button press machine. This type of covered button became the standard for home use and is probably most familiar to consumers today.

Today, quality *passementerie* buttons are readily available from both large and small producers across Europe, and countries such as India and China, among others, are also supplying the needs of clothing designers. There has also been an increasing interest in the traditional techniques of the thread-wrought buttons of the seventeenth and eighteenth centuries, with many craft groups undertaking the fine art of heirloom button-making.

Modern interpretation of *passementerie*
buttons from Italy, using shoelace-type cord.
Large purple, 65mm ∅; 2000s.

Buttons made from natural materials may also
depict the natural world, in this case a stone
button made from wood, or a leaf button made
from bone. Large leaf, 33mm long; 2020s, India.

6

Buttons, naturally

I BELIEVE THE WORLD IS INCOMPREHENSIBLY
BEAUTIFUL, AN ENDLESS PROSPECT OF
MAGIC AND WONDER.
—ANSEL EASTON ADAMS, AMERICAN PHOTOGRAPHER

I can't think of anything more enticing than a long walk surrounded by nature. Pockets are a necessity in order to come home with small objects — a leaf, a feather, a pebble, a twisted root or twig. Their shapes and colours inspire me and fill the walls and ledges of my studio space. I like to imagine that the ancients were also so inspired, and the prehistoric artist who could make beautiful adornments was surely respected and admired. Anything that could be shaped or tooled could theoretically be used as an adornment or fastening. We know of button-like items that have been unearthed during excavations, made from bone, wood, teeth, stone and shell; some have seemed primitive, others have been heavily decorated. While button production evolved in a multitude of directions, encompassing new materials and techniques, making buttons from natural products remains an important part of today's industry.

Bone

Bone is a living tissue forming a skeleton within a body; collagen proteins create a soft connective framework and calcium phosphate minerals provide strength and harden

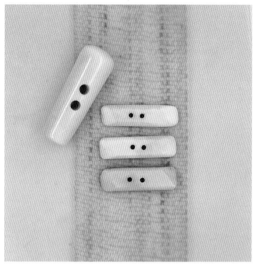

Bone buttons and toggle; toggles are turned on a lathe, while the elongated buttons are hand finished. Toggle, 32mm long; 2020s, India.

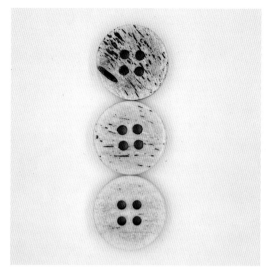

Simple four-hole sew-through bone buttons, each one showing the varying visibility of dark flecks. 23mm ∅; 2020s, India.

the structure. As a raw material, bone is both plentiful and readily available. Bones from larger animals can be very thick and suitable as a decorative carving material, and indeed, have been used so for thousands of years. Ancient cultures around the world have created objects (jewellery, amulets, etc.), tools and vessels from this organic matter. It can be easily carved with hand tools, and when polished it can be soft to the touch but retain its strength. Because of this, it is thought to be among the oldest of the materials used for button-making, especially after the introduction of the fastener to the European continent.

The processes used to create a bone blank suitable for button production, whether on a commercial or individual scale, are much the same. After cleaning the bones, they are boiled to soften them, then cut open with a saw. The soft tissue (marrow) is removed and the halves are pressed flat, either between two sheets of steel held together with clamps or by using a steel press. When the raw material is dry, blanks are cut for button-making in a 'cookie cutter' pattern. From the cut blanks, required thicknesses are sliced off. Slices cut closer to the outside of the bone are denser and ivory-like, while slices

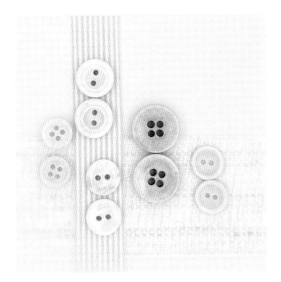

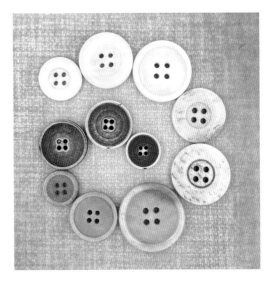

Small bone buttons such as these sew-through versions were used on undergarments for centuries. Small two-hole with rim, 10mm ∅; 1910s, Europe.

Bone suit buttons have once again become popular in recent years on quality men's clothing. This selection shows both polished and unpolished variations, in natural colour or henna or indigo dyed. Small buttons, 15mm ∅; 2020s, India.

cut closer to the hollow cavity are coarser and more porous. Because the connective tissues in the make-up of bones are supplied by tiny blood vessels, minute dark flecks are visible on polished bone. The shinbones of cattle are considered one of the better sources of raw material, but archaeological digs show that various types of bone have been used to produce buttons.

Perhaps some of the earliest buttons that emerged after their introduction to the European peoples were made from bone. As an ordinary raw material, commonly available in plentiful supply, primitively shaped buttons have been found in France dating back to the twelfth century. As buttons became more fashionable and extravagant, the lower classes could afford bone ones to at least get the quantity required to imitate their more affluent counterparts. Bone became one of the first raw material products to be mass-produced and sold, initially for rosary bead-making. The French town of Meru, and the surrounding area along the Loire Valley, was the main production area of European bone buttons. Millions of five-holed buttons were produced there during the eighteenth century, increasing to thousands of millions of four-holed examples from the nineteenth century. The expansion in mass production of this article corresponds to the changing attitudes towards clothing, especially as undergarments became increasingly popular. Utilitarian, inexpensive bone buttons were a perfect fit, as well as an economic saving for the upper classes who chose to display more expensive fastenings on their outer garments. They were also the fastener used on many uniforms of the infantry; considering the quantities involved, they were a definite cost-saving measure for the military forces.

Birmingham produced buttons from bone and wood from around the fourteenth century. Birmingham's transformation from an English rural manor in the eleventh century to a major trading area from the fourteenth century was the result of market forces — where raw materials were traded, craftsmen were attracted to set up shop.

The area not only produced simple buttons but primarily the blanks, or moulds, for the eventual fabric-covered and embroidered buttons as part of the Birmingham textile industry. Later, the moulds would be used for the pressed or cast metal bone-backed buttons of the eighteenth century. Catgut, often oversewn with cotton or linen thread, formed a shank when crossed through four-hole button blanks and knotted on the face; a generous amount of resin cement was placed on top, securing the knot and the covering of metal, which was then crimped over the bone mould.

In Sydney, Australia, archaeological digs have found evidence of colonial bone button manufacturing during excavations as part of the Parramatta Justice Precinct development. During the 1790s, the site held the second convict hospital and associated convict huts. Out of especially cut pieces of bone, buttons were shaped with a hand-held steel instrument, which created the circular form as well as a central hole. These single-holed buttons were either worked with thread, covered with fabric or drilled

Dyeing bone buttons highlights the natural characteristics of the product. Toggle button, 30mm long; 2020s, India.

Buttons created especially for the tourist market depicting insects or stories, in this case The City Mouse and the Country Mouse. Round buttons have an insert of etched bone on a wooden base, 37mm ⌀; late twentieth century, India.

with a further two or four holes (producing three- and five-holed buttons) to be used as the common sew-through type. It is assumed these were made by convicts living in the huts or recuperating in hospital, or by the leaseholders — buttons were needed to fasten the garments made by the female prison population, a large part of whom not only provided the convict clothing but also manufactured the cloth. From the same period and into the nineteenth century, evidence of bone buttons has been found in sites in Britain related to military or maritime use where forts, prison camps, prison hulks and shipwrecks occurred, and made by convicts, prisoners of war, slaves or lowly members of the military.

While not produced in nearly the same quantities as the sew-through variety, nineteenth century bone buttons with a metal shank were also popular. The disks were left plain or decorated with a simple ring engraving and fitted with a nail head, or stout pin, shank. Some metal-shanked bone buttons were fitted at the back with a drilled brass shank, the face either left blank or carved. Prisoners of war, biding their time, made some of these carved buttons — designs were simple, as bone was not considered a very desirable medium for carving by more affluent society, possibly because of its modest origin and common association. It was, however, used widely as a base for the more exclusive, and expensive, veneers of mother of pearl, tortoiseshell, ivory, ebony and horn. Bone buttons rarely have self-shanks, other than perhaps those made by ancient peoples, made out of necessity, or in more recent times, by the craft or tourist industry. Bone buttons have, and continue to be, dyed or inlaid with other materials. Bone does not give off an odour when heated, offering a handy way to prove that imitators are not the natural bone product.

Today, India is an important supplier of bone as a raw material, and bone (and horn) buttons and products. The product range for bone buttons is from ordinary shirt buttons or tailor's buttons for suits, to more elaborately carved and shaped buttons. In nearby Nepal, there is also a longstanding artisan tradition of handcrafts and needlework. I have been working with a Nepalese family who produce bone buttons and needlework accessories for more than twenty years; the quality of their workmanship has created a lasting bond and friendship.

Ivory

In contrast to the common, easily accessible material of bone, ivory sits at the opposite end of the scale. Due to its rarity, it holds an elevated place as a precious material, and as a consequence was among one of the oldest materials used for small sculptures, objects and amulets. Stone Age finds of mammoth ivory figurative carvings have been dated to around 38,000 BC, and elephant ivory from predominantly East Africa has supplied markets in the Mediterranean, Western Europe, the Persian Gulf, India and China for at least the past 2000 years. Ivory, like bone, is made up of calcified animal tissue, but the similarities end here; ivory has little connective tissue and no blood cells,

Stone Age finds of mammoth ivory figurative carvings have been dated to around 38,000 BC, and elephant ivory from predominantly East Africa has supplied markets in the Mediterranean, Western Europe, the Persian Gulf, India and China for at least the past 2000 years.

and is essentially a large tooth that extends beyond the lips. There are a few mammals that have tusks, such as the walrus, narwhal, hippopotamus and wild pig, but the word is mainly associated with ivory from the elephant family, including both the extinct mammoth and the elephant-like mastodon.

Teeth (and tusks) grow from embryonic cells that create a dental organ which produces the four main parts of the structure: the pulp cavity, surrounded by dentine, surrounded by cementum, and capped off with enamel. These grow in thick, even, perpendicular layers. In elephant ivory, the tusk is predominantly dentine throughout its length and thickness, surrounded by an external layer of cementum, with enamel covering only the very tip. Enamel is too hard to carve, and must be removed by grinding before carving, as in hippopotamus tusk.

Elephant ivory is a smooth, creamy white material that ages to a deep honey colour over time. It has a natural beauty that makes it attractive, along with the characteristics of being easy to carve despite its hardness, has good durability and a high polish finish. However, the product's acquisition leaves a lot to be desired. Elephants are hunted solely for their tusks, a practice that has seen a drastic decline in their numbers, made them extinct from certain regions, put others on the endangered species list, or led to an evolutionary change in the remaining animals. As elephants with the longest tusks are killed, smaller tusked elephants remain in the breeding cycle and pass on these characteristics to their offspring. Elephants use their tusks to forage for food, and it is unclear what consequences this may have on their survival. Unless an elephant sheds its tusk, removal results in the death of an animal.

Many civilisations (including Egypt, ancient Rome, ancient Greece, Russia, Japan, China and India) embraced the art of ivory carving as part of their culture. Because of the characteristics of ivory, many art works and sculptures remain — it is not a precious material that can be melted down

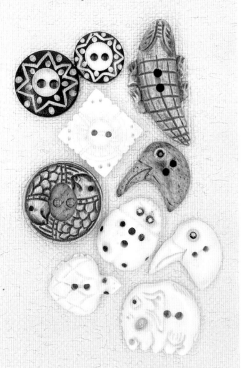

A selection of natural or dyed carved bone buttons, some with black horn inlay as eyes or ladybeetle spots. Double fish, henna dyed, 26mm Ø; 1990s, Nepal.

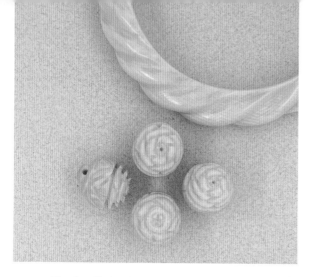

The family heirloom bangle pictured shows the fine patterning of real ivory. Buttons shown are made from bone, in the style of historical rosary carving, 15mm Ø.

Ivory carved buttons were once popular among the wealthy; this example in bone is reminiscent of the style. 48mm x 34mm, late twentieth century.

and used again, and it does not become brittle and break down. By the late medieval period, ivory carving in Europe was centred around Paris and Dieppe; while it was not a major art form, it was a highly specialized one, making and exporting small boxes and objects (including buttons), and religious ceremonial and utilitarian pieces, including rosary beads, across Europe. You may recall, from previous chapters, that the trade of the *buttonniers* (button-makers) was initially placed within the trade of rosary bead makers.

In Germany in the sixteenth, seventeenth and eighteenth centuries, ivory carving was an ardent practice of noble society, notably within the House of Hapsburg where Holy Roman Emperors Rudolf II, Ferdinand II and Leopold I, among others, were passionate about the craft. While idleness was the accepted etiquette for the ruling class, a small-scale turning bench provided an opportunity to fill the days. By the 1780s, Franz I, Count of Erbach-Erbach, was the driving force behind the introduction and development of a thriving ivory carving industry to the German Odenwald area. During the first half of the nineteenth century, elaborate carvings of hunting scenes were the favoured themes. One of the most widely respected and influential carvers of Erbach during this time was Ernst Kehrer (1816–76), whose delicate micro-carvings of deer, horses and dogs encircled by detailed foliage and rococo-style framing are found in brooches. Buttons with similar themes were popular, with the ivory carvings often used as the central inlay of a metal, or other, surround. Towards the second half of the nineteenth century, hunting scenes gave way to floral motifs — wreaths, bunches and eventually single flowers — the buttons being carved with a self-shank in the same material.

Another form of decoration on bone and ivory is scrimshaw. Scrimshaw was a popular art form made by scratching images and patterns with the use of a sharp needle-like object, popular among sailors on whaling ships, and the Indigenous peoples of the northern and Arctic regions. Common surfaces were the objects at hand — teeth and bones of whales, tusks of walruses, exposed mammoth tusks. The medium was polished, designs scratched onto the surface, and brightly coloured or black ink rubbed into the etched line work. Most objects, including buttons, decorated using the scrimshaw technique are from around the nineteenth century, although buttons for the tourist trade continued.

Nineteenth century changes in Europe and North America — particularly the Industrial Revolution and growing middle class — created an increase in demand for ivory products. Processing of the raw material could be done on an industrial scale, and East African elephant ivory was preferred due to its colour, texture and favourable working properties.

Consumption of ivory was growing, including as handles for cutlery, piano keys and billiard balls, and household objects including buttons. Its high cost and availability problems, caused by changing environmental and geopolitical circumstances, led manufacturers from the 1800s on to search for, and develop, alternative synthetic materials. Regardless, estimates based on nineteenth century trade records show that in the latter half of the century, 8000 to 30,000 tusks per year were exported from the region.

Efforts to safeguard the elephant by banning the use of ivory were established in 1989 by the Convention on International Trade in Endangered Species (CITES), and today elephant ivory carving is illegal in much of the world. Mammoth ivory, on the other hand, is still legal,

Contemporary scrimshaw on a bone button, turned into a brooch by jewellery designer Tenille Evans, Sydney, Australia. Bone button with black horn inlay, 33mm long; 2000s, India.

and has been in use since the seventeenth century, when fossil mammoth tusks were discovered in Siberia, and exported to Europe and China. Today, the Yukagir people of Arctic Siberia, once fisherman and reindeer hunters, have taken up hunting for mammoth tusks on the remote Kotelny Island. They make the journey on the frozen ice to the island and then wait for several months until the ice (and increasingly, the permafrost) starts to melt, revealing its hidden treasure. Tusks can also be found in Arctic Canada. On a summer trip to the Arctic with my brother in 2019, we visited the towns of Inuvik and Tuktoyaktuk, part of the Inuvialuit Settlement Region of the Canadian Northwest Territories. Always curious, we spoke with many of the locals regarding their life and work. Culture and traditions remain part of their lifestyle within a modern world, and needlework and carving are among them. Of course, I was on the hunt for buttons, but was surprised to see the beautiful mammoth ivory sculptures. We were told that occasionally, and ever more frequently, tusks appear in the melting permafrost.

Occasionally, buttons made from mammoth or walrus tusk have been created for the tourist market, particularly in Alaska in the early twentieth century. The depictions of Arctic animals carved in a simple, stylized form, are often adorned with etched line work and filled with pigment to create facial features and/or decorate the body. Other buttons, whether with sew-through holes or self-shank, have themes of Indigenous daily life. All of these have been produced for the tourist market. Expert carving of ivory buttons has also come from the Far East, where Chinese and Japanese carvers created intricate patterns. These were mainly for the export market, as their traditional clothing did not dictate the use of buttons.

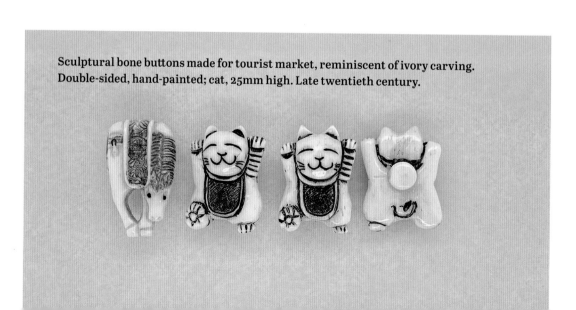

Sculptural bone buttons made for tourist market, reminiscent of ivory carving. Double-sided, hand-painted; cat, 25mm high. Late twentieth century.

These sculptural hand-carved owl and pussycat bone buttons are reminiscent of historical ivory Japanese *netsuke*. The small round buttons are made from ivory, with a self-shank and etched landscape scene; on face; 14mm ⌀, mid-twentieth century.

Tortoiseshell

I've always had a strange relationship with tortoiseshell. I grew up with antique combs from China, and despite their beauty, knowing they were made from real turtle always gave me a sad feeling. I have, however, had several pairs of imitation tortoiseshell eyeglasses throughout my lifetime, so much so that others called it my signature look. I have found a few antique tortoiseshell buttons when rummaging through old button boxes, but whenever I am offered new buttons or other products made from the real thing, no matter how beautiful they may be, I always refuse.

The word tortoiseshell is thought to have come into English usage in the seventeenth century. Various sources quote earliest dates from 1595 to 1605 for both the noun and adjective. Considered a luxury item, this semi-transparent raw material can be polished to a smooth, soft finish. Turtles were hunted in ancient Egypt and the ancient Far East for their shells to be used as a veneer inlay and for jewellery and small objects (such as combs). Through trading routes, tortoiseshell eventually found its way to Europe from the early 1500s, its use continuing over the next few centuries. As a precious material, it was seldom used for buttons until the late seventeenth to early eighteenth century, and then was often left undecorated to showcase the beauty of the material, decorated with paste or pearl borders, or inlaid with precious metals. A revival in the Victorian period, along with industrial methods of preparation, saw an increase in its use.

Despite what the name suggests, the natural material that came to be known

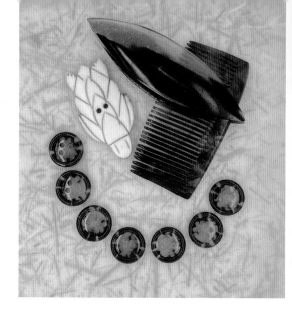

Despite what the name suggests, the natural material that came to be known as tortoiseshell comes not from land-based tortoises but from a species of marine turtle, namely the Hawksbill turtle, *Eretmochelys imbricata.*

Hawksbill tortoiseshell was used to make household objects including hair combs and tatting shuttles (pictured). The (anatomically incorrect) bone turtle-shaped button depicts the formation of the scutes that make up the tortoiseshell. The beauty of the shell, and its declining numbers, eventually saw replica material used for items such as these imitation buttons. 13mm ⌀.

as tortoiseshell comes not from land-based tortoises but from a species of marine turtle, namely the Hawksbill turtle, *Eretmochelys imbricata*. The Hawksbill is a migratory turtle and can be found in all the world's tropical and subtropical oceans. They roam the open water seeking the foraging areas of the ocean's coral reefs, and upon reproductive maturity (which takes twenty to 40 years) they enter shallower waters closer to land to breed, returning to nest on the beach of their birth. The only surviving species in its genus, the hunting of this animal specifically for its beautifully coloured shell has led to its listing as critically endangered under the International Union for Conservation of Nature (IUCN) Red List of Threatened Species.

Evolved from primitive reptiles, turtles have developed a hard, bony shell that encases their organs and protects from predators, open at the front end (anterior) for the head, neck and forelimbs and at the back end (posterior) for the hind limbs and tail. The back (or dorsal) shell is known as the carapace, and the underside (or ventral) shell is known as the plastron. The carapace holds the vertebrae and rib cage of the animal. During turtle evolution, the ribs have flattened out, and all connecting tissue, including that of the vertebrae, has turned into bone and fused onto dermal plates beneath the skin. To protect the shell further, a fibrous keratin protein — the same structural material that makes fingernails, hair and feathers — form into scutes (or plates) on top

Layered and pressed tortoiseshell buttons (left) compared to its imitator in pressed and painted corozo material. Buttons, 19mm Ø. Tortoiseshell, late nineteenth century; corozo, early twentieth century, 'SWORD MAKE — MADE IN ENGLAND'.

of the skin. In the case of the Hawksbill turtle, thirteen overlapping scutes — five down the centre and four on each side — make up the carapace. These are attractively marked with streaks, splotches and marbling in colours from yellow, amber and red to brown and black, and it is this unique shell pattern, when removed from its bone structure and dried, which is known as 'tortoiseshell'. The plastron is made up of the clavicle and pelvic bones fused to the dermal plates, in the same way as the carapace, although the plastron keratin layer (consisting of 22 scutes) is honey coloured throughout, and in the nineteenth and twentieth centuries was referred to as 'blonde tortoiseshell'.

The French were probably the first Europeans to develop methods of working the raw material. Shells cut in half and fire lit from below allowed for the scutes to detach from the carapace (the most prized portion) and the plastron. These were further softened in boiling water, scraped clean and laid between planks of hardwood (to avoid damage) and flattened in a metal press. Further advances in technology in the late nineteenth century led to more widespread use of tortoiseshell, despite its high cost, and in many ways this was the precursor of the plastics industry.

Buttons made from tortoiseshell were now shaped in compression moulds. Inlays could be pressed into the face of the button while still hot and in its pliable state, or left plain to emphasize its beautiful colours. Inlays included finely decorated designs in precious metals of silver or gold, pearl shell materials, or other highly regarded embellishments of the day. Most of these buttons are fitted with a backplate and loop shank cemented on the underside. Considering the expense of the product, and its increasing popularity going into the nineteenth century, early plastics production was geared towards finding artificial means to recreate tortoiseshell, and ivory — both being luxury items with challenging supply chains and progressively in short supply. This did not stop the trade in tortoiseshell, however, and this material was used in luxury buttons produced in Europe into the early twentieth century.

Horn and antler

Like bone, horns and antlers have been used for decorative objects, including buttons, since prehistoric times. Both raw materials come from large, hooved mammals called ungulates, and can be further divided into two groups, the cervid or bovid family. Antlers are branched, bone tissue structures found on most mammals in the cervid (*Cervidae*) family (deer, elk, moose, etc.) and occur in males, and the females of some species (e.g. caribou/reindeer). Growth begins from the antler's tip, at the top of the

A selection of crosscut antler buttons surrounding a hand-carved bone button with caribou silhouette. The buttons on the left are from Canadian caribou, the top right ones are deer horn from Tasmania. Caribou buttons, approximately 20mm ⌀; 2019, Northwest Territories, Canada.

The large crowns pictured are often intricately carved for buttons or jewellery items, while the buttons shown are cut lengthwise from the discarded antler. Rough small buttons, pictured top right, are staghorn, approximately 20mm ⌀; Scotland.

skull where two bony protrusions called pedicles are found. A specialized layer of tissue covered in short soft hairs (aptly called velvet) contains veins and arteries that feed nutrients to the growing bone structure. As they reach their peak growth the antlers begin to harden, the velvet dies and is rubbed off by the animal onto trees, shrubs, rocks and grasses, exposing the dead bone structure beneath. Rubbing the antlers brings them colour, staining the outer edge. Antlers also serve a purpose: they attract female deer for mating, and are a defence against other males or predators. They are shed annually and regrow each year. Size and longevity is dependent on food supply, nutrition, the animal's health and genetics, and in the case of reindeer (known as caribou in North America) males and females shed at different times of the year — males at the end of the breeding cycle, and females after they have given birth. Shedding is a two- to three-week process; the tissue between the antler and the pedicle slowly breaks down, loosening the antlers until they fall off.

In Europe, the use of antlers for button-making was a popular pastime, especially in the northern areas where traditional costume was used by hunters and mountain- or forest-dwelling folk. The emergence of tourism in these areas from the second half of the nineteenth century led to others appreciating the clothing style, particularly the handcrafted buttons that adorned them. In button-making, when the antler is discarded the burr thickness is cut away (crosswise) first, as this is considered the most precious material. The burr forms from the pedicle in a rosette-like widening and sits on the forehead of the animal. The slightly bizarre looking edge, with its many pearl-shaped protuberances, only adds to the appearance. Buttons made from this section have been carved with intricate hunting scenes or sculpted animal heads, reminiscent of ivory carving, and mostly have a self-shank. More often than not, for button-making much of the rest of the antler is cut along the length, producing more simple sew-through styles where the dense, brown stained outer layer is used on the surface, sometimes as a decorative treatment carved to show the white bone beneath. As the antler is a bone, the central core is often porous. Having said that, today antler buttons are commonly found as undecorated, crosscut, simple two-hole buttons; the outer edge is smooth as it reaches towards the tips, creating free-size, freeform buttons.

Horns are live bone tissue structures found on most mammals in the bovid (*Bovidae*) family (cattle, goats, sheep) and occur in all males, and in the females of some species. Unlike antlers, horns grow from the base (not the tip) and do not shed annually. Instead, the symmetrical pair starts growing from birth, is kept throughout the

ABOVE LEFT: Solid horn tip toggles and horn crosscut buttons showing growth rings. Blonde two-hole crosscut button, 35mm ∅; 1990s, Europe.

ABOVE RIGHT: Classic style horn buttons in various natural horn colours, tooled or left plain. Large button, four-hole with rim, 35mm ∅; mid-twentieth century, Europe.

LEFT: Goat tips made into buttons. The hollow tips are finished at the end with a horn end cap. Largest toggle pictured, 105mm long; 2020s, India.

animal's lifetime, and does not regrow if the horns become damaged or are removed. A fibrous keratin protein forms a conical shell around the bone core, extending into a solid keratin tip. This outer coating is the horn's raw material. Bovids use their horns for defence and dominance, but they are also beneficial tools for digging and stripping bark. As they grow, they may curl or spiral, but never branch.

Early horn buttons are made of natural horn, polished to reveal their natural beauty with colours varying from cream, to brown, to black, and often encompassing all three. Working with horn was a specific craft, controlled through the guild system in Europe, with companies of 'horners' formed in the City of London (1284) and York, and also in Paris. A horner would prepare the horns, first sawing off the solid tips. Similar to the preparation of bone raw material, remaining horn pieces were soaked in water for several weeks to remove the bony core. Heated to soften them so they could be cut lengthwise, they were prised open and any core residue scraped away. For the creation of flat pieces suitable for comb and button-making, these pieces were then placed between hot metal plates in a press.

As horn-working was divided by these two stages, horners were described as either being a horn turner (utilizing the solid tips) or a horn presser or breaker, who produced the semi-manufactured flattened horn. Craftsmen from a variety of trades purchased these flat sheets to create their products, and any buttons came mostly from the offcuts of the comb makers. In these early days before industrialization, hand-worked buttons were turned from sheet material (known as plates) or the solid tips. A slender sliced tip could make long toggle-type buttons or could be sliced crosswise to create a series of natural, varying-sized ones. As the solid tip varies in length from animal to animal, it is often uncertain how much solid material is in each horn. The popularity of natural horn buttons (and hair combs) grew during the eighteenth century, but it was the nineteenth century development of the commercial processing of this raw material that allowed the industry to flourish.

As a material for button-making, horn ticks all the boxes. It is flexible without being too soft, rigid without being brittle, and when heated becomes a semi-transparent material that keeps its shine almost indefinitely when polished. As industrialized production evolved, more of this raw material was used.

In the button-making industry, both the horn and hoof material of cattle is used. The hoof is a keratin covered tip of the toe of an ungulate; in the case of bovids, a single toe is protected by this layer. Horn and hoof pieces are brought to a plastic state by

The popularity of natural horn buttons (and hair combs) grew during the eighteenth century, but it was the nineteenth-century development of the commercial processing of this raw material that allowed the industry to flourish.

directly applying heat, boiling in water, or soaking in an alkali solution, and cut open while still pliable.

A second production method developed in the mid-1800s was the introduction of the commercial processing of every piece of horn, particularly hooves and scrap material, creating a manufacturing process with little, or no, waste. Raw material was ground into a powder, mixed with protein binders (often egg or blood albumen) and dyed black to create a compound that became the first attempt at button production from plastic. Horn buttons, in greater numbers, became a utilitarian fastening for common clothing. Finely detailed dies (covering themes of everyday life, classical heads in relief, flora and fauna) created exquisite buttons, now rare to find. These black horn buttons, many of which were made in France and Britain, could be worn with the mourning dress that was fashionable in the latter half of the century.

Unlike cattle and buffalo, whose horns are generally smoother on the outer wall, the horns of sheep and goats are generally more textured. Because the horns of bovids grow throughout their lifetime, there are distinct growing cycles — growth stops during the winter months and starts again in the spring. Especially in the case of sheep and goats,

Moulded black dyed horn button, stamped 'L.C.J. & T. — CAEN'. Caen is located in the province of Normandy, and was known to have a factory that made buttons from horn. 24mm Ø, France; late 1800s.

distinct rings clearly mark the division between these growth cycles. Horn tips of sheep or goats, with their quirky spirals and highly textured outer wall, make for attractive toggle-type buttons that may be left hollow or finished with an attached horn end.

Both natural horn and antler buttons are still produced today. Antler buttons remain mostly in small studio production, but modern horn buttons can be found in both large- and small-scale production. There are several producers worldwide who create the button blanks, suitable for commercial mass production. Modern milling machines create the classic tailor's button, adorning the suits of quality clothing where the natural product is on show in all its polished glory. Others, who use a combination of modern technology and hand-carving, create stylish, aesthetically pleasing accessories using both the natural material and/or decorative techniques to great appeal.

A selection of leather buttons showing a variety of treatments: rolled, stitched, pressed, stamped, decorated with escutcheon or rubber surface covering. Grey rolled leather button, 23mm x 23mm square; 1950s, Europe.

Leather

In the slaughter of animals for food, not only were bones an important raw material, but so were hides that produced leather, and horns and hooves. In early rural settings, leather and bone may have been made into crude buttons, perhaps out of necessity and as a readily available resource. By the sixteenth century in Europe, leatherworking was a well-respected art form. With the advent of the modern book in a smaller, more portable version, book covers made the transition from wood to pasteboards (layers of paper glued together) covered in leather. It is plausible that expert bookbinders may also have made leather buttons — leather can be decorated in a variety of methods such as chasing, tooling, stamping or embossing with or without gold. In later years, thin leather was used to cover buttons in the same way as fabric, or it could be adhered to a shaped or tooled metal base and shank.

The knotted leather buttons that are a familiar fastening on tweed jackets were invented in early nineteenth century England. Originally produced with a leather loop shank, in more contemporary times these have mostly been replaced with a metal shank — the leather shanks have a tendency to break open with wear and tear. Over the years, I have bought and sold several types of knotted leather buttons, made with leather strips of a width suitable for the scale of the button. The thickness (as opposed to the width) of the leather strips determines the overall finish — a more bulbous, knotted look is created with strips of approximately 3mm thick, while a finer look is achieved with strips of less than 1mm thick. The finished leather buttons are usually painted with a coloured lacquer or, in some cases, are left in their natural leather state — these

are left to age gracefully from a light tan colour to a deep, rich brown. The leather knots were woven by hand, then compressed in a steel mould to complete the finished button. Factories — such as the Worcester Button Company, the original maker of leather knot buttons — employed staff to knot and finish these buttons. B. Sanders & Sons,

ABOVE: A variety of classic, leather knotted buttons. Large brown button, 44mm Ø; 2020s, Italy.

RIGHT: A selection of freeform wooden buttons, crosscut or length cut. Large two-hole crosscut button showing growth rings, 45mm Ø; 2020s, India.

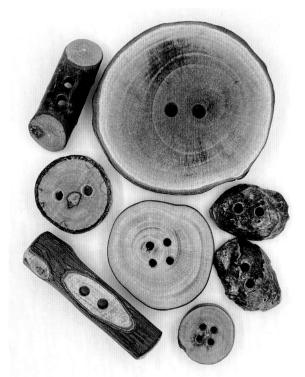

A selection of wooden blanks for button-making. Large
size, 25mm Ø; early twentieth century, Europe.

who later acquired the company, continued production alongside their regular output
of fabric and metal buttons. As the spread of this style of button continued to other
countries, in Australia outworkers were often used to create the leather knots, bringing
these to the small business that would press-mould them into their desired shape and
size, and finish them with dye and varnish.

Contemporary leather buttons may be made entirely from leather strips, fine
leather adhered to a cardboard backing or, more often than not, fine leather adhered to
pressed leather as a backing for extra thickness. Interestingly, the knots are still made
by hand before being pressed into shape, and the knotted or woven-look leather button
remains a popular fastening today.

A customer once questioned me about whether some of our buttons were actual
leather, so I took one apart, to verify its authenticity for myself and said customer, and
also because I was curious as to how they were made. A single leather strip is woven in
such a way as to produce a knot; nowadays, before the knot is pulled tight, a flat piece
of cardboard (or plastic) that holds the metal wire shank is inserted prior to the final
pressing stage that forms the finished button.

Wood

The word 'polymer' comes from the Greek *poly* (many) and *meros* (parts/units), and the
most plentiful organic polymer on this planet is cellulose. Wood, in the form of trees,
is an organic material made up of a combination of long-chain cellulose fibres and
complex organic polymers (lignin) that together create a structural composite material
product that is both strong in tension yet resists compression. Wood has been used for
millennia, both as an important fuel source and as an important construction material.

While I can imagine that a short stick may have acted as a toggle-type fastening in prehistoric times, its versatility, accessibility and potential to be easily shaped made wood one of the many sources for button-making, whether in its own form or as part of a construction of other buttons. Every variety of wood has been applied to button-making, though where wood is the primary focus or where strength is required, preference is given to harder, closed-grain woods such as boxwood, apple, maple, walnut and mahogany.

While early wooden buttons could be thought of as crude and for the common folk, wood (and bone) was used as the support in the making of early *passementerie* and cloth-covered buttons from the seventeenth century. The wooden forms (or moulds) were made by turners, who created lengths which would be cut crossways and drilled with one or more holes depending on the needs of the craftsmen who covered the blanks with cloth or fibres. Eighteenth century wood- and bone-backs, as they are called

LEFT: Various woods are used for button-making, prized for the natural beauty of the raw material. Large wooden two-hole button, approximately 62mm Ø; 1950s, cedarwood, Canada.

BELOW: A selection of modern laminated buttons using an assortment of woods. Large flat rectangular buttons, 40mm long; 2000s, Germany.

by collectors, used the same style of moulds for their finished buttons, although these were covered with a pressed or cast metal cap. Like bone, wood was also used as a base for other more precious veneer overlays, where the inferior base was completely covered. With the increasing demand for buttons in fashion, some buttons from the eighteenth and early nineteenth centuries were undecorated wooden ones, with the beauty of the polished natural woodgrain as the primary focus. These simple turned forms were attached by way of a pin shank or were drilled through with sewing holes. During the Victorian period, hardwood buttons became more decorated.

Wooden buttons were decorated using a variety of techniques. Marquetry involves a series of veneers assembled in a pattern to completely cover the base. Intarsia is where the wood surfaces are cut or hollowed out to receive inlay material. During the Victorian era, marquetry and inlays were often of tortoiseshell, ivory, silver or other metals, as well as ceramics, although the use of wood as an inlay material was not as common and probably only made as a special order. Metal escutcheons were also favoured as an embellishment to the simple turned forms, or the fine polished hardwood could be used as a background for open-worked metal designs. Wood could be lacquered, painted, lustred or dyed in various shades to bring out the natural grain patterns. The technique of laminating offered interesting decorative features and could mimic inlay work — lengths of different coloured woods are glued together and cut across to reveal the pattern.

A change in wooden button decoration came about in 1847, when Scotsman, Andrew Smith, presented a new collection, 'Breadalbane' wooden buttons, from his Birmingham workshop. Made from the wood of the Scottish mulberry fig tree, these hardwearing buttons were decorated by methods not used before — pencil and ink pictures, and/or separated patterns and prints.

Trends in the second half of the nineteenth century favoured metal picture buttons, pressed metal buttons featuring a scene or story. Some of these were made using fine metal stamped with a pattern, on a wooden base. By the 1880s, astute manufacturers offered a version of picture buttons made from wood composition. Pulped or powdered wood was mixed with fillers and a binder, then pressed or

Wooden buttons on sample card from Bohemia. The name of the firm is rubber stamped on the back, although some of it is illegible; besides wooden goods, it is unclear what other articles they produced. Buttons by Anton Lugner, Holzwaren & ?, Tachau (Böhmen), largest size 36mm Ø; late nineteenth/early twentieth century, Bohemia.

moulded; although the mixtures varied depending on the producer, some makers (such as *Albert Parent et Cie* in Paris) were able to create particularly detailed designs with a fine wood grain. (This style of manufacture is not to be confused with *bois durci*, which will be discussed later.) Decorations could also be stamped onto natural wood, although the definition of the stamped design was not always clear and could wear away.

Wooden button blanks, produced as inserts for *passementerie* buttons and later for home-style crochet and fabric-covered buttons (the mainstay of the wood and bone button industry), declined in production towards World War I, particularly due to the changing fashions. However, the period after World War I is said to be the heyday of the wooden button, with shortages of other raw materials leading to an increase in natural material use in button production. During the 1920s and 1930s, vast amounts of inexpensive wooden buttons were produced for the children's clothing market, hand-painted with decorations of colourful dots, flowers, etc. At the other end of the spectrum, enormous wooden buttons (60–70mm) adorned fashionable overcoats. Of particular note are buttons made by sculptor Henri Hamm (1871–1961), a student of the Académie des Beaux Arts in Bordeaux, who settled in Paris in 1902. His fondness for oversized object design produced some wonderful contemporary patterns that were created using both machine and hand-carving.

Today, wood remains an important part of the button-making industry. In countries that have a strong handcraft economy (such as India and Nepal), wooden buttons in light or dark hardwoods (locally known as toona, kadam, babool and guava) are not only turned to mimic modern tailor's buttons, but also hand-shaped and carved into myriad styles. Some European countries favour olive wood (*Olea europea*) as a medium from which to create wooden buttons. This hard, dense, strong wood has attractive contrasting lines of brown and honey. Since the trees are an important food source, the wood is acquired in the form of harvested branches through pruning, making it perfect for small objects such as buttons. While hardwoods are best for button-making, popular craft buttons in softer woods are found everywhere. As wood is porous, softer woods may not hold up to the wear and tear we expect from a hardwood fashion button.

Bamboo

Bamboo is a relative newcomer in the manufacture of buttons, but as a material it is highly sustainable due to its rapid and prolific growth. While not technically a tree, this woody grass shares similarities with wood in that it is a natural composite material, although the high presence of silica in bamboo is a factor in its ability to be strong yet light. As well as a fuel source, it has been used as a construction material, as a fibre for cloth, and as a pulp for papermaking. There are more than 1000 species of bamboo plant, of which about 100 are used for economic purposes, particularly the thicker walled species. The culm, or stem, of the bamboo plant is used in manufacturing. From the stem base, the diameter of the plant is pre-determined and it grows vertically upward, creating perpendicular intranodes along the way that give strength to the stem. The smooth length between the nodes is called the internode, and this length is shorter near the base of stem, providing needed strength as the plant grows. Each intranode is sandwiched between a set of two rings; the lower is the scar formed as the

Hand-carved wooden buttons have been popular since the 1940s. Round blonde wooden button with self-shank, 36mm ⌀; 2000s, India.

Olive wood is ideal for button-making and its warm honey glow and growth rings are a natural asset to the individuality of each button. These examples from France are decorated with laser etching. Large two-hole button with half checkerboard surface texture, 30mm ⌀; 1990s.

sheaf leaf falls away, and the upper is the scar formed after the growth of the intranodal tissue concludes.

Bamboo's manufacture to a raw material is much like other natural products in a round, hollow state: the pieces must be opened and/or made flat. Generally, mature bamboo of five to six years old is used, and poles must be split and cleaned after being freshly cut, as the green bamboo is easier to work than the hardened, dry bamboo. Single splits create wide panels, while multiple splits create widths for easier handling according to its final use. The inner layer is removed, or planed away, and the pieces are cured in preservatives and water for several days before being air-dried for a couple of months. In the case of buttons, more recently the intranodes have also been used as a source material. This would probably entail the internodes to be cut away from the intranodes before the bamboo stem is split.

The buttons I have come across utilize all parts of the bamboo structure and are predominantly waxed and left in their natural state, showcasing the raw beauty of the bamboo plant. Some bamboo pieces have been planed on both sides, allowing

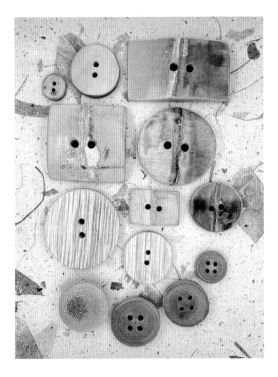

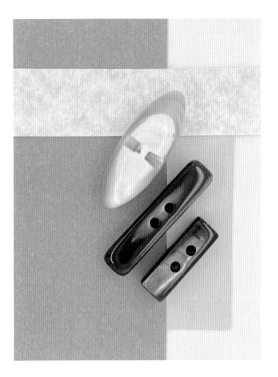

This selection compares the various elements of the bamboo plant used in the making of buttons. Large two-hole buttons, 38mm ⌀; 2000s, India.

Buttons made using the hinge area of the bivalve shell. Large two-hole button, dyed brown, 40mm long; 2000s, Italy.

for a double-sided flat disc, showing the striped walls of the internodal areas. Others, cut from the same part, have the outer curved side left intact. The intranode, with its hard, natural scar, is a design feature that makes for an instantly recognizable bamboo button. Less so are the buttons created from the intranodal material itself, but the fine dot pattern is the giveaway.

Shell

Shells are an obvious form of natural embellishment, their shiny and lustrous surfaces designed to catch the eye of passers-by, a gift from the sea. How difficult is it to walk along a shoreline and not stop to pick one up, marvelling at the wonders of nature before returning it to the sand? It is no wonder that some of the earliest finds of buttons as a decorative enhancement, found in what is now Pakistan, were carved from shell dating back to between 2800 BC and 2600 BC. Indeed, many of the coastal Indigenous and Islander communities around the world frequently used shells in their ceremonial costumes or to denote social standing. While many of the shells were not necessarily

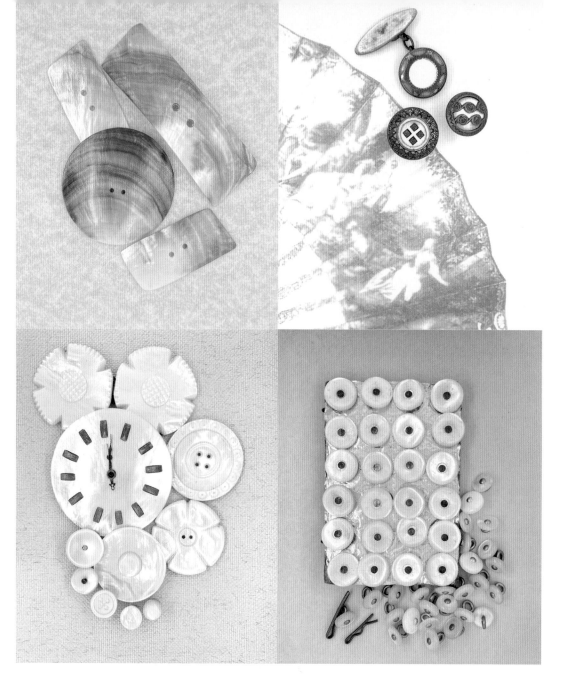

TOP: The growth rings of the shell are shown on these akoya shell buttons. Large round two-hole buttons, 52mm ⌀.

ABOVE: This beautiful selection of buttons and buckles from the late nineteenth century showcase the glory of the *Pinctada maxima* shell. Large shell 'clock face' buckle has brass hands and gilded indices, 62mm ⌀, European.

TOP: Mother of pearl and semi-precious stones were used as an inlay in nineteenth century metal buttons. Cuff button, jade surround with mother of pearl central 14mm ⌀, backmarked.

ABOVE: Metal pin-shanked mother of pearl buttons. Buttons attached to foil covered cards with R-clips, 13mm ⌀; nineteenth century, European.

It is no wonder that some of the earliest finds of buttons as a decorative enhancement, found in what is now Pakistan, were carved from shell dating back to between 2800 BC and 2600 BC.

used as buttons, the shell button became an adopted method of embellishment for some.

A shell is an external skeleton (exoskeleton) that covers the soft body of the mollusc. Molluscs can be divided into two groups: those having two shells with a hinge, the bivalves, and those having one shell, the gastropods. Like bones, the shell structure is mostly calcium, although in this case in the form of calcium carbonate; shells have only a very small percentage of protein (not more than 2 per cent) and are not made up of cells. Instead, molluscs have an organ in their body called the mantle (generally, the part that protrudes from the shell) that contains the ingredients necessary for shell construction. Molluscs continue secreting proteins and minerals to continuously grow the exoskeleton during their lifetime as their body grows.

The process of shell building is called biomineralization. First, a layer known as conchiolon (an uncalcified layer of protein and chitin, a structural polymer) is deposited by the animal at the outer border of the shell, followed by the extra-pallial fluid secreted by the mantle, creating a crystallized form of calcium carbonate, the mineral calcite. Shells grow at the same time in two directions — in length and in thickness. All shells are made of the mineral calcite, and this prismatic, porcellaneous layer is where the term 'porcelain' comes from, after the cowrie shell with its unique polished layer found both inside and outside the shell. Some shells produce a third inner calcified layer, adding thickness in the crystallized from of calcium carbonate, this time in the form of the mineral aragonite, known as the nacreous layer. The minerals calcite and aragonite have the same chemical compound, $CaCO_3$ calcium carbonate, but the atoms within the minerals are configured differently, leading to different structures and appearance. The porcellaneous calcite, while just as smooth, is much duller in appearance than the inner, pearly iridescent layer of aragonite nacre.

This nacreous layer is in charge of keeping the inner shell surface smooth and protecting the soft tissues of the animal from foreign objects or parasites, by enclosing any abnormalities in successive layers of nacre. Nacre is found inside some top snails and abalone, and in pearl-producing shells where the nacre can result in lumps attached to the interior of the shell, creating what are known as blister pearls or free pearls found within the mantle tissue. Hence, the name 'mother of pearl' is commonly referred to all shells that create a nacreous layer. In the button world, the pearl-producing bivalves are termed 'mother of pearl' while all other shells, even the nacre-producing cone shells, are termed 'shell'.

Mother of pearl and shell material has been known throughout Europe since the sixteenth century, with both the Makassar and trochus shells in use. The opening up of further trade with Asian markets brought more, and consistent, quality raw material in the eighteenth century. The shell known as Makassar was actually the silver-lipped *Pinctada maxima* and the black-lipped *Pinctada margaritfera*, fished from northern Australian waters; fishermen from Makassar (Sulawesi, Indonesia) arrived annually to fish for trepang (sea cucumber), trochus shell (sea snail) and pearl shell, which they traded with Chinese merchants. Camping along the entire northern coast, they employed local Indigenous people along the way — Northern Territory rock art depicts these journeys from at least the sixteenth century. The Australian pearl industry began in the mid-1800s, initially along the Western Australian shoreline, and by the 1900s the shell was of greater value than the pearl — world markets were using the shells for cutlery handles, inlay work and millions of buttons.

Up to and including the eighteenth century, mother of pearl and shell buttons were meticulously made by hand using the jewellery tools of a fret saw and hand engraver. Hand-engraved patterns were sometimes rubbed with silver or gold dust to enhance the design, or the natural shell was used as a lustrous background for a painted image or pattern of paste stones. By far the most striking are those that have been intricately carved and saw-pierced, and lightly embellished with precious metals or paste or steel-cut stones. Most pearl buttons of this century were predominantly fastened with a metal pin shank.

Shells were first introduced to the ancient art of cameo cutting during the Renaissance period and again in the eighteenth century, when the discovery of Pompeii and surrounds sparked renewed interest in the antiquities. While the ancient Romans used stone and glass as a medium, the Italians initiated the use of shells as an accepted and popular cameo material in the early nineteenth century. Shells commonly used were those that produced banded layers of colour, such as the non-nacreous helmet shells (of the Cassis species *Cyprraecassis rufa Cassio madagascarensis*), and the tiger

TOP: Machine and laser tooling are used to enhance the beauty of the natural shell. Large square two-hole button has a laser engraved pattern to expose the colourful layer of the black-lipped mother of pearl shell, 50mm x 50mm; 2000s, Italy.

ABOVE: Mother of pearl buttons in geometric shapes, all shanked buttons with self-shank or four-way brass box shanks. Large hexagonal button, 27mm ∅; early twentieth century, Europe.

TOP: A selection of modern black-lipped mother of pearl buttons, made using a variety of methods — machine- and laser-tooled buttons from Italy, hand-cutting and engraving from Indonesia. Large intricately laser-cut and engraved button, 30mm ∅; 2000s, Italy.

ABOVE: Hand-engraved buttons from the early nineteenth century. Large pinwheel design has brass loop and plate shank, 34mm ∅; Europe.

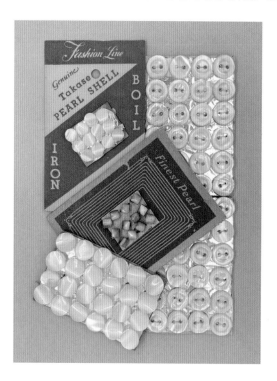

Two-hole and self-shanked buttons as presented on foil-backed cards. Shanked buttons are trochus shell (*takase* in Japan); purple dyed, pyramid shaped small buttons 'Finest Pearl', 4mm Ø. Japan, early twentieth century.

cowrie, among others. Following the success of the Wedgewood-style buttons, cameo buttons in the newly acquired, nacreous black-lipped pearl shell, with its lustrous rainbow layers, were popular in the second half of the nineteenth century. Engravers within the jewellery trade made the buttons — initially hand carved, the reliefs were elaborate in their detail. The introduction of machine tools allowed for an increase in numbers produced, but although the designs remained flattering the line work was coarser.

Towards the end of the nineteenth century, à jour work (hole work) became a fashionable method of pearl button decoration. Some of the earlier, less complicated work was made using a fret saw through drilled holes. Later, drills were used exclusively for more elaborate designs. Intricately carved and à jour work buttons were also popular in Jerusalem, where the traditional handicraft of shell carving was introduced from Italy in the fifteenth century. In the 1990s, I met with one such contemporary carver and purchased his entire collection of more than twenty pieces of exquisite buttons, approximately 40mm in diameter. I'm sad to say that I sold them all, without even taking any photographs or keeping one for myself, but the memory of our conversation about the rich history of the carving remains intact.

The *Pinctada margaritifera*, or black-lipped pearl shell, stands equally next to the *P. maxima*, the only difference being the colour of their pearl and shell. Because of their thickness and strength, both species are frequently used for tooled button designs, from the classic tailor's style with a rim and four holes, to more intricate patterns. This pearl-producing oyster is found in waters of the Indo-Pacific marine realm, from the Persian Gulf to French Polynesia, with successful aquaculture occurring in Fiji, among other countries.

In the first half of the nineteenth century, Vienna and Prague were the main European production centres due to developments in polishing, using hydrochloric acid, with the addition of water on machinery for shaping and drilling. The new processes led to the further spread of the shell button industry to Germany, France and England. Artisan-made pearl buttons were still available, but the Industrial Revolution and the mechanical use of hydroelectric power allowed for mass production by the end of the century. Trading partnerships brought different shells onto the market: the *Turban marmoratus* green turban snail was a widely used nacre-producing shell, but *Trochus niloticus* 'mother of pearl snails' were a preferred choice and were sold virtually all over the world. The changing art and design trends in the early twentieth century, from the nature-inspired Art Nouveau to the more geometric forms of Art Deco, led many continental European pearl shell button-makers to embrace new shapes. Greater interaction between art and industry brought a more functional style to everyday objects, and buttons were introduced in shapes (e.g. diamond, hexagon) that had previously not been seen. They were now found on all aspect of clothing, women's and men's; such was the rich appeal of the shell material that it lent a feeling of quality to garments, even being used on the renowned carpenter's guild clothes.

The engraving of shell buttons progressed from purely hand-engraved to the introduction of hand-operated engraving machines. This led to a more even depth of line work, although ornamentation remained at the discretion of the maker. More of the shell was also being used; the thick centre was used for larger and/or carved buttons, while smaller buttons were processed from the outer, finer edges. Shell buttons competed with, and eventually overtook, the bone button as the standard undergarment or household linen choice. While many millions of these unadorned buttons were produced, they were later replaced by the emergence of the corozo button industry.

By the second half of the nineteenth century, Birmingham became a centre for pearl button manufacturing in Europe, with larger manufacturers supplying the raw material to smaller tradesmen. At its peak, at least 2000 people were employed in the pearl button industry, using 1800 tons of various shells in a year, not including the toolmakers and the cottage industry of women who sewed the buttons onto foil-covered cards. Austria was a major competitor in price and quantity, and France held the lead in the elaborately finished high-end market.

A curious use of pearl buttons originated in London in the 1880s. The wealthy West End society became accustomed to parading on Sundays in the fashionable parks, wearing their best attire and pearls. The costermongers imitated their style by sewing lines of mother of pearl 'flashers' (fishing lures) onto their clothing and doing their own parading, known as the 'Lambeth Walk'. These street traders were an organized group, with elected Coster Kings and Queens representing their neighbourhoods and helping those among them who had come across hard times. During their parade, they would raise funds for the less fortunate. Henry Croft, a ratcatcher and street sweeper from Somers Town in London, was very taken by the traders' outlook and style, and covered a shabby dress suit and top hat with more than 50,000 mother of pearl buttons — sewn in patterns, symbols and slogans — joining the costermongers on their fundraising activities. His outfit drew attention everywhere he went. Soon after, the traders began decorating their suits in a similar fashion, wearing these outfits especially whenever they were fundraising. Women decorated their dresses and coats, and they collectively became known as the 'Pearlies'. Coster Kings and Queens now became the Pearly Kings and Queens, spelling out on their outfits their title and area of representation, as well as adding symbols of good luck in buttons. Today, the Pearlies are still active in their fundraising and community awareness service, carrying on the work started by their ancestors, passing the title through familial ties.

Another modern use of mother of pearl buttons as decoration and embellishment

Pearly Kings and Queens use pearl buttons to create patterns, such as flowers, good luck symbols and words on their clothing.

Northwest coast First Nations people use pearl buttons as part of the decoration on their ceremonial robes. This Kwakwaka'wakw button blanket (<u>k</u>ange<u>x</u>tola) was made prior to 1940 and features the central crest of the thunderbird, with coppers on either side. Image courtesy of Museum of Anthropology at UBC, Vancouver, Canada; Kwakwaka'wakw button blanket, Object Nb3.1413, photographed by Derek Tan.

can be found on the ceremonial button blankets of various First Nations peoples from the northwest coast of North America. I remember as a child going to a museum and being hypnotized by the exquisite details of these robes. It was only later as an adult that I discovered the history, true meaning and power that these blankets convey.

Original ceremonial robes were made from a variety of materials — animal skins and furs, woven from mountain goat and dog wool or cedar bark and other vegetable fibres — and were often decorated with shells such as dentalium (a long tooth or tusk-like marine mollusc) and pieces of the highly prized abalone. The Europeans brought manufactured cloth in the 1700s, and in the 1800s the Hudson's Bay Company had set up trading posts in Masset, Haida Gwaii (1825) and Fort Rupert (1849) on the northeast coast of Vancouver Island, trading woollen blankets for furs. Eventually, the woollen blankets began to replace most others and were decorated using dentalium, abalone pieces and strands of cedar bark. 'The sewing of buttons to decorate the blanket,' wrote Daisy Sewid-Smith in her book *Robes of Power*, 'began when a Kwakw<u>a</u>k<u>a</u>'wakw man saw an Englishman wearing a buttoned suit. These men, we later learned, were called "Cockney Pearlies" from England.' These mother of pearl and abalone buttons were acquired through other traders.

Button blankets are a coded legal document passed through matrilineal descent. They communicate rank and status, are generally decorated with the family crest, and display clan histories and the associated duties, rights and privileges of the wearer. They can be thought of as sculptural totem poles, worn as powerful statements of identity, and are beautiful objects made by talented artists. A potlatch ceremony preceded the

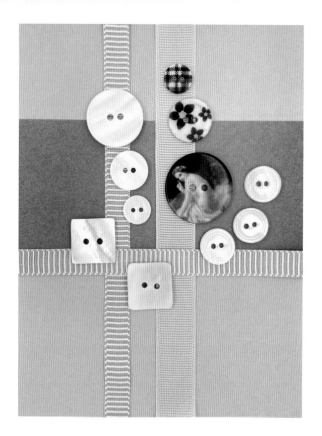

Today, China leads the world in freshwater shell button production. These buttons are mainly round, mostly two-holed (although four holes may be specified) and millions are unadorned, the attraction being in the smooth white or cream natural finish. This also provides a base material for decals. Large button with bathing woman decal, 28mm Ø, 2000s.

gifting of such an auspicious item, but the 1884 to 1951 government ban of these proceedings did immense damage to the traditional identities and social relations of Indigenous peoples. While potlatches still exist in some communities, dancers and others now also use button blankets as an educational tool for both Indigenous and non-Indigenous people.

In the early 1870s, a German lathe worker and button-maker, John Frederick Boepple, was given a box of North American freshwater pearl mussels, which he found very suitable for button production due to their thick nacreous layer. Following the death of his wife, he moved to the United States and eventually settled in Muscatine, Iowa, where he found the best shells for his work along the Mississippi River. In 1890, American protective tariffs made imported pearl buttons more expensive, giving Boepple the incentive to start the Boepple Button Company. Others soon followed him, transforming the small Iowa town into the 'pearl button capital of the world.' The American shell button industry was huge; between 1901 and 1910, around 35,000 tons of shells were processed. The peak production year of 1916 saw an output of 6 billion buttons across factories primarily from Iowa, New Jersey and New York. Around 20,000 people were employed in the industry, not to mention the toolmakers and women who sewed the button cards. Unfortunately, the great demand for pearl mussel shell led to rapidly depleted American fishing grounds. Japan had entered the button market in 1908, selling Chinese pearl mussel and trochus snail products at a lower cost, and despite protective tariffs against Japan in 1923, changing fashions saw a decline in the industry with worldwide demand ceasing in the 1940s with the introduction of the

The *P. maxima*, or silver- or gold-lipped pearl shell, was, and is still today, a major source of high-end raw material. Farmed for its pearl, the animals have nuclei inserted into their shell to ensure the growth of the gem; after grafting of nuclei, pearls are removed and nuclei inserted a number of times until the mollusc has reached its limit of productivity. At the end of its commercial pearl-giving life, the shells are harvested for both meat and shell. Due to its thickness and size, being the largest of the *Pinctada* genus, it has the scope to produce many quality products from each shell. The largest commercial sources of these shells are found in the northern and northwestern waters of Australia, with breeding farms also found in the Philippines and Indonesia.

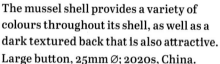

The mussel shell provides a variety of colours throughout its shell, as well as a dark textured back that is also attractive. Large button, 25mm ⌀; 2020s, China.

A selection of high-end laser cut and engraved, or inlaid with crystal, buttons using *Pinctada maxima* as the raw material. Large button, 34mm ⌀; 2000s, Italy.

cheaper, plastic buttons.

Today, pearl and shell buttons still have a place within the button industry. The attraction of the natural product is in the material itself. Apart from the tooled versions, where the shell has been manipulated to the constraints of a design, natural surfaces are often polished and left as is — their beauty lies in nature's wonder. Mother of pearl shells commonly used in button-making are often the same shells used in the jewellery industry and are the by-product of the pearl industries. Periculture, where shells are farmed and cared for within strict environment surroundings, ensures that stocks do not become extinct as has happened with many species of the freshwater pearl mussels from the Mississippi River. It is now internationally recognized that to sustainably manage marine populations for commercial harvest, genetic conservation must play a key role.

While equipment for manufacturing pearl and shell buttons has progressed since the nineteenth century, some similarities remain. In Italy, the semi-manufactured shell blanks are cut manually with a water-cooled diamond tubular (disc) cutter, then passed through a series of diamond smoothing discs on a conveyor belt for rapid removal of

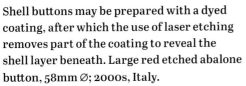

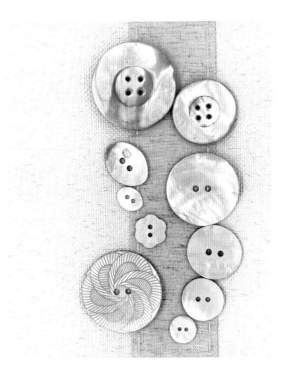

Shell buttons may be prepared with a dyed coating, after which the use of laser etching removes part of the coating to reveal the shell layer beneath. Large red etched abalone button, 58mm ⌀; 2000s, Italy.

A selection of modern and vintage akoya shell buttons. Large etched 2-hole button, 34mm ⌀.

imperfections. Blanks are then carefully selected and graded, and chosen for different applications depending on their thickness. Turning machines are used for the shape and design of the finished buttons. The same machinery is used to produce polyester buttons, with the turning speed lowered to accommodate the shell's hardness. It can be operated semi-automatically or automatically, the disk face identifiable by photoelectric cells. A mixture of water, powdered pumice and clay removes the hardness of the edges. If the buttons require further whitening (often necessary after the previous treatments) they are first emerged in water and then hydrogen peroxide. Finishing is a two-step process: first, water and sulphuric acid to bring the buttons to a semi-glossy stage, followed by final tumbling in fine granules of corozo to achieve the mother of pearl iridescence. Many shell buttons today, often those made in the Asia-Pacific region, are still cut and carved by hand using motor-powered tools.

Dyed shell buttons have been popular since the twentieth century. As the shell material is ultimately a protective exoskeleton for the animal inside, it takes a lot of dye and many, many hours, for the colour to penetrate the armour. In more recent times, I've noticed many manufacturers are choosing a different way to colour shell buttons.

A coating is applied to the buttons, either in a high gloss or matte finish, and it is the coating that accepts the dye treatment, saving time and costs. This solution has some drawbacks — the coating may chip away, usually through rough care or laundering, leaving the button looking rather unsightly. Some makers use a combination of dyed coatings and laser etching technology for stunning results.

A smaller yet commercially important pearl-producing shell is the *Pinctada fucata martensii*, or akoya, a by-product of the Japanese and Chinese cultured pearl industry. The iridescence of the natural nacre has pastel colours of pink, blue and green on a white background. Buttons that have been acid treated to darken the colours are referred to as 'smoke' and have a darker blue/grey background. Because the shell is smaller and the nacreous layer

ABOVE: Interesting freeform buttons, displaying the vivid colour patterns of the abalone shell. Largest button in rough oval shape, 50mm long; 1960s/1970s, North America.

RIGHT: The undulating surfaces enhance the vibrancy of these abalone shell buttons. In the mid-twentieth century, buttons were dyed to intensify and add deeper tones to the product. This selection includes buttons from the 1920s to recent times. Large round two-hole button, 45mm Ø.

finer, the shell's natural curvature remains a feature of the buttons produced. Larger sized buttons will inevitably be curved, while smaller sized shirt buttons, cut from the edges of the shell, may be flatter. China and Japan now successfully farm the akoya and besides the harvest of its pearl and meat, many millions of buttons are produced from the shells and sold worldwide.

Another nacre-producing marine snail is the abalone, from the taxonomic family *Haliotidae*. Abalone marine snails are found in almost all parts of the world, with the exception of the Pacific coast of South America, the Atlantic coast of North America, and the Arctic and Antarctica. They are mainly harvested for their meat.

For more than 10,000 years, North American Indigenous people collected abalone, probably at low tide, both for the meat and the shells. Shells were used whole as vessels or cut into pieces for inlay or to embellish objects of daily life, including jewellery and talismans. Prized by many Indigenous cultures for their shimmering, rainbow colours, there is evidence of widespread trade of the shells throughout pre-colonial times. The red or Californian abalone *Haliotis rufescens* is the largest of the species, and is the type mostly used in the button-making industry.

During the San Francisco gold rush of the mid-nineteenth century, Chinese workers who came to labour in the gold mines and railway construction discovered the bounty of abalone in the nearby waters. The harvest of abalone meat was cooked, salted and dried and sent back to their home country, while the shells were considered worthless and discarded on the beaches. By 1880, a small meat export industry developed; by 1890, 200 tons of abalone meat was exported to China. Before long, the Japanese followed suit and soon took over the monopoly.

The first European settlers in North America were not interested in abalone, either as a source of food or embellishment. But during the 1870s an Englishman working in San Francisco identified its potential and set up a small factory to process the shells for inlay, in the tradition of Indigenous tribes of the west coast such as the Pueblo, Navajo and others. By 1890, the thriving American mother of pearl industry took interest in this product, and shells were transported to the American button factories as well as further afield to the European continent. With several hundred tons of shells exported each year, they became a commercially important source of income for California. The decline of this population (due to the large demand for the meat) started in the twentieth century, before World War II, and by the late 1990s the industry recorded losses of 90 per cent. This led to quotas on both size and quantity, but the efforts of

Paua shell buttons from New Zealand, and paua inlay on mussel shell base from Indonesia. Small buttons on card, 9mm Ø; 1990s.

Paua Shell by Tui
Golden Bay, N.Z.

marine biologists have successfully replenished stocks, and the red abalone is now commercially harvested through aquaculture, mostly off the waters of southern California.

Many gastropods of the genus *Haliotis* are endangered, yet their harvesting remains culturally important for many Indigenous people, both as a food source and decoration. Restrictions are now in place against commercial export of, for example, the whole shells of the paua, or *Haliotis iris*, found only in New Zealand, even after the introduction of aquaculture production. Māori people used ashes and pumice stones to polish the outer shell, revealing the deep blue, green, bronze and pink colours arranged in a vibrant structure often compared to the harlequin pattern of opals. The shells were used as inlay work for jewellery and objects made from stone and wood, including the walls of community houses. Paua shell buttons are prized and sought after, such is the innate beauty of this colourful shell.

The cowrie shell, from the family Cypraeidae, is a small to large sea snail found in the Indo-Pacific region and was prized by many Indigenous cultures, viewed as a symbol of fertility, birth and wealth. For many African peoples, they were used extensively as a form of currency, and after the sixteenth century this usage spread to other parts of the world, particularly along the trade routes from Africa to South and East Asia. The shells were left intact, with the value based on a shell's weight.

Cowrie shell buttons have become more readily available since the late twentieth century, with the largest and most colourful of the species, the tiger cowrie (*Cypraes tigris*), being the preferred type. Its outer shell displays splotched markings that vary

Paua shell buttons are prized and sought after, such is the innate beauty of this colourful shell.

LEFT: Many different types of shells are used in button-making, although not necessarily on an industrial scale. Small producers use the materials available, showcasing the natural beauty on offer. This selection includes the many shades of the tiger cowrie and green turban, as well as handmade buttons using the base of a cone shell: 35mm ⌀, 2000s, Indonesia.

BELOW: A selection of Victorian era black glass buttons in the style of jet buttons from Whitby.

from warm tones of chocolate to cooler tones of grey blues on beige. While earlier eighteenth and nineteenth century buttons from this shell were often carved in cameo style to display the banded layers beneath, today's buttons are mostly cut to shape and drilled with sew-through holes — the beauty lies in the natural shell pattern. Despite periods of abundance of tiger cowrie buttons, the shell is not as plentiful as it once was and it is endangered in some parts of the world due to loss of habitat.

Jet and gemstones

Jet is a gemstone, mostly associated with mourning buttons and jewellery worn by Queen Victoria after the death of her husband, Prince Albert. But it has a much richer history that far precedes this era. Formed in the Jurassic period, it is the fossilized wood of the ancient Araucaria tree, a family of conifers that once grew in rainforests spanning both hemispheres. Catastrophic weather events around the world facilitated the formation of jet and in the Whitby area caused the trees to be swept into the sea and become encased in the sedimentary mud of the sea floor. A number of contributing factors assisted the fossilization process to form what is now called Whitby jet, with deposits found along a 12-kilometre stretch of coastline surrounding Whitby, as well as through the cliffs and under the moors. This gemstone is known as hard jet, a consequence of carbon compression and salt water. Jet occurs in many other parts of the world, including continental Europe, notably Spain and southern France. It was known in the Roman Empire province of Lycia, found near the estuary of the river Gages (now the Antalya region of Turkey), from which the European name for jet, *gagat*, is derived. However, the gemstone from these areas is known as soft jet, a consequence of carbon compression and fresh water.

Early finds of Whitby jet buttons and toggles have been attributed to the Neolithic Beaker people. Slightly later, during the Bronze Age, jet's use expanded to jewellery beads and necklaces. The stone was easily carved with the primitive tools of the time, and must have been valued for the natural allure of its rich blackness, as well as its perceived magical status — rubbing the surface creates a static charge that attracts small particles, which are thought to protect the wearer from evil.

Amber and tiger's eye buttons from the 1990s. The natural chatoyance, or lustre, of tiger's eye is caused by the reflection of inclusions within the stone; 20mm x 20mm, Germany.

During the Roman, Viking and medieval periods, the use of Whitby jet continued. Artefacts uncovered from the Roman city of Eboracum (now York) show an increased use of jet, including a workshop with tools and jet discards, and many more items of jewellery have been found in burial sites. The Romans already knew about jet, and they no doubt brought supplies from Spain and other parts of their empire to the markets of their new cosmopolitan northern city. Like the Romans, the Vikings were also partial to jet, creating both jewellery and non-jewellery pieces; Whitby jet artefacts can be found

Early finds of Whitby jet buttons and toggles have been attributed to the Neolithic Beaker people.

in the Scandinavian countries, as a result of the Vikings' trading networks. During the tumultuous medieval period, Whitby and its famous abbey became the centre for religious activity, and this determined the use of jet — jewellery and ornaments of this time had strong ecclesiastical designs. Throughout these periods, the use of Whitby jet was small in scale and limited to the supply of the raw material found along the coastline and under the cliffs.

The modern Whitby jet industry started around 1800. A retired naval pensioner, Captain Tremlett, who had seen amber beads turned on a lathe during his travels to the Baltic, was interested in experimenting with the turning of jet material; both raw materials are mineraloid gemstones. He enlisted the help of experienced jet workers, Robert Jefferson and John Carter, and a turner, Matthew Hill, to develop a commercial business. By 1850, around 50 jet workshops had been established. The successful promotion of Whitby jet items at the 1851 Great Exhibition in London was instrumental in publicising the area and its unique gemstone, and the acquisition of pieces by royal members (Queen Victoria and the Empress of France) led others to take

These coral and selenite buttons were made using various methods — coral beads adorn this handmade button, on a covered button base, 40mm ∅; reconstituted coral is pressed into moulds to create these small amulet animal buttons, 20mm long; dyed selenite is faceted to create high-end buttons, large size 34mm long with metal shank. China, Mexico, Europe.

Non-precious stones such as agates and soapstone have been made into buttons on a small scale. The freeform agate stones from Germany have been tumble-polished and a metal shank added; the soapstone buttons have been handmade by craftsmen in Ghana, Africa, large size 27mm Ø.

up the renewed trend. With Whitby jet now in higher demand, beachcombing supplies became exhausted and jet deposits were now mined; shafts cut horizontally into the cliffs and hillsides under the moors produced more raw materials. The death of Prince Albert in 1861 sent the Queen and her subjects into a collective mourning, and demand continued to grow. By the 1870s, the heyday of the commercial trade, there were some 200 workshops creating jewellery and buttons.

Some turned to other sources for their jet. Imported Spanish jet arrived in Whitby, but due to the differences between hard Whitby jet and soft foreign jet, the quality and reputation of jet buttons slipped. It didn't help the industry that cheaper imitators now entered the market. Black glass from Bohemia and France offered a less expensive product to the British people, who wanted to join their Queen in the fashion of the day. Indeed, the term 'French Jet' refers to black glass buttons. Other imitators were vulcanite, a form of vulcanized rubber (not to be confused with the mineral vulcanite). It was known under the brand name of Ebonite, referring to its black colour and its proposed use as an ebony wood substitute.

Changing tastes and fashions following the death of Queen Victoria eventually led to the decline of the Whitby jet industry. Today, the craft consists of a small group of artisans who meet demand with the Whitby jet supply found due to erosion. However, the products from the nineteenth century still command high prices today. Despite their excessively elaborate style, which might not coincide with modern tastes, they show an amazing level of craftsmanship and skill.

Further use of natural gemstones in button-making is left in the artisanal studio or in the experimental realm. In the nineteenth century, France experimented with slate as a material, and the firm of Clay's in England did manufacture a quantity, but these

Various gemstone buttons. Amethyst beads are sewn onto a covered button; amethyst freeform polished stone with attached metal shank; reconstituted malachite animal amulet buttons; lapis lazuli buttons with sterling silver bezel. Large round button, 29mm Ø; 1990s, Peru.

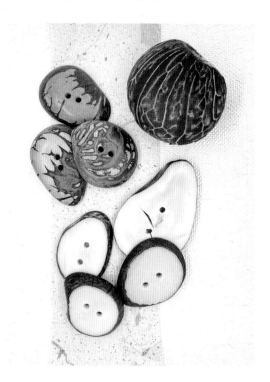

The tagua nut is cut into slices to create button blanks for further tooling or be drilled for attractive freeform buttons such as these. Large freeform two-hole button, 60mm long; 1990s, Peru.

An original box of 'stone nut' corozo buttons from the early 1900s, *garantiert faden nicht schneidende löcher* — 'guaranteed thread holes will not cut thread'. Black dyed buttons, 15mm ⌀; Germany.

are very rare today. I have purchased or commissioned buttons made from natural materials such as amber, agate, amethyst, boulder opal, tiger's eye, soapstone and selenite, to name a few, but never in commercial quantities. Some suppliers have simply tumbled small, irregularly shaped, uncut gemstones and attached a metal shank on one side. My own personal collection of tiger's eye buttons, shaped into squares and drilled through, were the result of the company's experiment with the raw material. They refused to supply more than the amount they had on show, explaining the unfortunate common occurrence of breakage both in the shaping and drilling processes. Other issues to consider with natural gemstones are their hardness and durability — they have not undergone rigorous testing and are generally not suitable for many forms of laundering. For example, while they look spectacular, lapis lazuli buttons do not like immersion in water as this can eventually dissolve the gemstone.

Corozo

A new raw material that found its way to the button-making firms of Europe was the tagua nut, otherwise known as vegetable ivory or corozo. This hard, dense nut of the

Corozo was a versatile material that could be stamped with designs, dyed, painted to imitate tortoiseshell and even inlaid with crystals or hand-painted ceramic beads. All buttons have a self-shank; large round button, 20mm ∅.

The naturally occurring growth patterns of the tagua nut may be further enhanced by dyeing; since the dye only penetrates the surface, the use of carving allows for stunning effects. The natural skin of the nut may be left intact to enhance the look of the finished button. Large red carved buttons, 32mm ∅; 1920s/1940s, Europe.

female tagua palm, plentiful in the northwest of South America, had been used for carvings for centuries. Tagua's introduction to Europe was somewhat different — it was used as ballast on German sailing ships coming from Panama and Ecuador. In the 1830s, after being discarded on the wharves of Hamburg, it was discovered that the material had a uniformity and ease of working similar to elephant ivory, and some 30 years later, in the 1860s, the corozo era began. During the second half of the nineteenth century, some billions of vegetable ivory buttons were made.

Worldwide, the most important source of vegetable ivory is still South America, namely Ecuador. The native plants, of which there are six species, come from the aptly named genus *Phytelephas* — elephant plant — in reference both to its size and the ivory-like similarities of the nut. The nut is pure cellulose (containing starch, protein and nutrients), storing food for developing plant embryos, and before maturity it has an edible, milky liquid centre. An edible fruit covers the outside, and the fruits grow in large clusters within a spiny, woody outer casing (known as an epicarp). As the fruit ripens, the spiny casing breaks down, allowing the fruits to fall to the ground where they are removed from the nut by foraging animals, or are removed manually during

harvest. The resulting core, varying in size from 2 to 10 centimetres but generally in the size and shape of a hen's egg, has a brown, cracked outer skin (resembling an avocado pit) covering the creamy white meat of the nut. The exposed nuts are left to harden for at least two to three months, during which time they slightly shrink and a small hollow may form in the centre.

Tagua nut carvers of decorative objects make certain they avoid getting too close to the possible void, or incorporate it into their design. Apart from buttons, tagua nuts have been used for creating jewellery, decorative sculptures, knife or umbrella handles, chess pieces and dice.

I use the terms 'tagua', 'vegetable ivory' and 'corozo' interchangeably; when English speakers first discovered the material, the term vegetable ivory was coined due to the similarities it shares with elephant ivory. It is the nut of the tagua palm, and native South Americans refer to the material as tagua. But when used in the modern button industry it is now known worldwide as corozo.

The nuts have a tightly closed, marbled wave-like grain, enabling a shiny polish. Because of its density, it required hacksaws or fretsaws and files in order to work it, leading to the term 'stone nut' in the German (*steinnüss*) and Dutch (*steennoot*) languages. German manufacturing began with experiments of the raw material in the early mid-nineteenth century, attributed to Herr Schlick, who engaged

English manufacturers began experimenting with vegetable ivory raw material from the 1850s and displayed their products at the 1862 International Exhibition.

Berliner woodturners to experiment with the so-called 'unusable waste material' for the purposes of creating handles for umbrellas and canes. The results were so favourable that by 1859 several woodturning shops converted to the production of *steinnüssknöpfen*. By 1860, corozo had reached the now steam-powered button-turning mills, with production spreading to North Saxony and into the Bohemian towns. Until World War I, Germany was the world leader in corozo button production, creating quality products that were exported widely across the globe.

English manufacturers began experimenting with vegetable ivory raw material from the 1850s and displayed their products at the 1862 International Exhibition. Once again, Birmingham was at the centre of production. Trade with the United States started button-making in that country in 1864; by the 1880s, Rochester, NY, was the centre of the vegetable ivory button industry and, until plastic buttons became common, 20 per cent of all buttons produced in the United States were made from this natural product.

The French eventually caught up with their British rivals, starting their corozo industry in 1870. A year earlier, the button-manufacturing firm of Tacchini & Fanti, in the Bergamo region of Italy, acquired German raw material and started their own production; merging 25 years later with *Società Anonima Manifattura Bottoni* (SAMB),

Coconut shell has a long history as a material for making household objects, but the button trade probably only started using it in the twentieth century, initially for the tourist market and later as the staple for the ubiquitous Hawaiian shirt. Today, it is used as a sustainable base for decal decorated buttons: large William Morris decoration style button, 40mm ∅; 2020s, India.

COCOANUT BUTTONS
MADE BY
NATIVES OF THE ISLES

Carved - Polished
by Hand

they ramped up production on an industrial scale. At the 1900 Paris *Exposition Universelle*, SAMB won a gold medal for their buttons, of which they Italianized the name to *bottoni di frutto*. Both Germany and Italy, in 1895 and 1910 respectively, set up firms in Ecuador from which they acquired their raw material, increasing the tagua industry in South America.

As the central void of the tagua nut can only be determined once it is cut into, in nineteenth century Europe the button blanks were processed using a variety of methods. In Germany, the nuts were cut in half and drilling and boring tools were used to make blanks. In Italy, thin slices of the nut were processed. In France, four slices were cut from the exterior and a one-step technique produced a finished back and smooth fronted, half-finished button blank.

The peak of the first wave of production of vegetable ivory buttons was from the 1870s to the 1920s. Then in 1940 this material, along with glass and pearl shell, was replaced by the advent of inexpensive plastic buttons. Until then, corozo was made using a variety of techniques for maximum effect. In some styles the outer brown skin was left intact, allowing for imaginative tooling to produce a two-tone effect. Dyeing enhanced the natural whorls of the grain, and because the interior colour remained intact, tooling provided a colourful two-tone effect. Due to the waste produced by the manufacture of these buttons, methods of salvage and re-use were investigated, and in some respects this was the forerunner of the plastic button. Offcuts of tagua were finely

In my capacity as a jeweller, I meet and work with opal miners and dealers who have delighted in creating buttons for me. As precious gemstones, these are definitely *not* machine washable; nonetheless they are sought after by a select few who appreciate Australia's national gemstone. All buttons shown are boulder opal from Queensland. Shank buttons are treated opal matrix, large round button 26mm Ø, with sterling silver shank; 2000s, Australia.

ground into powder, washed and formed into a thick slurry, then pressed into a mould under heat and pressure. Methods of stencilling, painting, embossing, stamping and engraving enhanced these pressed buttons.

The attraction for natural materials resurfaced in the 1970s, and the tagua industry made a progressive recovery. Coming into the 21st century, the tagua nut has again sparked interest in button-making and other decorative industries, as more sustainable and ethically sourced materials are desired. As a substitute for elephant ivory it not only responds to animal welfare issues but also presents alternatives to deforestation for farming by stimulating the local economies that benefit from the tagua trade. There are now South American companies who not only supply raw button blanks of corozo but also manufacture the finished button product themselves.

Today, corozo buttons are made from the true nut material, where the grain is on show as a feature of its own merit. They can be designed as sew-through or shanked buttons, from simple tooling to intricate laser carving and bespoke laser etching. Hexagonal drums, containing a foaming agent and abrasive, tumble polish the buttons until the required smoothness is achieved. One of the current worldwide uses of the waste material is in the cosmetics industry, where tagua powder has thankfully replaced plastic microbeads as an exfoliant.

The use of natural raw materials in button production may have started from necessity, but the innate beauty that nature produces has an instant appeal. The decision to choose natural buttons often goes hand in hand with quality or beloved projects. When situations arose where supply was interrupted, or worse, depleted, the quest to create alternatives began. Industry pioneered new materials that for a time dominated the accessory industry, leading natural button production to stall into an almost 40-year-slumber. Since the 1980s, a slow but steady rediscovery and appreciation of these natural materials has led the button industry back into careful manufacture, with more global awareness of species origin and a sense of conservation. Buttons made from natural products always require more handwork, and therefore often come at a higher cost than commercially mass-produced ones. They are seen commercially on high quality clothing worldwide.

Plastics can mimic
natural products,
or create all-new
products. This buttons
and buckle set imitate
mother of pearl and
gold inlay, each piece
individual. Large
button 34mm ∅,
polyester; Switzerland,
late 1990s.

7

The plastics evolution

… JUST BECAUSE WE ARE NO LONGER IMPRESSED BY PLASTICS DOES NOT MEAN THAT PLASTICS ARE ANY LESS IMPRESSIVE.

—IAN HOLDSWORTH, PLASTICS HISTORICAL SOCIETY

Today's general public considers plastic a scourge — a cheap and nasty product that ends up in our landfill and waterways, polluting the earth. Indeed, plastic has permeated every aspect of our lives, and many of us in the developed world irresponsibly throw it away without any consequence. However, when it was first invented it was greatly prized and, as long as the correct form of the material used was fit for purpose, it was an asset to many and showed great longevity.

Fundamentally, plastics are primarily mouldable organic materials that can be grouped into two distinct classes, thermoplastics and thermosetting plastics. Thermoplastics soften and flow when heated, are usually shaped by heat and pressure, and retain their shape when hardened and dry. If reheated, they will soften and flow again. Thermosetting plastics are soft to begin with, but during the moulding process, through heat and pressure, an irreversible chemical reaction takes place; thermoset plastics do not re-soften, will char before melting, and are generally harder (and often more brittle) than thermoplastics. The nineteenth century was a period when chemists experimented with numerous plastic formulations using a variety of organic substances, which in turn led to the discovery of the first semi-synthetic material.

While the initial push to invent plastics was to create a substitute for costly natural decorative products (such as those made from ivory, mother of pearl and tortoiseshell), it soon found uses as an electrical insulator and later was an important material during the war effort. Along the way, its use in reproducing luxury items as affordable products played a small part in creating a more egalitarian society, and button-making joined the technology ride.

Although the first semi-synthetic plastic was officially exhibited in 1862, the word 'plastic' was only officially recognized by the British Plastics Federation and the British Standards Institute in 1951. However, since its nineteenth century introduction, there followed a frenzy of experiments, developments and applications, so much so that in 1979 the amount of plastic produced in the world was greater than the amount of steel. The Plastics Age had arrived. Chemically, plastics are made up of long chain polymers; smaller molecules (monomers) react with each other under the right conditions to create repeating units of chain structures — polymers. Besides the base polymer, a colourant improves the visual look and other additives aid in the manufacture or improve the working function of the product.

Some natural products have plasticity and can be readily shaped, and early experiments were made using the natural materials of horn and tortoiseshell, often described as the original plastics. Both are a natural thermoplastic material, and have long been used for making numerous accessories and household items.

Papier mâché

Another type of plastic that has a long history is papier mâché, made with mashed paper and glue or starch. Originating in Imperial China, the technique was introduced to, and developed in, France probably in the latter part of the seventeenth century (hence the French name), and soon after adopted by Germany and England. The term describes many objects made using different methods, all having the common factor of mashed up paper and a type of glue, press-moulded and cast into the required shape. In 1772, an Englishman by the name of Henry Clay patented a product he named, 'paperware', which revolutionized the industry. His method of creating strong sheets of papier mâché was as follows. Rag paper sheets were coated on both sides with a glue and flour paste and compacted in a metal press; after pressing, the sheets were saturated in linseed oil for waterproofing, and lastly dried in an oven at the high temperature of

Luxury buttons designed and manufactured from thermosetting polyester plastic.
So many elements of hand-manufacturing have gone into these unusually faceted
and dyed buttons. Large green and black, 30mm ∅; late 1990s, Italy.

about 540°C (1000°F). This durable material was in demand for architectural, decorative
and furniture objects, and eventually also buttons.

Henry Clay trained as a printer and was an industrial innovator who established
the japanning industry in Birmingham. Japanning, the popular varnishing finish,
was used on wood, and also papier mâché, creating a shiny black (also red or green)
surface that could be painted. When Clay's patent expired in 1802, others took up
his technology. As a thermoplastic material, the sheets produced could be used in
machines similar to those used to produce horn buttons. Buttons were usually made
with shanks — metal loop shanks inserted into a hole drilled especially — or, less often,
moulded self-shanks. Many buttons were elaborately decorated with gold leaf and over-
painted with an asphalt-based pigment (asphaltum), or finely painted in colours, as well
as gold, encompassing chinoiserie and contemporary themes of the day. Wafer thin
pieces of pearl shell could also be applied to the surface in ornate, mostly floral patterns,
before being finally varnished. The French company of *Albert Parent et Cie* included
papier mâché buttons in their collection of exquisitely produced buttons.

Early on in my button buying, I purchased hundreds of domed papier mâché boot
buttons. All of them were finished with a polished layer of black japan, a mixture of
molten asphalt, natural resin varnishes, drying oils and turpentine. Some were simple,
unadorned buttons, some had pin shanks, and a very few had a small pearl shell disc on
top, attached with a pin shank. Over the years, costume departments of the Australian
film and theatre industry purchased most of these authentic nineteenth century items
for the corresponding period articles they made. While papier mâché buttons continued
into the early twentieth century, their heyday was during the Victorian era, particularly
during the years 1835 to 1875.

Bois durci

Bois durci (hardened wood), a form of wood pulp moulding, was the invention of Frenchman, François Charles Lepage, who patented his product in 1855. He declared that his substance could be a substitute for any hard or plastic medium, such as wood, leather, bone and metal. Waste materials were the main components, namely sawdust and animal blood collected from the abattoir. The sawdust from hardwoods, preferably ebony and rosewood, could be mixed with other powders (from vegetable, mineral or metallic sources); the blood albumin could be mixed with any glutinous or gelatinous matter. Raw material was created by soaking the dry powder in diluted albumin and, when thoroughly permeated, left to dry and then ground into a powder again. The material was formed into its final shape using compression moulding (under heat and pressure in preheated steel moulds), resulting in a remarkably dense thermoset casting with fine details and a glossy finish.

Papier mâché box displayed with British-made boot buttons, 9–11mm ∅; circa late 1800s.

Lepage sold his patent to Alfred Latry, who established a Paris factory, *La Société du Bois Durci*, and manufactured small decorative objects (such as inkwell stands, desk sets, combs, plaques, jewellery, buckles and presumably some buttons) which he sold in his Paris store, A. Latry & Cie. Items were exhibited at the London International Exhibition in 1862, and the Paris *Exposition Universelle* in 1867. In the late 1890s, *La Société de Bois Durci* was taken over by MIOM (*La Manufacture d'Isolants et Objets Moulés*) who continued making a form of *bois durci* until around 1920.

Shellac

The refined secretions of the tiny lac insect are an unlikely source for the only commercially harvested natural resin of animal origin: shellac. It takes about

This display of contemporary buttons, uses dyed sawdust with a resin binder to create buttons imitating the *cloisonné* style. While much cruder than the *bois durci* items produced in the nineteenth century, they nevertheless utilise the wood in a similar manner. 30mm x 30mm, cushion cut; early 2000s.

15,000 lac insects around six months to create just under ½ kilogram (1lb) of shellac.

When collected, heated, cleaned and filtered, shellac produces a brittle thermoplastic substance. It has been harvested since antiquity and was brought to Europe in the thirteenth century where it was predominantly used in a lacquer form, as a paint pigment, varnish or protective coating on paintings and wood, or made into a compound to form a sealing wax. Further experiments in the later nineteenth century led to mixing molten shellac with fillers, such as ground wood (and later slate and mica), producing a compound that could be moulded by heat and pressure. These shellac compounds were capable of replicating very fine details, and although only small amounts of buttons were produced it was used to make intricate jewellery and other objects (mirror backs, small boxes, picture frames). Shellac's fine reproduction qualities were put to good use after the mid-1890s, when shellac mixed with ground slate and carbon black was used to make 78 rpm gramophone records; this use of the compound remained in place until the 1950s, when it was replaced by vinyl. However, it was shellac's attributes as an excellent electrical insulator, and the need to find a substitute for the rapidly expanding electrical industry of the twentieth century, that eventually led to the first fully synthetic plastic.

Rubber

After Italian explorer Christopher Columbus' second voyage to the Caribbean in 1493, the Western world was first introduced to rubber, but it would take over 200 years for the origin of this material to become known. European explorers, who later mounted

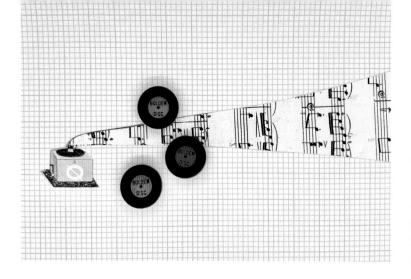

Until replaced by vinyl, shellac — due to its fine reproduction qualities — was used for the manufacture of gramophone records. Two-part injection-moulded nylon buttons, Golden Disc buttons 16mm Ø; 2000s, France.

scientific expeditions across the globe, brought back with them a previously unknown raw material collected from native trees. In the Americas, in countries where the native rubber tree grew, archaeological finds show the use of latex rubber in a stabilized form from as early as 1650 BC; Mesoamericans made playing balls and other objects and, later, the Mayans and Aztecs also used latex as a waterproofing medium by either impregnating textiles or coating containers. In South-East Asia, locals used gutta-percha for knife and other tool handles. These two materials captured the imagination of early scientists in the eighteenth century, and plastic innovators in the nineteenth century.

Rubber is a natural polymer that has thermoplastic and elastic properties, an elastomer. In its relaxed state, the polymer chains appear disordered, but when stretched the molecules align into an ordered arrangement. The material comes from the milky white liquid known as latex, found in the ducts or in the cells of rubber-producing plants.

In 1736, French naturalist, explorer and adventurist Charles-Marie de La Condamine sent samples of natural rubber, or *caoutchouc* as it was known in French, back to his homeland, although he could not unlock the mysteries of how to use it. Later, in 1770, English chemist and philosopher Joseph Priestly noted that a piece of this new material could easily rub out pencil marks on paper, and coined the English word 'rubber'.

Real progress of the rubber industry came in the early nineteenth century through the experiments of two Englishmen, chemist Charles Macintosh and inventor Thomas Hancock, and American manufacturing engineer, Charles Goodyear. Macintosh's 1823 rediscovery of coal-tar naphtha as an effective solvent for the material led to his rubber solution being spread between two layers of fabric, resulting in the 'mackintosh' waterproof garment. Hancock, who had been cutting strips from imported rubber for use on clothing and footwear, invented a masticator for the waste cuttings; through friction, his 1820 device was able to bond the rubber scraps into a mass that could be reused in further manufacturing. As colleagues and later partners, the two solved some of the obstacles of working with natural rubber, but their products remained unstable. While natural rubber is malleable, it becomes sticky with heat, and rigid and brittle with cold; stabilizing the material was key to its commercial success.

In the 1830s, Charles Goodyear was experimenting with ways to stabilize rubber for use in manufacturing, which eventually led to his 1839 discovery that the addition of sulphur and heat treatment produced a material that was durable, less sensitive to heat and had a characteristic bounce. He called it 'fireproof gum'. At the same time, Thomas Hancock came to a similar conclusion, perhaps through Goodyear's work, calling the process 'vulcanization' after Vulcan, the Roman god of fire. Hancock patented his vulcanization technique in late 1843, beating Goodyear's patent of early 1844. Both exhibited their sampling of hard rubber-embossed items at London's Great Exhibition in 1851, using the names Vulcanite or Ebonite.

Amasa J. Goodyear, the father of Charles and Nelson, was an inventor, manufacturer, merchant and farmer; among the many diverse articles he produced were ivory, shell and pewter buttons, so both sons were equipped with the knowledge of small item manufacturing. In 1851, Nelson Goodyear patented an improved vulcanization process and allowed two American companies — the Novelty Rubber Company of New York and New Brunswick, N.J. (N.R. Co.) and the India Rubber Comb Company of New York (I.R.C. Co.) — the use of his patent under licence to manufacture

These playful, modern 'rubber' tyre tread buttons are made from silicone, a man-made material derived from the element and compound of silicon metal and silica sand, respectively. Perhaps an homage to the Goodyear Tire & Rubber Company? Large button, 36mm x 21mm; 2000s, France.

Following the death of England's Prince Albert, moulded, hard black rubber jewellery items and buttons were produced to fill the demand for mourning fashion accessories.

buttons and other products. After his patent expired in 1870, another two companies joined in making hard rubber buttons, the Dickinson Hard Rubber Company of Springfield, MA (D.H.R. Co.), and the American Rubber Company (A.R. Co.). The Novelty Rubber Company produced the widest variety, mostly black, in many shapes, sizes and patterns, including various shank types and two- and four-hole sew-throughs; pictorials, geometric and textile patterns, flowers, animals, and military buttons for the American Civil War were among their collection.

Considering the popularity of rubber buttons in the United States, they were not popular in England or Europe, allegedly due to the smell. Hardened, natural rubber buttons seem to have been manufactured solely in the United States. The European vulcanite probably progressed to include a variety of mixtures including the addition of shellac or other fillers. Following the death of England's Prince Albert, moulded, hard black rubber jewellery items and buttons were produced to fill the demand for mourning fashion accessories. While they were unlike the top-quality handmade Whitby jet objects, black rubber composition was considered an acceptable, more affordable alternative, especially owing to its intense black colour that could be beautifully polished.

Rubber remains an important resource today, although modern rubber buttons are no longer made of natural rubber, and South America is no longer the source of cultivation. Two factors led to the collapse of the South American industry. In 1876, English explorer Henry Wickham smuggled about 70,000 seeds from the Amazon for germination in Kew Gardens, of which about 2500 progressed to seedlings and were sent to English and Dutch colonial plantations in South and South-East Asia. And in the early twentieth century, South American rubber trees became the victim of indigenous leaf blights, ending their cultivation. Today's larger rubber plantations are found in Thailand, Indonesia, Malaysia, India and Vietnam (all originating from the seeds taken from South America), where they are unaffected by local plant diseases.

Although these buttons with textile and floral patterns are pressed from corozo material, they are reminiscent of coexisting styles made from black rubber. Large button, 20mm ∅; late 1800s/early 1900s, Europe.

Rubber buttons are no longer made from natural rubber or gutta-percha, but from synthetic rubber derived from oil-based products, or silicone. Today, they are mostly used for active sportswear clothing. While contact sports clothing styles have progressed, these replica 'rubber' shirt buttons are commonly found on the classic-style cotton jerseys worn today. Black silicone buttons, 14mm ∅; 2000s, France.

Gutta-percha and balata

In 1656, English botanist John Tradescant returned from his travels to South-East Asia with many botanical specimens, among them gutta-percha, which he called mazer wood. At the time, this strong and somewhat flexible wood was considered a curiosity, but some 200 years later the West discovered its true potential through the efforts of Dr William Montgomerie, a surgeon with the East India Company. During his initial posting in Singapore, in 1822 Dr Montgomerie noticed the local people made machete handles and other domestic utensils from a native tree gum, the *Palaquium gutta*. Following a posting to Bengal, he returned to Singapore and reacquainted himself with the material, experimenting with its possible uses. He learned its Malay name, *gettah percha* — *gettah* meaning tacky gum, and *percha* the name of the tree. In 1843, Montgomerie sent samples and documents outlining his findings to both the Medical Board of Calcutta and the Royal Society of the Arts in London.

The French were also making inroads to South-East Asia, and in 1845 diplomatic envoy Théodore de Lagrené brought a quantity of this new material to the French Ministry of Commerce. By 1847, huge advancements in determining the physical and chemical characteristics, as well as the machinery to work it, saw multiple patents taken out, both in Europe and the United States. This new raw material could be plasticized in hot water and easily moulded and upon cooling, maintaining a tough yet flexible form without the need for vulcanization.

Another source of gutta-percha, known as balata, comes from trees found in Central and South America, the *Manilkara bidentata* or common name bully tree. Both trees come from the same taxonomic family, *Sapotaceae*. The name balata comes from the Caribbean where local people used the word to refer solely to the gum found in the trees. Gutta-percha contains 70 to 75 per cent gum and 6 to 10 per cent resins. Balata contains equal amounts of gum and resin, although the gum found in balata is identical to that of gutta-percha.

Gutta-percha is a thermoplastic natural polymer, chemically the same as rubber. However, as an isomer of rubber, it has a different molecular shape, giving it different properties; gutta-percha is durable, but is comparatively unelastic. Collection of gutta-percha latex is also different. In contrast to rubber, which has a network of latex tubes, the latex from the gutta-percha tree is found in the cells of the bark and leaves, and is therefore not collected by tapping as is used for rubber. Initially, whole trees were cut down to extract the latex, potentially leading to complete destruction of stocks without replenishment. Later it was found that the leaves held the best quality latex; these are ground to detach the gum threads from the leaf tissue and washed repeatedly in boiling water. This mass is then washed in cold water, causing the gum threads to adhere to each other, rising to the surface while the saturated leaves fall to the bottom. Unlike rubber, which turns into a sticky, unworkable adhesive when boiled, gutta-percha is not sticky and when soft is easily handled. The gum pieces are collected and sieved several times through a fine mesh before going into the masticator that kneads it together like dough. From here, it is ready to be moulded into any shape or form.

Once gutta-percha's properties were understood — including its excellent

Chicle, the gum from the sapodilla tree *(Manilkara zapota)* is thought to contain both rubber and gutta-percha, but was mostly used as the main ingredient of chewing gum in the late nineteenth century. Two-part nylon injection moulded buttons, 18mm x 5mm; 2000s, France.

insulating properties, especially for electrical wires, and the fact it is biologically inert, which meant it could be used in the medical profession — it became so popular it was considered the ultimate material, especially in Victorian England. An 1848 patent by Englishman R.A. Brooman shows a number of machines to process the material, multiple ways of improving its properties, and an extensive list of items made with gutta-percha, including buttons. The ease of working gutta-percha meant it could be shaped by pressing into cold moulds or by extrusion. Its low water absorption meant no visible shrinkage when drying. Softened material repeatedly passed through a series of rollers (calendar rollers) produced sheets of gutta-percha; air-drying was all that was needed for the material to become hard enough for ordinary purposes. Adding metallic fillers, exposed to low heat (100–150°C/212–300°F) under pressure, allowed it to be tempered if required, giving it a metallic finish.

Rubber and gutta-percha buttons were not hugely produced over a long period of time, considering the other materials used in the industry, but the machinery that was developed and repurposed to work these new materials was significant to further developments in the plastics industry. Thomas Hancock's masticator, and later calendar rollers and spreading machines of the 1830s, as well as Henry Bewley's 1845 extrusion machines for gutta-percha tubes come to mind. Small fancy goods items from rubber and gutta-percha were most popular in the latter half of the nineteenth century, but even with changing fashions their use continued up to the 1940s, after which all rubber was requisitioned for the war effort.

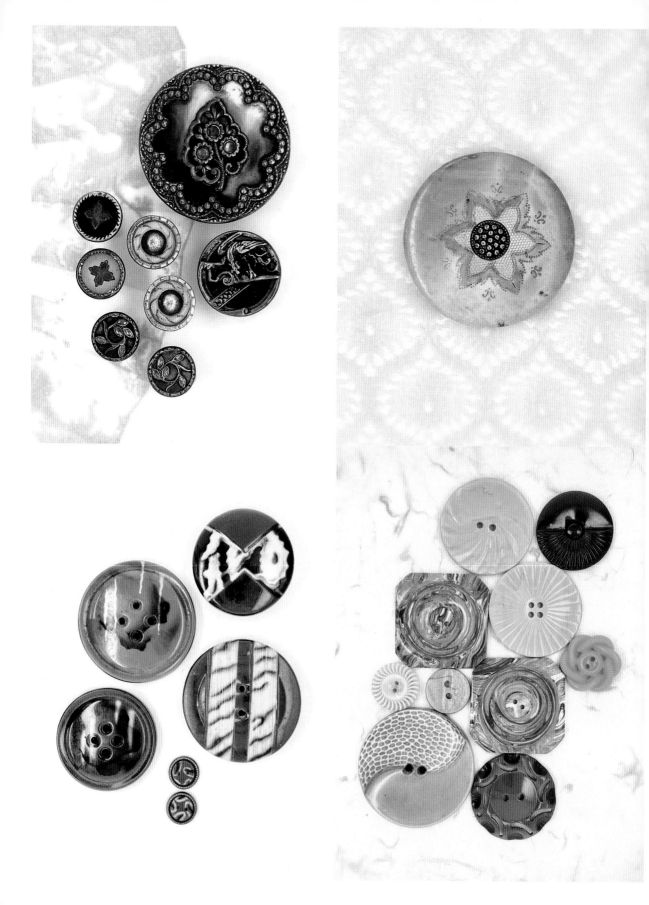

OPPOSITE FROM TOP LEFT: Twentieth century hand-painted celluloid 'tight tops' with lacquered steel backs; small shirt buttons with brass rolled rim. Large teal button, 38mm ∅; shirt buttons, 10mm ∅.

An early 1900s celluloid button, made in multiple layers: a blackened gold gilt escutcheon is attached to a silver gilt-faceted sheet, covered by a celluloid layer with gilded decoration and pierced flower pattern, pressed into a steel back. This top is then pressed into a blackened steel back plate with self-shank. 45mm ∅; France.

A group of late 1800s/early 1900s metal buttons with celluloid inserts, painted to imitate natural materials or colours. The brass face material is combined with black lacquered steel backs and wire loop shanks. Large button, 31mm ∅.

A selection of pressed celluloid buttons, showing some of the colours and treatments of the celluloid material. Large beige yin yang style, 43mm ∅; twentieth century.

Semi-synthetics

The cellulosic family: cellulose nitrate (CN) and cellulose acetate (CA)

Who would have thought that natural cotton would be the starting point for the world's first semi-synthetic plastic? Biological processes that create natural polymers exist in plants and animals (including humans) and can be found in silk, wool, proteins and DNA. A very common natural organic polymer is cellulose, the substance that creates the cell walls of plants. The waste product from the growing textile industry was the starting point for the first semi-synthetic cellulose plastics.

In 1845, Christian Friedrich Schönbein, a renowned German chemist working in Switzerland, accidentally discovered cellulose nitrate in his kitchen when he used his wife's apron to wipe up nitric and sulphuric acid he had spilled, turning it to a liquid. He continued experimenting, influenced by the 1938 work of French chemist and professor Théophile Jules Pelouze whose *pyroxyline* (from the Greek *pyro* 'fire' and *xylon* 'wood') was a result of wood fibres, paper or rags dissolved in concentrated nitric acid to produce a highly flammable cellulose nitrate, or nitrocellulose. In 1846, Schönbein patented his formulas in both England and France, sending samples to his friend Michael Faraday in England — paper and/or vegetable fibres, made transparent and able

The nineteenth century saw materials such as natural ivory and tortoiseshell become increasingly scarce and expensive, and the challenge was to find good substitutes.

to be formed into various shapes. His interests lay in creating guncotton, a replacement for gunpowder, but that's another story. French chemist Henri Bracconot had preceded both Pelouze and Schönbein. In 1832, working in Nancy, Bracconot conducted experiments preparing potato starch, sawdust and cotton with nitric acid, calling it *xyloidine* and hoping to create coatings, films and shaped articles.

The nineteenth century saw materials such as natural ivory and tortoiseshell become increasingly scarce and expensive, and the challenge was to find good substitutes. Experiments with new materials and technologies, at a time when chemists didn't really understand the structures of what they were producing, were definitely trial by error. Alexander Parkes was one of the experimenters, a man with a wide range of training, skills and interests and a true materials technologist. During his lifetime, his insatiable curiosity and ingenuity led to some 80 patents, including his important contributions as a metallurgist: he devised a method of electroplating fragile objects, invented a number of alloys, and his method of de-silvering lead is still in use today. However, it was his work in the rubber industry that was the catalyst for his future invention, the world's first semi-synthetic plastic.

Parkes worked in the rubber industry in its early days, and by 1846 the vulcanization of rubber had become standard practice. A good problem solver and innovative thinker, all of his experience with the materials, techniques and processes of handling rubber, including the new technologies (calendaring, spreading, and extrusion machines) were put to good use when he learned of Schönbein's work. In Parkes's experiments, the volatile nitrocellulose was first diluted in ether to create a somewhat less flammable 'collodion', and Parkes's knowledge of sulphur chloride helped him generate the plasticiser necessary to create a new thermoplastic product that he named after himself, Parkesine.

From 1856 he took out the first of several patents in the development of his Parkesine, concentrating on its properties and possible uses. He later enlisted the help of his chemist brother, Henry Parkes, to develop ways of making it look more attractive; Henry invented dyeing and marbling techniques that mimicked tortoiseshell and many different woods as well as an array of bright colours. Parkes's mixture of cellulose nitrate (derived mostly from wood flour and cotton waste) and plasticisers produced an exceptional substance, which was hard as horn yet remained flexible like leather. It was also capable of being cast or stamped, painted, dyed or carved. Parkes formed the New Parkesine Works with business partner Daniel Spill, but by 1868 it was in liquidation. Parkes was unable to replicate the same quality of material in a commercially viable way, and his use of poorer quality raw materials in order to maintain a low price point was his eventual downfall. However, his experiments using various mixtures of cellulose nitrate, alcohols, camphor and oils predated the development of the first commercial plastic: celluloid.

The search continued for new substances to reduce the dependency on natural raw materials and their associated supply and quality control issues. Chemists, individual inventors and entrepreneurs across Europe and the United States, without any understanding of the formation and structure of the polymers they were creating, continued with experiments, carrying on from those before them. In the United States,

Twentieth century 'tight tops' and 'bubble tops' were a common type of celluloid button, where the celluloid face was pressed onto a metal backing. This selection of hand-painted buttons have foil inserts to create added glow. Large purple button, 50mm.

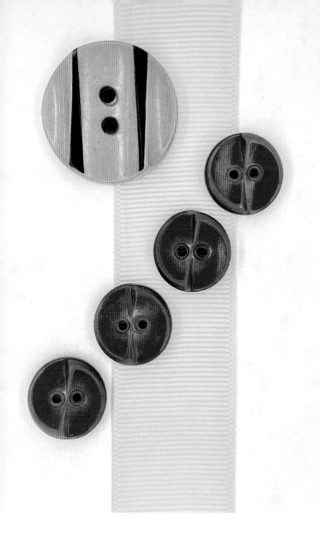

John Wesley Hyatt was perhaps motivated by a $10,000 prize offered in 1863 by the company Phelan and Collander for anyone coming up with an alternative for their ivory billiard balls, although his interests took him further afield than just the one application. Together with his brother Isaiah S. Hyatt, their experiments eventually led to the first commercially successful thermoplastic cellulose-based product, overcoming some of the problems that caused so much trouble for Parkes and Spill. Isaiah called it 'celluloid'. A patent was taken out for their invention in 1870, and in 1872 the name was trademarked. John Wesley Hyatt made an important contribution to this new plastic technology by inventing a machine that could fabricate celluloid sheet material, using Hancock's 1840 slicer to slice from large moulded blocks. He was already using equipment that had been developed for the rubber industries — Samuel Peck's screw press, Hancock's masticator, Bewley's extruder and Samuel Peck's hydraulic press (1816). Manufacturing began in 1870 with celluloid dentures at the Albany Dental Plate Company, to be superseded three years later by the Celluloid Manufacturing Company. Their expanded product range was advertised as an inexpensive alternative to natural ivory, horn and tortoiseshell, among other materials.

The Hyatts wanted to expand overseas, sending representative Amasa Mason to England and France to establish joint ventures there. They were successful in France, and the *Compagnie Franco-Americaine* (later to become *Compagnie Française de Celluloide*) was opened in 1875 outside Paris. The company's celluloid articles were exhibited at the Paris 1878 *Exposition Universelle*, where they not only showed the wide range of colours and applications but also attracted investment for expanding the industry, with several companies later to produce this new semi-synthetic plastic material.

Removable collars and cuffs, from fiercely starched linen or celluloid, were attached to the shirt with specially made buttons. While technology was racing forward, classic mother of pearl collar and cuff studs were still *de rigueur*. Circa early twentieth century.

In England, Mason's efforts to enlist L.P. Merriam in a venture with the Hyatt brothers was not successful, but Merriam's interest in celluloid continued and he later got together with Daniel Spill. After the collapse of the New Parkesine Works, Spill continued work in London, improving on Parkes's formulas, forming the Xylonite Company in 1869. Despite struggling to create a market, and the eventual 1874 closing of the company by its directors, he maintained faith in the product and continued. In the same year, he relocated and began the Daniel Spill Company, producing 'Xylonite' and a white form, 'Ivoride', with Merriam setting up the manufacture of products next door. Despite none of their ventures having proved financially stable so far, together they took on partners and established the British Xylonite Company in 1877. In this same year Spill took action against Hyatt in the United States, claiming violation of Spill's US patents. The dispute lasted several years, in 1880 finding for Spill, but progression to a higher court eventually found for neither; the 1884 decision found that Alexander Parkes was the inventor of the process using camphor and alcohol, and that there were no restrictions on the use of these processes by others. Anyone was free to use them. Afterwards, the word celluloid started use as a generic term for this product.

The turning point for early celluloid manufacturers around the world was the mid-1880s' success of celluloid collars and cuffs. Removable collars, starting with the ruff, had been in existence since the sixteenth century, and were initially reserved for the ruling class as a sign of aristocracy. The changes to society brought on by the industrial age brought back the use of removable collars (and cuffs) but this time for a different market. Purportedly started by an American woman in the late 1820s, who removed the collar and cuffs of her husband's shirt to launder and later re-attach them, the trend caught on and soon companies started making removable collars and cuffs for a variety of clientele, particularly the growing cohort of office workers who became known as 'white collar' workers. For these workers, shirts could now be washed less frequently, and replacement of collars and cuffs was more cost effective than buying a new shirt. For the aspiring gentleman, detachable collars allowed one to keep up with the latest styles. Initially made from firmly starched linen, the discovery of celluloid made it possible to create collars and cuffs interlined with linen that could be easily cleaned with soap and water. The trend soon followed in Europe, which embraced the resulting social changes.

The success of hair combs, and later collars and cuffs, made from celluloid was an incentive for others to join the market. Germany followed France's success with celluloid manufacturing,

The French eagerly took up the manufacture of celluloid buttons, an inexpensive alternative material for everyday use. Haute Nouveauté buttons, 26mm ∅.

The turning point for early celluloid manufacturers around the world was the mid-1880s success of celluloid collars and cuffs.

and by 1900 England, the United States, France and Germany all had significant celluloid industries. In Germany, the 1880s saw the establishment of new firms, or the restructure of rubber factories to include the new celluloid fabrication. The expansion of the industry led it to overtake all other European countries with celluloid production, with mergers of smaller companies beginning in 1904. By 1916 many of the firms formed the *Interessengemeinschaft der Deutschen Teerfarbenfrabriken* (Syndicate of German Coal-Tar Dye Manufacturers), sharing knowledge, markets and production while remaining independent. In 1925, the syndicate companies were officially merged into one company, renamed the *IG Farbenindustrie AG*, and by the late 1920s it had become an international company, for a time dominating worldwide production.

Another European innovator of celluloid was the family company of Mazzucchelli. Started in 1849 by father Santino, the tiny factory produced buttons and hair combs from horn, bone and tortoiseshell. By 1900, with many more workers, son Pompeo Mazzucchelli was attracted to the new celluloid material because of its aesthetic appeal and lower price, especially when compared to tortoiseshell. Initially importing sheet material from both France and Germany to create their products, in the early 1920s Mazzucchelli started producing their own celluloid. Soon other Italian firms followed both production of material and products.

After World War I, more countries began celluloid production, including the Soviet Union and Japan: the Okhtenski Chemical Factory (1926) in Leningrad (now St Petersburg) and the Dai Nippon Celluloid Company in Japan. Japan had the edge — the natural camphor needed to fabricate celluloid was locally produced and of a high standard, labour costs were cheaper, and there was government support of export and shipping costs. By 1935, Japan was the world's largest producer of celluloid.

Early use of celluloid in the button industry started around the mid-1870s. This new thermoplastic material was embraced for the new opportunities it presented in terms of manufacturing as it could be used in a solid, plastic or fluid state. Transparent celluloid was used for the popular lithograph buttons of the time, imitating the glass inset in metal buttons, or as a coating for metal tops. It could be produced in any variety of colours and could be perfectly matched to fabrics.

Independent celluloid button production progressed in the 1880s — mother of pearl could be imitated by adding small particles of lead phosphate to the raw material, and the new aniline dyes (synthetically produced in the 1850s) hand-painted onto celluloid sheets closely resembled the effects of horn and tortoiseshell. This had an immediate effect on the efficiency of material used. Delivered in uniform sheets, it was more cost effective than the natural products of mother of pearl, horn or tortoiseshell as there were no colour or quality inconsistencies and manufacturers could calculate in advance the material needed for production. The same dyes and pressure moulds that were used for metal buttons were now used for celluloid button production, the only change being the necessary prior heating of the plastic material in order to avoid breakages during the cutting, moulding and stamping processes. And, most importantly, the new products generally had the same properties as those they were emulating in both rigidity and their ability to be easily polished. Celluloid moved from insert to main structural material in button-making, with inserts of mother of pearl, or other material, a common decorative feature. During the 1920s, when women took to the new short hairstyles, the hair comb industry floundered. However, celluloid remained the most common plastic, and buttons and other decorative items (e.g. toiletries) from celluloid continued until the mid-1940s.

Celluloid did have one major drawback: it remained a somewhat volatile substance. Working conditions in celluloid factories were dangerous, with long hours (55–80 hours per week!) and the risk of fire or explosion; after the cellulose has been reacted, great care must be taken when removing the acids with water — dry cellulose nitrate is combustible. Early factory fires in Newark, London, Berlin and Mannheim were often due to impure, and therefore unstable, manufacture of cellulose nitrate. Stringent safety measures were put in place to alleviate some aspects of production,

OPPOSITE FROM TOP LEFT: Mock horn and tortoiseshell celluloid buttons. Large button with mother of pearl inlay, 57mm ∅; 1920s.

Early injection-moulded celluloid buttons with hand-painted accents. Large button, 28mm ∅; twentieth century.

Pressed ivory coloured celluloid, tinted with colour. Large pink button, 33mm ∅.

Hollow celluloid buttons in two parts, with celluloid back and either self-shank or metal loop shank; dyed or metal painted finish. Large silver button, 34mm ∅; twentieth century.

An elaborate and labour-intensive group of designer celluloid buttons, using stamped forms and extrusion in these multi-layered examples. Large button, 27mm Ø; twentieth century.

but dramatic cinema fires and loss of lives caused by celluloid motion picture film continued. The search was underway for another plastic substitute. Casein-formaldehyde and phenol-formaldehyde resins were in development, but in terms of cellulose-based plastics, the answer was eventually 'non-flamm' celluloid, or cellulose acetate.

In 1865, French chemist Paul Schützenberger created the first cellulose acetate, reacting wood pulp with acetic anhydride, but was unable to replicate the method on an industrial scale. Eventually the techniques were improved, and in the early 1900s, chemists were able to make cellulose acetate photographic film, with Swiss chemists Henri and Camille Dreyfus, and German Dr Arthur Eichengrün among them. The next decade saw various trials, failures and eventual successes, and the first production of cellulose acetate on an industrial scale was in the form of dope used to coat the wings of aeroplanes in World War I, a replacement for the flammable cellulose nitrate lacquers.

Cellulose acetate rod and sheet material started production in the early twentieth century. High clarity transparent sheet was used as a substitute for glass, until replaced by acrylics. It was used in many products (including as a layer in safety glass), although celluloid continued to be the favourite for decorative items (including buttons) because of the beautiful, natural effects that could be mimicked. The breakthrough in the use of cellulose acetate was through new techniques, namely the injection-moulding process.

Compression moulding and injection moulding share similarities in that both processes involve heat and pressure. The difference with the injection-moulding process, as developed by Eichengrün, is the addition of a hopper and the screw within.

The plastic material (and dyes, if applicable) is placed into the hopper, where the screw moves the moulding powder through the barrel; the material is mixed together with the action of the screw and as it moves down the barrel becomes molten and is injected into the mould chamber. Both heat and pressure can be accurately and exactly controlled, allowing for the rapid production of multiple objects that are identical in shape and size, with minimal labour. While injection-moulded cellulose acetate buttons were produced, it is the injection moulding process itself, used later with other forms of plastic, which sparked the imagination of button designers in the following decades.

This material and the injection-moulding process also caught the eye of Ole Kirk Christiansen, who in 1934 changed the name of his Danish wooden toy company to LEGO (from the Danish *leg godt* meaning 'play well'). In 1949, LEGO manufactured its first plastic brick from cellulose acetate, the forerunner of today's iconic brick.

As new materials came into being, particularly after World War II, cellulose acetate production gave way to the newer petroleum-based plastics. However, one company continued with their cellulosic plastics alongside other production, one being Mazzucchelli 1849, now one of the major worldwide manufacturers of cellulose acetate products for the eyewear and design industries. The creation of the incredibly diverse

Many later celluloid buttons were post-formed with hot pressing. This selection is unique in that they are manufactured in two parts before being put together. Large green button, 38mm Ø; twentieth century.

patterns of this beautiful product is still done by hand by skilled plastics specialists. Cotton linters are commonly used to make cotton flakes (or powder); they are squeezed through a giant press, forming a transparent paste that becomes the base for future process. This paste is put through warm rollers (calendaring) several times until the desired thickness is achieved, like making pasta. Organic dye powders are mixed with acetone and smeared onto the cellulose sheet, then rolled up and fed through the warm rollers again and again until the colour is mixed uniformly throughout. Next, the coloured acetate is chopped into small cubes and put through warm rollers again, creating a patterned sheet of acetate. To create a solid piece of material, several sheets are placed on top of each other and, through compression, they are formed into a solid cube. It is from this cube that sheets are cut, with each sheet being left to air for several weeks to allow all solvents used in the process to evaporate. The result is a high quality, labour-intensive luxury product.

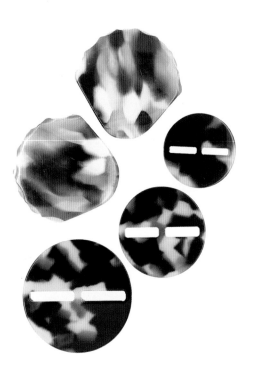

These modern celluloid acetate buttons from sheet material were made around 50 years apart using the same process. Large sew-through button, 35mm Ø; 2010s, Europe.

Casein-formaldehyde (CF)

Plastics made from plants, and now milk? In the search for new products as substitutes for horn, ivory and tortoiseshell, another natural product was looked to, namely the protein found in cow's milk, casein. Casein has also been used in non-food applications, since antiquity in glues and paints; it has a viscosity that can be thinned with water to suit the need, and dries to a matte finish, making it ideal for mural painting. Some more recent artists of note that have used casein in their work are Edvard Munch and Andy Warhol; Munch used casein as

Brightly dyed casein buttons
with tunnel shank. Large
orange button, 22mm ⌀;
twentieth century, Europe.

Casein has the ability to be tooled in a variety of interesting shapes. Large baby blue button, 32mm Ø; twentieth century, Europe.

Polished and satin finish Galalith casein buttons. Large striped button, 28mm Ø; twentieth century, France.

one form of binder when mixing his paints for both his 1893 and 1910 versions of *The Scream*, as well as other works and sketches on canvas, and Warhol used casein paints for some of his early 1960s work, a medium used by commercial artists of the time of which he was one.

My first experience with rigid casein was in the 1980s, during my time in the Netherlands. Many of the vintage buttons purchased for the shop were made from casein in many and varied forms and colours. On one outing to the smaller towns near Amsterdam, we visited a small casein manufacturer; the owner took us around the factory and showed us the finished product in sheet and rod form for buttons. When I returned to Australia to open my own button venture, I made a point of visiting suppliers here. Brian Wilson, from Melbourne manufacturer Maxart Buttons, was very helpful, gave me a tour of their factory and showroom, and I was pleasantly surprised to find packaged casein sheet material in their Cheltenham warehouse from the very same

Galalith casein buttons in solid, mixed block or marbled colours. Large purple 42mm ⌀; twentieth century, France.

White casein could be overdyed and cut back to create extra details. Large brown with diagonal stripes, 32mm ⌀; twentieth century, Europe.

manufacturer I had visited in the Netherlands. Serendipity!

Experiments with casein protein as a solid plastic material began in the late nineteenth century, but early patents did not include a hardener and the resulting material was impractical. In 1897, two Germans were experimenting with casein polymers, Ernst Wilhelm Krische and Adolf Spitteler. Krische owned a small printing and bookbinding and manufacturing company in Hanover, and was commissioned to create washable white writing boards. He tried coating cardboard with a thick layer of casein, but it became soft when wiped clean with water and warped when dried. Spitteler, a chemist from Prien (Bavaria), made a chance discovery in his lab, anecdotally together with a 'cat helper'. It has been said that Spitteler's resident lab cat knocked over a bottle of formaldehyde during the night, with the contents pouring into a bowl of milk on the floor. Returning to the lab the next day, Spitteler found the milk had turned into a hard, horn-like substance. Further experiments led him to realize the potential of this new material. Krische sought out Spitteler, and their collaborations led to them taking out patents for their discovery in Germany in 1899, and in the United States in 1900.

Casein-formaldehyde was introduced to the world at the 1900 *Exposition Universelle* in Paris. Patents for the manufacture of this new plastic were taken up in Germany by *Vereinigten Gummivarenfabriken*, and in France by Pellerin and Orosdi (*Compagnie Française de la Galalithe*) who gave it the trade name '*Galalith*' from the Greek *gala* (milk) and *lithos* (stone). Both invested their energies in producing solid casein as a plastic raw material rather than as a coating, and by 1904 the two companies merged to become the *International Galalith Gesellschaft Hoff & Co.* Until the beginning of World War I, this was the only company which successfully manufactured casein plastic, using the now universally adopted 'dry method' of production.

In England in 1909, Russian student Victor Schutze from Riga patented a different method of manufacturing solid casein from milk curds. The Syrolit Company was set up in Stroud, Gloucestershire, using this new 'wet process' method, producing a casein plastic they called *Syrolit*. Unfortunately, the wet process was not practical, and by 1913 the company was facing bankruptcy. A new company was formed on the same premises, renamed *Erinoid*, and in 1914 the factory was modified to a version of the dry process. The lack of competition during the war years allowed *Erinoid* to gain a foothold in the casein plastics market, and by the end of World War I both Galalith and Erinoid were trade names commonly known in the industry.

Cow's milk contains about 3 per cent protein, 80 per cent of which is casein. The raw material is not only a natural product, but also a by-product of the dairy industry. From 1914, the casein protein was extracted from skimmed milk; the milk is skimmed of its fat, and the use of heat, and acids or rennet as the enzyme, causes the casein to form into curds. The curds are washed in water, mixed with an alkali to make water-soluble caseinates, and dried to form a powder. Plastics are based on rennet casein. The dry casein is mixed with water until absorbed, and this paste is then fed into the hopper of an extruder. The moderate heat action of the hopper screw binds the materials into a dough that is extruded under pressure. The resulting rod is either left as is before being hardened, or placed side by side in trays where a heated hydraulic press forms the casein into sheet material. To produce a hardened material suitable for manufacturing, the resulting shapes were immersed for long periods of time in a solution of 5 per cent formaldehyde in water — a 25mm (1 in) sheet could take up to a year — and left to dry.

Design and production constraints kept its application to a narrow field; casein

The heyday for casein buttons was the 1920s to 1930s — in 1926, 55 per cent of the world's buttons were made from casein.

is neither a thermosetting nor a wholly thermoplastic material. Despite its limited moulding ability and only reasonable electrical insulator capabilities, it was relatively heat resistant to a laundry iron and withstood dry cleaning. Like celluloid, it could be produced in a wide range of colours and finishes. Colouring prior to extrusion ensured colour consistency of the material, and the addition of fish scales produced a pearlized effect, providing an almost endless colour palette including exotic tortoiseshell or horn patterns. This was especially important considering the timeframe to prepare the finished, hardened material. Unlike celluloid, which could be thermoformed from thin sheets, casein was cut from thicker sheet material or sliced from rods, and most items machined due to the distortions that occurred during the hardening process. Moderate stamping and shaping with the use of a hot press was achievable. After machining, polishing was either in the form of mechanical abrasives or a chemical dip polish. The button and buckle trade was the main user of casein plastics, and the changing fashion market meant that pale coloured stock, easily penetrated by acid dyes, could be readily surface-dyed to meet the need. Two-tone effects could be created by further machining surface-dyed buttons, exposing the base colour below. Other items of note made from casein plastics were knitting needles, fountain pens and mechanical pencils, knife handles, costume jewellery, and dressing table wares.

The heyday for casein buttons was the 1920s to 1930s — in 1926, 55 per cent of the world's buttons were made from casein. The material flourished in the decorative arts trade where firms across Europe embraced the new plastic, and it remained the material of choice until after World War II. New producers in England introduced trade names, such as Lactoid and Dorcasine, and the Casein Plastics Association (originally the Artificial Horn Manufacturers' Association) was formed to represent casein-formaldehyde manufacturers' collective interests. When World War II closed the supply of raw casein granules from Europe, the CPA sourced its product from Argentina, assuring continued supply for the button industry charged with producing buttons for the military. By the 1950s, there were more than 80 listed casein-formaldehyde

plastics manufacturers worldwide, all with individual trademarks. France had the largest number of companies, followed by Germany, the United Kingdom, Italy, the United States, Austria, Japan,

FROM LEFT: Overdyed and cut back casein buttons. Large polka dot style, 30mm Ø; twentieth century, Europe.

These square, stacked white and black casein buttons have a peek-a-boo cut-away corner as detail. 23mm Ø; Europe.

Modern casein buttons in a matte red finish. Large button, 40mm Ø; 2010s, Europe.

Czechoslovakia, Mexico, the Netherlands, Russia and Switzerland, respectively. Product names included Argolit (Czechoslovakia) and Casolithe (Netherlands), Calliperle (France) and Corozite (Italy), Moskalit (Russia) and Satolite (Japan) were among the many.

In the United States manufacturers explored the commercial market of casein plastics only after the original patents had expired. It was first produced and sold under the name of Aladdinite (1919), after which others followed, producing Karolith, Erinoid and Kyloid. However, its success lay in the button industry, and mergers of casein factories with button manufacturers began after 1928; the Aladdinite and Kyloid plants were taken over by the Button Corporation of America; the Erinoid Company of America and the Karolith Corporation (with others) became the American Plastics Corporation, calling its product Ameroid. Casein plastics were not as popular in the United States as they were in Europe, namely for two reasons — the American climate meant that the drying of casein-formaldehyde was as long as the curing process, and competition began from the new cast phenolic resins.

After World War II, casein use began a slow decline as new petroleum-based plastics began to surface. Although factories in England and Europe continued making improvements in processes for casein manufacture into the 1950s, many larger companies ceased production by the 1980s. Today, caseinates are made in countries that have large dairy concerns; New Zealand is the top producer, followed by Ireland, France, the Netherlands and Denmark, respectively. As a solid material, casein is used almost exclusively to produce high-quality buttons, most of the ones I have purchased coming from the European countries. Often described as the most beautiful plastic, casein buttons have a character unlike others; the material is denser than polyester, and matte finished buttons have an almost soft, velvety feel. It remains one of my favourite plastic mediums in button form.

The synthetics

Bakelite and beyond

During the late nineteenth century, alongside semi-synthetic cellulose- and casein-based plastics, experiments in the first man-made, truly synthetic material using phenols were taking place. Phenol is a volatile crystalline solid, and until the advent of the petrochemical industry in the mid-twentieth century (when it was produced synthetically) it was derived from coal tar, a by-product of the production of the solid fuel, coke. German chemist Friedlieb Ferdinand Runge was the first to extract an impure form of the chemical, calling it *karbolsāure* (carbolic acid) in 1834. Two years later, French chemist Auguste Laurent coined it *phène*, and by 1841 he was able to condense it in its pure form; his fellow countryman, chemist Charles Gerhardt, coined

Unusual rough-shaped phenol-formaldehyde (PF) buttons in deep brown and deep red: coarsely faceted buttons have self-shank; log shaped button has wire loop shank. Log shape, 28mm long.

the name *phénol* in 1843. In England, experiments for the use of phenol were in the antiseptic realm — carbolic acid was used in England for the treatment of sewage, and later Sir Joseph Lister introduced phenol in methods of antiseptic surgery, publishing his results in the *Lancet* in 1867.

Phenols were only used in the emerging plastics field some years later. Author Morris Kaufman traces the origin of the industry to a paper by Johann Friedrich Wilhelm Adolf von Baeyer, where von Baeyer noted that aldehydes and phenols reacted to produce resinous substances. The work was notable in academic and industry circles, but research was not taken further at the time due to costs and manufacturing processes. It was not until formaldehyde became an inexpensive, commercially available product (almost two decades later) that experiments recommenced, with chemists and entrepreneurs across Europe looking to create a material that, simply put, could either replace shellac as a varnish, or replace celluloid as a plastic.

German chemist Carl Heinrich Meyer was the first in the world to condense phenol and formaldehyde (with the addition of an acid) to create a synthetic resin in 1902. His shellac substitute was patented and manufactured in the same year by employee, Louis Blumer, whose lacquer and glue was marketed as Laccain. (Baekeland would later call his version of this resin Novolak, both names a nod to the lac beetle.) Austrian chemist Adolf Luft was aiming for a hard plastic material like celluloid, but his 1902 material was too brittle for commercial possibilities. English electrical engineer, James Swinburne, was acquainted with Luft's work, and recognized that phenol resins could be suitable as a heat-resistant electrical insulator, setting up the Fireproof Celluloid Syndicate to continue the research. From 1904 to 1907, Swinburne, together with a group of celluloid engineers, eventually created a successful hard lacquer, only to be beaten to the British patent office by Leo Baekeland.

Dr Leo Hendrik Baekeland was a chemist whose first patent for workable phenol-resin technology marked the beginning of the modern plastics industry. Born in Ghent, Belgium, in 1863, in 1889 he left an academic career and moved to the United States to join a photographic company. A brilliant academic, chemist and entrepreneur, he co-founded the Nepera Chemical Company to manufacture his invention of photographic printing paper, Velox, selling the company and the rights in 1899 to George Eastman for a substantial sum of money. Having the resources to follow independent research of his choosing, in 1902 he also turned to finding a synthetic substitute for shellac, and in the process discovered a mouldable thermosetting plastic, overcoming the technical

Beautifully carved PF in classic black, including unusual victory torch, all with wire loop shank. Small round button, 28mm Ø.

difficulties that others had encountered in making solid phenol-formaldehyde mixtures.

Dr Baekeland called his phenol-formaldehyde polymer 'polyoxybenzylmethyl-englycolanhydride', or Bakelite. He had the means to take out patents for his inventions, including the important heat and pressure hardening process of his Bakelizer, and protect his intellectual property both in the United States and internationally. At the same time, he began manufacturing Bakelite from his converted barn/home laboratory, hoping that his product, which did not burn or melt, could be used for smokers' articles and buttons. He also found that the use of fillers could add other attributes to his product. By 1909 he completely understood the technology of working with his mouldable phenol resins. His intention was to license his patents for others to manufacture into products. In 1910, he opened the first factory near Berlin in Germany, the Bakelite Gesellschaft GmbH and later the same year, the General Bakelite Company in Perth Amboy, New Jersey. In the following years, more factories

ABOVE: Various shades of carved PF in cherry amber, dark amber and honey amber. Large flower buttons in mottled honey amber, 40mm Ø.

LEFT: Beautifully carved PF in classic brown, all with wire loop shank. Small round button, 28mm Ø.

and licensees in other parts of Europe and Japan spread Bakelite throughout the world. Bakelite's properties were increasingly sought after by the growing electrical and automobile industries, ensuring a global market.

The moulding process for small objects in Bakelite could be done in about two minutes. Bakelite's only drawback was its limited choice of colours, available in dark brown, dark green, dark red and black. The relatively high temperatures used in the curing process caused the resin to darken. Regardless, Bakelite as a 'material of a thousand uses' was an important material, and was an international success.

Alongside the moulded material, there existed a small market for blocks of unfilled cast resin that could be turned on a lathe and carved for the smokers' market (pipe stems, cigarette holders) and other household items. One of Baekeland's employees, Lawrence Byck, began experimenting at home with embedding things (photographs, small objects or artworks, etc.) into the resin, and after World War I, Baekeland allowed Byck to open a subsidiary company on the premises, the Embed Art Company. Byck used the transparent material for jewellery and other personal items, creating pendants, paperweights, etc. in amber, ruby, emerald and jet colours until 1928, after which demand for the moulding materials took over.

Red PF buttons including an unusual stacked version: black, on red, on black. Large four-hole button, 55mm ∅.

Bakelite as a 'material of a thousand uses' was an important material, and was an international success.

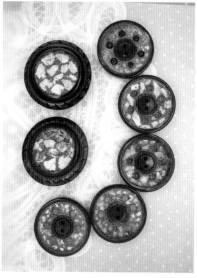

Turned PF buttons in the form of bobbins. Black button has added thread motif, 37mm long.

Bakelite with embedded shell chips set in gilded grout, sew-through versions also with coloured glass cabochons. Large black, and amber, buttons with wire loop shank, 45mm ⌀.

In response to finding a product that could compete with celluloid in the decorative goods market, German chemist Dr Friedrich August Raschig was probably the first to produce a commercially available, clear phenol casting resin, in 1909. Others in Germany, France and Belgium were also experimenting, taking out patents, and the use of catalysts different to Baekeland's advanced the independent phenol-formaldehyde industry there. The goal was to create a material that could be used as a substitute for shellac, copal/amber and ivory, and the resulting products did so and more.

Like casein, the heyday for the thermoset casting resin was between the world wars. The 1925 *Arts Decoratifs et Industriels* exhibition held in Paris showcased the new Art Deco style to the world, and the new easily worked casting resins of phenol-formaldehyde responded well to the new style. The bold colours and geometric shapes of Cubism were very popular, as well as intricate carvings. High society accepted the new material, especially after fashion houses promoted the material in both their jewellery and clothing accessories — Coco Chanel's beads and bangles accentuated the simple black dress, and Elsa Schiaparelli's whimsical buttons were used on everything from hats to swimwear. By the mid-1930s there were more than 300 listed trade names, with over 70 specifically listed as providing sheet, rod or tube material for the button, bead and jewellery industry: in Germany, names such as Leukorith, Utilit, Lor-Wal-Lith, Ornalith; in England, names such as Bexite, Metduro; in other parts of Europe, Formit, Eolit (Austria), Durolit (Belgium), Cristaloid, Similex, Nobeline (France), Ivrite (Italy), Haefelyte (Switzerland), Solith (Czechoslovakia). The American Catalin Corporation of New York City was among the first in America to take advantage of expiring patents, trademarking

Bakelite-Gesellschaft, Berlin,
trinket box, with various 28mm
sew-through PF buttons.

ABOVE: Bangles and whimsical buttons were also made from PF material, as in these bird and anchor examples. Large two-hole sew through green bird, 42mm Ø (wingspan) with French-knot linen thread eye detail; 1940s, United States.

RIGHT: PF buttons: geometric shaped butterscotch colour with tunnel shank, and two-tone carved brown and grey marbled button with wire loop shank, 50mm Ø.

'Catalin' in 1927. Their range of fifteen colours included amber, jade, onyx and marble. Besides Bakelite and Catalin, names such as Jewelin, Gemstone, Marblette were among the new trademarks. The new companies helped bring Art Deco to the masses, in what was an undeniable consumer boom in affordable and desirable products.

Cast phenolic resin was predominantly used as a turnery material, and as such was produced in shapes suitable for turning and lathe manufacture. The final thermoset material was made without any fillers, and was cast into rods, sheets, tubes or specialty shapes from which buttons, buckles, beads and other decorative items could be shaped and carved using a variety of tools. It could be sawed, sliced, machined or turned, or carved into intricate shapes; finishing in large tumblers produced a glass-like polish. One advantage of the cast resin was its colour; another was the ease with which it could be worked. It could be manufactured into a water-white clear thermoset material, which could be carved from behind and hand-painted for an engaging effect. The addition of dyestuffs or pigments produced a range of colours from transparent rich hues and opaque colours including ivory, to marbled throughout. It could also be formed to create multicoloured blocks.

Bakelite — which produced iconic twentieth century designs such as the GPO telephone, the Purma camera, Ecko AD36 radio, and later the colourful Catalin radios and all those glorious fashion accessories — eventually lost its edge, as new, cheaper plastic formulations were developed that were easier to manufacture. Today, the term bakelite is often used to encompass a wide range of formerly trademarked materials, such as Catalin, Jewelin, etc. as it is often difficult to distinguish between the various phenol-formaldehyde resins unless they are stamped.

The amino plastics

Plastics made from plants, from milk, and now body fluids? In the search for new cast resins, in contrast to the dark phenol-formaldehyde mouldings, an important discovery was made — the amino plastics. Urea is the waste your body produces when it metabolizes proteins and it leaves the body through urine. However, before feelings of horror set in, urea has been synthetically produced on an industrial scale since 1870. Synthetic urea is produced by the reaction of ammonia and carbon dioxide, with the resulting carbamate salt heated to form urea.

Simple leaf shapes, and drilled and hand-painted utilitarian buttons made from PF. Round buttons, with coloured polka dots, 22mm Ø.

Popular urea-formaldehyde products in mottled colours, shown here as buttons and picnicware. Buttons, some with hand-painted decoration, 22mm Ø.

Lively and pastel colours of melamine-formaldehyde allowed for utilitarian buttons at competitive cost. Large green button, 23mm Ø; United States, late 1940s.

In the search for new cast resins, in contrast to the dark phenol-formaldehyde mouldings, an important discovery was made — the amino plastics.

In 1773, French chemist Hillaire-Marin Rouelle was the first to isolate urea. Some 55 years later, it was the first organic compound to be synthetically made, by German chemist Friedrich Wöhler in 1828, although as with most pioneering organic chemical experiments he was trying to prepare something else. It took another 36 years for urea and formaldehyde to come together, and it was not until after World War I that urea-formaldehyde resins were further investigated. Eventually Edmund Rossiter, at the British Cyanides Company, developed the first commercially successful amino resin thermosetting material of its kind, marketed from the 1920s as Beetle, Beatl and Bandalasta.

In 1834, German chemist Baron Justus von Liebig was the first to isolate melamine, although it remained of academic interest only, until the 1935 discovery (in both Germany and Switzerland) that it forms valuable resins when mixed with formaldehyde. In the United States, Monsanto and American Cyanamid & Chemical Corp. were also working on the same reactions, and by 1939, American Cyanamid was commercially producing products made from this improved amino resin. MF resins, in comparison to UF resins, share similarities, but MF allowed for fillers that could withstand higher temperatures (initially asbestos, now fibreglass) and gave it improved benefits over its urea-formaldehyde cousin, with more resistance to heat, acid and electricity; and importantly, it was better able to withstand water and detergents. Although there are many formulations to produce melamine, it is now mostly manufactured from urea.

The new amino-based resins were widely sought after. UF is a non-transparent water-white or white base, while MF is a transparent clear base. Their attraction was their ability to be made into light, bright colours (something lacking in the phenol-formaldehydes) and together with their other attributes they provided for a multitude of uses across a wide range of industries. As far as the button industry is concerned, UF resins are very much in common use today, from single-coloured buttons for the military to mottled buttons that imitate (extremely well!) natural materials such as horn. The two-stage method of manufacture, from semi-manufactured blanks to final heat compression, seems to be exclusive to button production. In the case of single-coloured buttons, the urea powder is coloured according to need, and compressed into pellets through the use of a machine adapted from the pharmaceutical industry for the button industry.

In the case of multicoloured mottled buttons, the urea powder is coloured and mixed into a paste, then passed through a rolling machine into sheets or preformed pieces. The different colours are layered or stacked, depending on the desired effect, and then rolled into a cylindrical shape. This is then put through an extruding machine, with a conical end that can be changed according to desired size, which cuts the material into pellets as it exits the process. The pellets are left to dry, to release any excess moisture. One-colour and mottled pellets are loaded onto moulds, where they are heat-pressed and given their final moulded shape. Some simple buttons are moulded and drilled with holes in the same machine, while others are moulded into an intermediate shape and then turned according to need — wide or narrow rim; rounded centre; matte centre,

The manufacturing processes of MF saw an increase in plastics used in the new market of children's buttons. Animal buttons such as these were popular, and had hand-painted accents to enhance the look. Duck buttons, 18mm ∅; United States, late 1940s/1950s.

Modern mottled urea-formaldehyde buttons in various configurations, some imitating natural horn-like materials in a variety of colours. Large mock horn button with wide rim, 25mm ∅.

We have the curiosity of chemists to thank for many of the world's inventions, especially in the realm of plastics, and these playful buttons honour their efforts. Rx bottle: injection moulded nylon, 26mm high; chemical flasks: decal on MF plastic buttons, 23mm ⌀ and 15mm ⌀.

shiny rim; shiny centre, matte rim; decorative centre, etc. — and holes drilled. The final finishing, where the buttons are trimmed, polished or glazed, occurs in a barrel tumbler.

The poly era

The interwar years were productive for the plastics industry, especially due to the scientific investigations of German chemist, Hermann Staudiger. During the first 60 years of development, chemists, or often people with no formal training, made discoveries in kitchens, home workshops or small labs, either by accident or through observation, with no understanding of the formation or structure of the result. They knew how, but not why, their substances worked. By the early twentieth century, chemists discovered that many substances (both natural and synthetic) were polymeric and they knew they were made up of large numbers of smaller units, but how they were arranged and held together was not yet known.

The chemicals derived from coal and agricultural sources were available in sufficient quantity; ethylene was derived from cotton and wood, phenols from coal tar, urea and formaldehyde from coking coal. Encouraged by new scientific discoveries, chemical companies began to form research teams led by scientists dedicated to finding new polymer formulations. These companies produced the raw materials for the emerging plastics industry.

Polymethyl methacrylate (PMMA, acrylic, Plexiglass, Perspex, Lucite, Acrylite)

One of my earliest experiences with acrylic, and the one I come back to every time I'm reminded of the material, is when my father brought home a set of flat squares with interlocking slots to create shapes and structures. As an engineer, I could see what had attracted him to make the purchase, both from his designer's point of view and as someone who explored new trends. It was 1970 and the transparent clear and brightly coloured glass-like squares were a marvel to me. Much later in life when my professional button adventure began, I gained newfound appreciation of the product and its dip into the world of fashion accessories.

This thermoplastic material traces its ancestry to German chemists in the late nineteenth century; the rubbery acrylates of Caspery and Tollens in 1873, the polymerization of methacrylic acid into a solid resinous substance by Rudolph Fittig in 1877, and further work by Georg W.A. Kahlbaum in 1880, whose polymethacrylate (PMA) predicted PMMA. In 1901, Otto Carl Julius Röhm was granted a doctorate for his thesis on the polymerisation products of acrylic acid, a subject he would return to several years later.

Röhm and his friend, banker Otto Haas, formed a company and the success of their product (a leather tanning agent) allowed Röhm to return to research in acrylic chemistry where he was initially looking to create a resin that would replace the inferior, yellowing celluloid that had so far been used as a sandwich material in safety glass. Instead he created an acrylic, shatterproof, glass-like plastic. Through the efforts

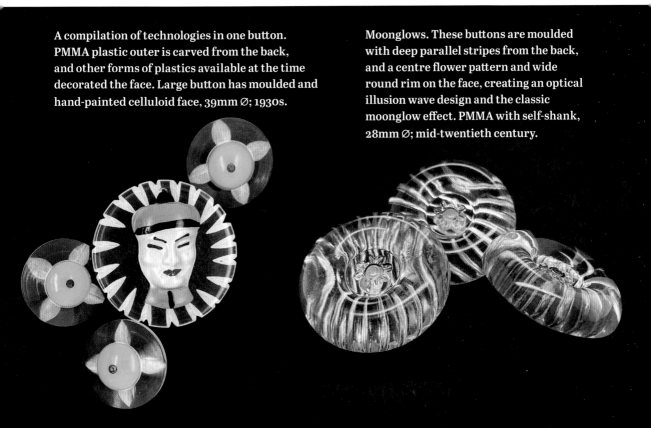

A compilation of technologies in one button. PMMA plastic outer is carved from the back, and other forms of plastics available at the time decorated the face. Large button has moulded and hand-painted celluloid face, 39mm ∅; 1930s.

Moonglows. These buttons are moulded with deep parallel stripes from the back, and a centre flower pattern and wide round rim on the face, creating an optical illusion wave design and the classic moonglow effect. PMMA with self-shank, 28mm ∅; mid-twentieth century.

Surplus wartime acrylic was sometimes used for making buttons, such as these sew-through and shank versions. The sew-through buttons are made from manipulated rounds, lightly heated and folded over. The fold-over squares have a brass stamping of a soldier in the centre, with a glued shank, 30mm Ø.

A collection of mid-twentieth century polished PMMA buttons, carved from the back to create depth in the design. Some are hand-painted within the carving to reflect the colour throughout. Large flower shape, 43mm Ø.

of employee and research chemist Dr Walter Bauer, the company received their first patent for this new plastic in 1928. Progress toward the acrylic resin we know today was made in the early 1930s, when Bauer, in Germany, and Rowland Hill, at ICI in England, made improvements in their product, eventually creating a clear plastic that could be used in place of glass. It was trademarked as Plexiglas in Germany (1933), and Perspex in England (1934). This lightweight glass substitute was useful for aircraft and automobile windscreens, and demand increased significantly during the lead up to World War II, where it was used exclusively for military applications.

Acrylic sheet has a high tensile strength, and is weather- and scratch-resistant. It was used extensively during World War II for moulding aircraft canopies and the nose cones of bomber planes. After the war, there was a surplus of these acrylic parts, and they were repurposed into various household items, among them buttons. Later, through the use of PMMA powders, the material could be processed through extrusion or compression moulding, cast into rods, sheets (or optical lenses), or through injection moulding into closed moulds.

When American company DuPont trademarked its Lucite, it also licensed its material to a wider audience, namely costume jewellery makers (including Trifari, Coro and Joseph H. Meyer Bros.) and presumably button-makers, based on evidence of Lucite buttons. Besides the clear, transparent form resembling glass or rock crystal, it was also produced in a variety of colours in clear, translucent and opaque material. After the war and into the 1950s, new materials were emerging: moonglow Lucite, with its distinctive moonstone shine, confetti Lucite, containing glitter trapped inside the resin material, and granite Lucite, where contrasting coloured fragments were dispersed throughout an opaque material. Lucite was more chemically stable than celluloid and cheaper to produce than Bakelite and, like the latter, it could be carved and easily polished.

Today, buttons made from PMMA are generally mass-produced using the injection-moulding process, where aluminium or steel closed moulds allow for fine details. Because the material is hard, water resistant and lightweight, it is an excellent substitute for glass and crystal buttons, especially where weight or ease of care is a consideration. Acrylic buttons are most popular in a variety of transparent colours, but are also available in translucent, opaque or iridescent colours. They may have two holes, tunnel shank or loop shank. Clear faceted, foil-coated buttons provide a less expensive, practical substitute for the more luxurious crystal styles.

Polyamide: nylon

My grandmother had a nylon lingerie factory in São Paulo, Brazil, and my mother, my sister and I benefitted from the most luxurious undergarments imaginable. I still have and wear some of the pieces, dating from 1966, a testament to the quality of the manufacture and the longevity of the material. When we think of nylon, we usually think of stockings or fabric or perhaps strings on musical instruments, but the first use of this new plastic was for toothbrush bristles in 1938 (replacing the animal hair that

Nylon buttons may be pigment dyed or, more often than not, manufactured in white that can then be easily dyed. These four-hole sew-through 'clown' buttons come in a variety of sizes; the back shows the hollowed-out design, using less material, and the clearly visible gate marks. Largest button shown, 80mm Ø; 2000s, France.

Nylon allows for playful design, often using components to create multiple-part, whimsical buttons and fine details. It also allows for mix and match colours to create opportunities within the colour palate. Daisy buttons, 24mm Ø; 2000s, France.

had formerly been used). Its inventor was Wallace Hume Carothers, an outstanding American chemist who worked as an academic at Harvard University until he was asked to head the new research laboratory at DuPont in 1928. His experiments were huge contributors to the growing polymer science, a vindication of Hermann Staudiger's work, and led to modern plastics technology.

During his short lifetime, Carothers contributed many important innovations including synthetic rubber (neoprene) and polyamide (nylon), and laid the foundations for further research into polyesters. Nylon's later appearance as a rigid material was not central to the mind of its inventor who was focused on its use as a fibre, and unfortunately Carothers died in 1941 before seeing the true success of nylon, now one of the most common of all plastics.

Nylon was another of the plastics that was commandeered for the war effort; as a fibre, it was used to manufacture parachutes (among others), particularly after the supplies of imported silk were cut off. However, in the 1950s, its use as a moulding compound took off. In 1946, American inventor James Watson Hendry made improvements to the injection-moulding machinery used for thermoplastics, and his design and subsequent refinements remain the most dominant type of injection-moulding machines used today. Nylon is the generic term used for a large group of polyamides, but all of them share the characteristic of being relatively easy to mould or extrude into most forms. Two forms of nylon — nylon6 and nylon66 — are used as engineering plastic (particularly if added fillers are used for improved features). They have good mechanical properties, chemical and abrasion resistance and also create inexpensive, durable buttons that can be washed and dry-cleaned freely. The injection-moulding process allows for multiple buttons to be made at one time, with a mould that has a main sprue and multiple runners leading to the finished article, making this type of plastic button easily identified due to gate mark/ejector pin marks often present on the final product. The buttons are removed from the runners, and the remaining 'tree' may be added to the next batch, usually with some new material — too much recycled material contaminates the button batch, producing articles that don't have the same properties as the virgin material in terms of dye-ability. Former button manufacturer, Maxart Buttons, used their recycled material to produce items for other industries. On a visit to their Melbourne factory, they showed me articles made for the interior of household goods (stereos, speakers, etc.) and for civil engineering, in the form of racks to space the reinforcing bars within a concrete road pour.

The natural colour of nylon is off-white, and while it is most widely available in natural, white or black, nylon buttons are also easily dyed with common dyes; for that reason, they are often moulded in white, allowing for different colours as needed, although dyes or lustres may also be added to the raw nylon pellets in a batch. The material is stable enough to be designed in components, providing button designers the creativity to make multiple part buttons that, when combined, easily become whimsical multicoloured fasteners. Many of my favourite children's buttons are made using multiple components of different colours, put together with careful and considered design elements.

Thermosetting polyester: unsaturated polyester (UP)

Those who have been surprised to discover nylon can be a solid, may now be further surprised to know that the largest percentage of plastic buttons are made from polyester, in solid form. Polyester is a general term including all polymers where the foundations are formed by the chemical reaction of polyfunctional alcohols and acids. French chemists Joseph Louis Gay-Lussac and Théophile-Jules Pelouze (in 1833) and Swedish chemist Jöns Jakob Berzelius (in 1847) were the first to form polyesters. Although they were unable to find a use for their discovery and moved on to other experiments, their work laid the foundations for later investigations.

Most of us encounter polyester as a fabric, or as the ever-present plastic drink bottle, both of which are made from the thermoplastic polyethylene terephthalate (PET). Buttons, however, are made from thermosetting unsaturated polyester, the formulations of which have their origins in the 1933 patent taken out by an American, Carleton Ellis. Ellis was an inventor and research scientist, writing extensively on synthetic resins and plastics. He discovered that when UP resins were mixed with a peroxide catalyst, they cured to become an insoluble solid. His subsequent 1940 patent on the subject, adding styrene to the mix, was the first mention of the material as a moulding material. Although Ellis's interests lay primarily in the development of coatings, his discoveries began the industry of polyester casting resins. Others would later expand on his mixtures and develop polyesters that could be cold cured at room temperature.

Thermosetting unsaturated polyester has many commercial uses. When reinforced with glass, it is among the strongest plastics in the world, used for boat hulls, road vehicles, etc. Unreinforced UP is used for, among other things, clear casting resins, coatings and buttons. Polyester buttons were introduced in the 1950s, and over the next decades slowly overtook other plastics used in the button-making industry. The material is hard wearing and can easily mimic natural products (mother of pearl, horn, ivory, tortoiseshell) as well as be used for wonderful artisanal creations.

To make buttons, the solid material is first made into a semi-manufactured form, in sheets, rods (or blocks) and blanks. Centrifugal cylinders are used to produce sheet material, and casting machines produce rods, using different processes. To create sheets, the resin, in liquid form, is prepared with accelerators and catalysts, and any colourings, pearl essence or other additions are made. The liquid resin is poured into the rotating interior of a large horizontal chrome-plated cylinder that has a lip at either end (so the resin does not escape). The centrifugal system allows for layered pouring, achieving bands of horizontal colours, or simultaneous pouring using multiple colours. When the resin reaches a gum-like consistency, the centrifuge is stopped.

Hand-mixed polyester sheet, cut to create these sumptuous high-end rectangular buttons. Large blue button, 38mm x 32mm x 10mm thick; 2010s, Europe.

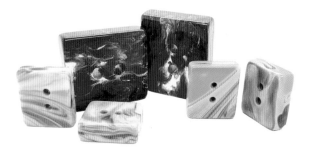

CLOCKWISE FROM RIGHT: Sheet material may be produced in many creative ways. Pictured are examples of marbled style with tunnel shank, and stacked solids that are tooled to reveal the extent of the colours. Large two-hole buttons, 15mm ∅; 2010s, Europe.

Polyester buttons imitating horn, tortoiseshell, mother of pearl and aged ivory. Cut from sheet or rod material, they are further tooled to produce the final results. Mock mother of pearl four-hole button in beige has a laser cut pattern on the rim edge, large size 38mm ∅; 2000s, Europe.

Some of the most beautiful plastic buttons, and those that are among my favourites, are ones that have been hand-finished. Here, Italian ingenuity takes the semi-manufactured product to create incredible shapes and effects, using artisanal techniques of shaping and carving. Some buttons can be overdyed, and carving into the polyester reveals the magic within. Or polished solid colours are carved to leave a matte pattern as detail.

The sheet is cut and carefully removed from the cylinder, where it is either taken to the punching machine to create button blanks or cut into rectangular sheets as a semi-manufactured product for button producers. To create rods, casting machines are used. Colour effects are achieved vertically, using fixatives in part of the pouring process. When the rods reach a gelled consistency, they are removed from the tubes. The rods are fed into machines with rotating blades to create button blanks or are supplied directly to button producers as a semi-manufactured product.

Machines specific to the button industry progressed from the 1950s, with highly specialized machines able to turn the blanks into an enormous range of varied button designs. After the blanks have reached the final stage of hardness, they are fed into fully or semi-automated turning machines, able to work on one or both sides of the button, as well as drill precision holes. (The same machines can be recalibrated and used to turn other materials, such as casein, horn and shell.) Final polishing of polyester buttons happens in a barrel tumbler, where wooden pieces are added to a liquid abrasive polishing medium. Many polyester buttons are prepared as pigment dyed material, but may also be left white and/or mottled. These can be overdyed afterwards, using special polyester dyes.

ABS (acrylonitrile-butadiene-styrene)

ABS is a thermoplastic that was created as a result of research and development in the United States after World War II. In the 1930s, in military preparation for war, German leaders saw the need for self-sufficiency when it came to rubber production. Having no access to rubber plantations except through imports, they concerned themselves with the invention of synthetic rubbers, the final elastomers based on butadiene and styrene. At about the same time, DuPont in the United States became interested in synthetic

The author as ABS plastic LEGO character, examining a sliced ABS button showing the fine metal deposit on the plastic base.

ABS metal-plated buttons offer a lightweight alternative to metal buttons, and are found in numerous styles. Large enamel button with silver rim, 38mm Ø; 1990s, Switzerland.

Clear ABS material, technically called MABS, can be injection-moulded to create a variety of lightweight buttons that imitate cut glass or crystal. Embedded flower buttons with faceted top, 30mm Ø; 2010s.

rubbers, but it was only during the 1941 occupation of the rubber plantations in the Far East that the industry took off, with government and chemical companies cooperating.

After the war, and the return to natural rubbers, there was an excess of styrene production, leading scientific research teams to create new forms of plastics. Many experiments were geared towards the injection moulding of polystyrene, the breakthrough coming when the aforementioned was mixed with elastic compounds, one of which was the thermoplastic acrylonitrile-butadiene-styrene (ABS). These three components, when brought together, create a good engineering plastic that can be easily injection-moulded; acrylonitrile units provide heat resistance, butadiene provides good impact strength, and styrene provides rigidity. ABS was patented in 1948 by Lawrence E. Daley (working for the US Rubber Company) and was first introduced commercially by the Borg-Warner Corporation in 1954. Incidentally, in 1963 LEGO modernized its brick design to include the now iconic interlocking studs on top and tubes on bottom, and since then all pieces of LEGO are made using ABS plastics.

The qualities of ABS plastics were also attractive to the button industry, and the early 1960s invention of electroplating metallic coatings onto ABS made them more so. Prior to this discovery, thick coatings were used to encase other plastic materials. However, it was found that oxidizing acid mixtures evenly etched the surface of the ABS material, thus facilitating bonding of a thin electroplated coating similar to metal plating. The fine details of injection-moulded ABS plastic buttons could now be metallized, and this form of button gained a strong foothold in the market, particularly leading up to and including the 1970s. In comparison to metal buttons, which were widespread during this period, metallized plastic buttons offered a lightweight alternative. These buttons continue to be an important part of button manufacturing; plating increases the strength of the button, making it more durable and abrasion resistant, as well as enhancing its aesthetic appeal.

Improvements in the plating of ABS plastic buttons have evolved into a streamlined, electroless plating process, using a chemical rather than electric current method. Once the buttons have been injection moulded and freed from the sprue, they undergo an etching process where microscopic holes are left on the surface to make bonding easier. After neutralizing, they go into a bath of low-concentration precious metal activator (for example, copper) that acts as a plating catalyst. From here, the buttons are individually hooked onto racks, and are dipped first into an accelerator bath and then on to the final plating solution. Buttons are then removed from their hooks and given a spin-dry before final drying in a heater for several hours. Typical metal plating colours for ABS buttons include gold, nickel, silver and copper.

Although many ABS plastic buttons are plated, that is not always the case. Unplated ABS buttons are somewhat similar to nylon buttons but have different properties. Both may be produced in their natural light colour (ABS is naturally ivory coloured) and dyed afterwards, or be pigment dyed directly when mixed with the

The fine details of injection-moulded ABS plastic buttons could now be metallized, and this form of button gained a strong foothold in the market, particularly leading up to and including the 1970s.

plastic pellets in the hopper of the injection-moulding machine. ABS is a less expensive material and has a lower melting point, making it more cost effective during the manufacturing process. It also is lighter in weight than nylon but is more or less equal when it comes to strength and abrasion resistance. However, I find that ABS buttons are slightly more brittle than their nylon cousins, with nylon having more flexibility, particularly when interchanging two-part buttons. ABS may also be manufactured as a transparent plastic. Clear ABS is produced by the copolymerization of methyl methacrylate (MMA) with the monomers of acrylonitrile, butadiene and styrene, where the formulations are altered to accommodate the MMA. Technically, this product is called MABS.

Button using recycled paper in thermosetting plastic. Dyed blue, 23mm Ø; 1990s, Germany.

Moving forward

Since the late 1980s I have witnessed a trend in button manufacturing to explore the possibilities of using recycled materials, or blending natural products into plastic buttons. Some of the earliest examples I came across were some rather odd-looking buttons that I was told had recycled paper mixed throughout as well as on the outer layer, with the result that the buttons looked quite messy in an interesting kind of way. Each button was an individual, and I was warned when I purchased them that they would eventually lose their loose top layer with laundering and/or wear. I did warn customers about this, but for those who purchased them, this did not seem to matter — the peculiarity of these items was foremost in their minds. At the time I had mixed feelings about them, but as I look at the few remaining buttons I have, I now appreciate their quirkiness and wish I had a complete set of each of the colour blue, mint green and peach.

An interesting field of research from the late twentieth century is bioplastics. Plastics research, it seems, is coming full circle to return to its origins, in an effort to

Buttons can be made from recycled polyester, binders and dyes. Large green button also contains organic material, 28mm ⌀; 1990s, Italy.

Polystyrene waste material, reimagined as high-end buttons by Sydney-based jeweller Tarn Smith in a variety of forms, sew-through or self-shank. Centre row, two-hole round buttons with sterling silver wire rim, 18mm ⌀; 2020, Australia.

reduce dependence on fossil fuels. For the first 80 years of the industry, plastics were made solely from biopolymers, and many of those from renewable sources — cellulose, casein, shellac and ebonite. Scientists have been reviewing the documents left by their early twentieth century counterparts, particularly the protein-based biopolymers of casein and soy, and the starch-based polymers of corn, sugar and rice. For instance, American automobile giant Henry Ford constructed a car made from soybean meal in 1941, showcased at a couple of Michigan fairs. Known for his inventiveness, his motivation at the time was also admirable in his desire to combine the benefits of industry with agriculture. Unfortunately, war prevented further models being built and the project was never revisited, however since the 1980s a resurgence of research in bioplastics has been gaining momentum.

Moving into the 1990s, European countries were more aware of environmental factors regarding manufacturing and many began re-using their scrap plastic material

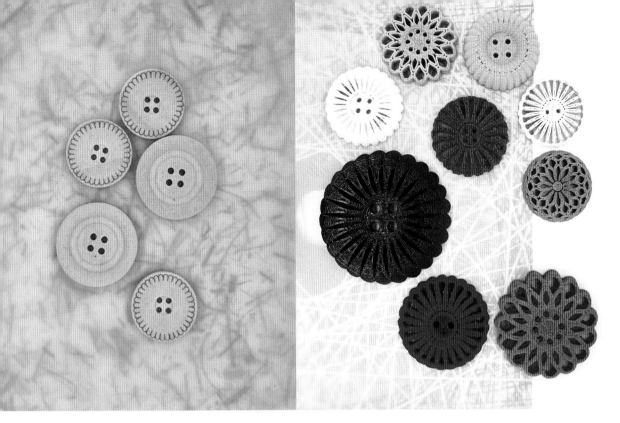

Buttons from recycled polyester, binders and dyes. Large button, 28mm Ø; 2010s, Italy.

3D printed buttons in various designs as imagined by Femke Roefs and Leoni Werle. Large hot pink button, 40mm Ø; 2020, the Netherlands.

in interesting and inventive ways. This practice continues today with perfected manufacturing processes that create buttons that are both interesting and unique, or undiscernible from those made from new materials. Most of these are made with the addition of thermosetting recycled fillers, bio poly resins, or in some cases a percentage of new polyester material. All have a minimum of 60 per cent recycled material, with interesting and surprising results, including the use of recycled paper, coffee grinds, cotton fibres, hemp and recycled polyester.

Sydney based jeweller Tarn Smith has recently added another aspect to his practice, using recycled plastics as precious materials. Smith completed his four-year jewellery apprenticeship at internationally renowned jewellery company, Cerrone, before moving on to a Bachelor in Design Arts at the Australian National University (ANU) in Canberra. As an educator I had the pleasure of working with him during his apprenticeship, seeing his creativity unlock to create some memorable pieces.

Later I had the opportunity to attend the ANU graduate show and witnessed the skill and thought process that emerged from his further work. I became very interested in his later work with plastics, how he used waste material to create 'fine jewellery' pieces, trading the traditional metal for remade plastic, or integrating the material as gemstones into more traditional work. He is interested in the concept of value; while the scrap material has no intrinsic worth, it is a laborious process to turn it into something desirable. I commissioned some buttons from Smith, and the results are intricately detailed simple forms using, what should be precious, discarded resources.

Apart from recycled material in buttons, another innovation to hit the fashion industry is 3D printing. As a jeweller, I am well versed in the practice of 3D wax printing and how the jewellery industry has adopted the technology in the 21st century, so I was intrigued to see the 3D plastic printing technology on display at the international fashion trade fair in Paris a few years ago. The technology of 3D printers has evolved to accept many materials, and has been used in applications from the frivolous chocolate and sugar works in the confectionery industry, to important biocompatible and sterilizable plastic and metal used in medical applications. Despite the ever-evolving range of materials that might be used in 3D printing, the most commonly used are ABS, polylactide (PLA) and polyvinyl alcohol (PVA). PVA, known to most of us as white wood glue, is used in 3D printing solely as a support structure material; it is easily dissolved away in water after the final processes of printing is completed.

PLA, also known as polylactic acid, is a biodegradable, thermoplastic polyester made from renewable sources such as corn starch, sugar beet or rice. It was first invented by Wallace Carothers in 1932, during his research into renewable plastics at DuPont, and was made from corn starch. However, Carother's bioplastic research at DuPont came to a halt as he was unable to find a commercially viable production method. Years later, in 1989, Dr Patrick R. Gruber was credited with inventing a feasible method and PLA can be now be produced inexpensively and on a large scale. Starches can now be processed into a biopolymer that looks, acts and performs like petroleum-based plastics. It is easily applied to the 3D printing process and available in a large range of colours.

The most popular and affordable process used in 3D plastics printing is fused filament fabrication (FFF), also known as fused deposition modelling (FDM™). The first step is to design a computer-aided drawing (CAD). The CAD data is sliced into layers and transferred to the machine, whereby the project is constructed layer by layer on a build platform. Thin filaments of thermoplastic and support materials are supplied on spools. In a method comparable to a glue gun, uncoiled material is fed into dual heated extruders that precisely deposit both support and thermoplastic material layer by layer in an ordered geometry, as the build platform moves down. The components solidify quickly when they come into contact with the build platform or the previously deposited layer. When the printing process is finished, the project is removed from the build platform and the support material cleaned away. This method leaves visible layer lines, which can be smoothed away using a variety of methods.

In my ongoing search for new products for my store, I came across some interesting buttons from Dutch designer Femke Roefs and German designer Leoni Werle. These two designers collaborated to produce miniature works of sculpture in button form. The inspiration for their design hails from the childhood toy the Spirograph, interpreting the two-dimensional designs into attractive three-dimensional works. The thing I like most about them is how they embrace rather than hide the layer lines that the fused deposition modelling process produces, demonstrating their skills as designers. They have used PLA as their printing medium, and because this material becomes flexible at around 60°C (140°F), it is recommended to hand wash at 30°C (85°F). For this reason, they are often sold in brooch form.

Plastic has now been made for over 150 years and is spread throughout our modern lifestyle. A question that may come to mind is why plastic was so fiercely researched and developed, and so widely accepted? The simple answers may be firstly to find substitutes for natural products either in decline or no longer widely available, and secondly due to the price and constant evolution of the product, which continues today. While plastic buttons are still manufactured to resemble their natural counterparts, the most exciting ones are those that utilize the material at its best in its own right. Button designers look to the various plastic qualities when planning new models with the choices of visual attractiveness, wearability and ease of manufacture coming into play. However, the environmental impact of plastics does play a role and will do so in the future. Despite the higher cost of bio-based resins, compared to fossil fuel-based ones, consumers are demanding change and many scientists are taking up the challenge.

Masculine virtue or feminine vice?
Button styles once used solely for
men's clothing are now (sadly)
considered feminine. Various
metal and enamelled buttons; large
button, 34mm Ø; 1990s, Italy.

8

Trends, themes and button quirks

I WASN'T A GREAT STUDENT, BUT I WAS
INTERESTED IN THIS THEATRE THING, AND
I COULD SPEND HOURS IN THE LIBRARY
RESEARCHING WHY THE CUFFS IN THE
EIGHTEENTH CENTURY HAD FOUR BUTTONS.
IT WAS MY HANDLE.

—JIMMY SMITS, AMERICAN ACTOR

Ever since the button reached Western society, this humble fastening has literally and figuratively been poked and prodded, enduring varying rules and regulations regarding its use and production. We often identify fancy buttons with women's wear, but fashion was originally a masculine affair, for which the ruling class instigated new styles and standards. Fourteenth century man not only set the guidelines for taste, but fathers and husbands managed and paid for the clothing of the women in their household. Together with lawmakers, they had a great deal of influence on female fashion and regulated feminine dress. However, women eventually modified their own garments to more closely resemble menswear, including buttons and the tighter fit, leading to accusations of challenging gender norms. As the centuries passed, the luxurious fashions of the

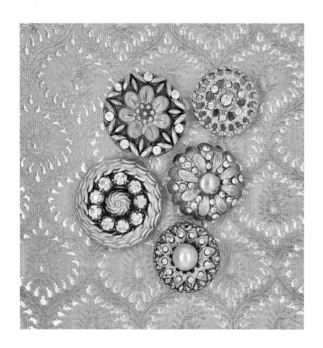

A selection of modern buttons reminiscent of the luxurious buttons made from gold and diamonds once favoured by those who could afford them. Large button, 28mm ∅; 1990s, Europe.

ruling classes, once a masculine virtue, became known as a feminine vice.

When the masses tried to imitate the ruling class, directives were put in place that dictated the number of buttons, and the materials used, by common folk. This in turn led to extravagant creations from precious metals and precious stones, in a series of one-upmanship by the ruling and noble classes. Kings, almost to the point of bankruptcy, have jealously coveted buttons, and flaunted their wealth on their clothing; France's Louis XIV (1643–1715) is purported to have spent the equivalent of $5 million on buttons during his 54-year reign, including the commission of a set of at least 100 diamond buttons. Although women, including royalty, were not meant to outshine their male peers, all that changed with Marie Antoinette, the queen of France's Louis XVI. She dressed and spent money as she pleased, and as a result prompted local industry and commerce to flourish, as courtiers and subjects copied her fashion style. While her extravagances eventually came to an unfortunate end as the French Revolution took hold, she played her part in the modern feminization of fashion.

As sumptuary laws were eliminated across Europe, fashions began to change more quickly. Where previously buttons were associated with the person, they now became part of the garment's design. The status of the button as a symbol of wealth and power was eroded and 'fashion' became accessible to anyone who could afford it. Button-makers had a wide variety of materials from which to make fashionable accessories and chose them according to the social standing, gender and age of their clientele. Buttons were utilized as both useful fastenings and decorative embellishments, and although they remained as a feature, they were more harmonious to the overall look. Coats were an essential part of men's dress and, for the wealthy, buttons were applied everywhere — on the centre front, on pocket flaps, or to hold large cuffs in place so as to show off

France's Louis XIV (1643–1715) is purported to have spent the equivalent of $5 million on buttons during his 54-year reign, including the commission of a set of at least 100 diamond buttons.

the sleeve decoration (lace or embroidery) that had become fashionable. Later, as coat sleeve fashions once again became more fitted, sleeve buttons took on a functional role, opening to allow the hand through. For the gentleman, the coat was also an essential form of clothing. Shirts that were utilitarian were worn as a form of underwear, and considered rude to show in public. Buttons allowed the sleeves of the coat to be rolled up out of the way while enjoying leisure hikes or working on the estate.

The end of the eighteenth and into the nineteenth century brought not only changing political freedoms across Europe, but also changes in the sphere of manufacturing due to the Industrial Revolution. There was a clear need for standardization of measurements and in the nineteenth century many countries adopted the *ligne*, or line, abbreviated as capital L or the triple prime symbol ‴. The name for this measurement comes from pre-revolutionary France and is based on a historic unit of measure, the *pied-du-roi*, or King's foot. Smaller increments were as follows: 12 *lignes* equalled 1 *pouce* (1 inch), and 12 *pouces* equalled one *pied-du-roi*;

Changing styles in men's coat fashions over the centuries has seen the button adjust accordingly. These twentieth century buttons are indicative of some of the various trends, from elaborate, large sized *passementerie* types, to insignia, to the now classic four-hole sew-through. Imitation horn, 20mm Ø and 15mm Ø; UF plastic; 2019.

The name for this measurement comes from pre-revolutionary France and is based on a historic unit of measure, the *pied-du-roi*, or King's foot.

however, the length of this measure was not standard throughout the country. After the revolution, France officially adopted the metric system (in 1795) based on multiples of 10. For conversion, in 1799, one *ligne* was the equivalent of 2.256mm. This measure is still used today in the watchmaking trade, for measuring watch movements, and for measuring the width of hat ribbon, and is not to be confused with the button measuring *ligne* derived from Germany, where 1.6mm is the equivalent of one *ligne*.

In Germany, eighteenth century button-makers had started using *ligne* as a measurement for button diameter, one *ligne* based on $^1/_{40}$ of an inch. Although there were discrepancies in lengths of an inch from area to area, the proportion has remained the same, and as formal lengths were adopted worldwide, the *ligne* (pronounced 'line' in English) has become a recognized form of measuring buttons in the trade where a smaller increment of measure is required. Therefore, 1 inch equals 40 *ligne*, equals 25.4 millimetres (mm), and 1 *ligne* equals 0.635mm. For conversion, button size in mm divided by 0.635 equals *ligne* size; *ligne* size multiplied by 0.635 equals size in mm. Buttons are always measured on the diameter. Buttons that are odd shaped are measured at their

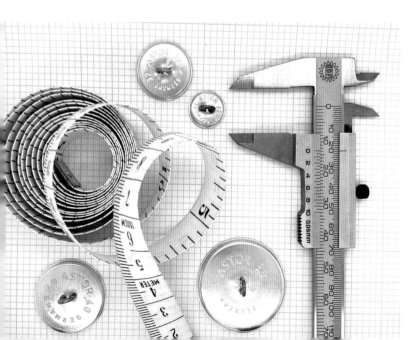

Buttons are often marked on the back with their measurement in *lignes*, as on these examples of button covering backs from Astor, and measuring tools of the button industry include *ligne* calipers, shown here with millimetre equivalent.

longest section; square buttons are measured diagonally from corner to corner.

As the 1800s progressed, men's clothing styles became more sedate, and the buttons became smaller in size and less of a statement. In the mid-century, the 'tailor's button' was introduced, a simple round button that advertised the name of the tailor, or firm, who made the garment. This button often had a central depression with initially two or four holes (eventually four holes became the standard) and a wide rim on which to impress or engrave the name of the garment maker. The modern men's suit jacket and blazer has its origins here, and as far as button treatment, things haven't changed very much since. Single-breasted blazers can have two to three buttons, or four to six buttons if double-breasted. The Nehru cut blazer has five buttons down the front. In a classic three-button jacket, there is the 'always, sometimes, never' protocol — always fasten the middle button, sometimes the top one, and never the bottom one. As far as sleeve button conventions, the number seems to be a sliding scale from casual to formal. I've seen traditional tweed jackets brought into the store with one, two or three buttons, with most having just two. Blazers often have three buttons, suit jackets often four. Bespoke suits have operating buttonholes, and often 'kissing' buttons, those that are sewn side by side with a slight overlap. Suits that have unopened buttonholes are often off the rack, and allow for any alterations in sleeve length.

Australian branded buttons; metal, horn or corozo 'tailor's buttons'. Tailors, merchants and outfitters not only made men's clothing, but also government uniforms: military, railway, postal service, police. Examples shown include J.H. Thomas from St Kilda (Melbourne); from Sydney, Messiter Ferguson, D. Jones & Co. and David Jones Ltd, R.C. Hacon, Murdoch's, Hordern Bros Ltd, W. Martin & Co. (Sydney and branches), Farmer & Company, Ltd, City Hatters; Lowe's Ltd — horn from Sydney and London and metal from Sydney and Newcastle; Maryborough. 'Kissing' buttons are from Gowing Bros Ltd (Sydney), 15mm ∅.

During the 1800s, the sewing machine was an important industrial development in fashion. Although it had been invented in the previous century and improved by

Can't beat 'em, join 'em —
buttons with zipper pull on
face. Large size 24mm Ø,
metal; 1990s, Switzerland.

inventors over the next several decades, it was mainly used in factories with varying degrees of efficiency. The first domestic sewing machine patented and marketed internationally, was that shown by Isaac Merritt Singer at the *Exposition Universelle* in Paris in 1855, for which he won first prize. However, it remained out of reach for most over the next couple of decades due to lack of agreement on patents, but by 1877 it became less expensive and more widespread within the modern household. Women could now make clothing for themselves and their family at home, getting ideas from a variety of sources. Men's tailoring and ready-to-wear businesses sprang up, as well as department stores selling ready-made garments not only for men, but also for women and children.

Paper patterns for domestic use were another development, and New York was the centre for the growing industry. The first full sized, folded paper patterns for sale to the public were those made available by Ellen Louise Demorest and her husband William in 1860. They held fashion shows in their home, selling patterns available in one size from the styles, eventually expanding to list them in their magazine, *The Mirror of Fashion*. Afterwards, Ebenezer Butterick started the Butterick Company (1863) with graded patterns in standardized sizes, followed by James McCall's McCall Pattern Company (1870), the Vogue Pattern Service (1899) and Simplicity Pattern Co. Inc. (1927). Together with the domestic sewing machine, paper patterns became a regular addition in family magazines, spurring the self-tailoring boom.

Paris remained the centre of Western fashion, and retailers flocked to Parisian couture houses to purchase garments, or designs reproduced on fashion plates, leading to expansion of the paper pattern industry, all with the support of the *Chambre Syndicale de la Couture* (Trade Association of High Fashion), originally formed in 1868. Heading into the twentieth century, and with the continued domination of Parisian haute couture, buyers had the option to buy the original garments (or sample *toiles*) or patterns, together with the rights to copy them, including all information relating to the fabric, trims and buttons.

The interest in leisure and sporting activities by women brought unconstrained,

Paper patterns enabled the latest fashions to be made at home.

ABOVE: François Victor Hugo, the great grandson of Victor Hugo, was a skilled craftsman who made buttons for the leading couturiers of France, and was one of the first artisans to work with Elsa Schiaparelli, creating the buttons with her signature on the front. Shown here, a twentieth century copy of his insect on a leaf creation for the fashion designer, along with other contemporary buttons influenced by his designs.

TOP: Large mother of pearl buttons in a classic style with wide rim and two holes. 33mm Ø; late nineteenth/early twentieth century, Europe.

ABOVE: Novelty buttons aimed at children began in the 1930s, and continue today with buttons made under licence or designed by manufacturers. Aimed at the younger market, or those young at heart. Pooh buttons from Disney; 14mm Ø, China.

looser dresses topped with fitted jackets and coats evolved from menswear. These centre-opening garments used large quantities of buttons in many sizes, leading an English contemporary fashion reporter in 1877 to claim that ladies had been affected by 'buttonmania', a trend that continued for some time. In the early 1900s, until disrupted by the war, buttons were everywhere on women's clothing, in all shapes and sizes, colours and materials, colour matching garments or in stark contrast. (I am reminded of the BBC One/Starz 2017 production of E.M. Forster's *Howard's End*, and the coat of Margaret Schlegel: full length with 28 large mother of pearl buttons in a double-breasted style — it was wonderful.) Many button styles were influenced by the Art Nouveau themes of nature, with stylized flowers and plants, birds, and women with flowing hair.

The war years, besides the obvious horrors, brought rations on fabrics and clothing, but the periods after had renewed vigour, especially for buttons during the 1930s and 1950s. In the years following World War I, dramatic changes occurred in women's fashions. Women, especially in Northern Europe and the United States, entered the workforce and opted for a comfortable yet stylish form of office dress. Coco Chanel was perhaps the biggest influence on women's fashions, from her simple lines and dropped waists of the 1920s to sleeker, elegant forms of the 1930s. Buttons often adorned her clothing as decorations as well as fastenings; she used skilled craftsmen to make buttons according to her designs, influenced by the Art Deco style and its geometric forms and bold colours, reproduced in enamelled metals or the new casein plastics. These same craftsmen made the accessories Chanel wore, introducing the costume jewellery trend during the 1920s and 1930s. Indeed, plastics and art movements played a huge role in the changing styles of buttons.

Button choices for clothing were about making a bold statement. No one was better at this than the inimitable fashion designer Elsa Schiaparelli, who is most well known for her fashions of the 1930s during her years in Paris. As discussed earlier, Schiaparelli's whimsical designs and buttons were an essential aspect of her aesthetic. Her collaboration with accessory designer Jean Clément, who worked exclusively for

Button choices for clothing were about making a bold statement. No one was better at this than the inimitable fashion designer Elsa Schiaparelli

Designers still use branded buttons using their logo or name to identify or differentiate their garments from others. Gold and black enamel Valentino buttons, 23mm Ø; 1970s, Italian.

Some of my favourite buttons are created or designed by European craftsmen, using hand finishes in artisanal studio workshops. This selection of buttons is made from bespoke mixed polyesters and individually hand-carved. Early 2000s, Italy.

'Madame Schiap', produced some of the most well loved styles: acrobats, ballerinas, spoons, ponies, lollipops to name a few, in a wide variety of materials enhanced by glow-in-the-dark paint. Among the many other designers to work with Schiaparelli were Roger Jean-Pierre, and Jean Schlumberger, who would later become an important designer at Tiffany & Co. In the book *The Jewels of Jean Schlumberger*, Schiaparelli is quoted as fondly remembering her time with Schlumberger: 'We used the most unbelievable objects: animals, feathers, caricatures, paper weights, chains, locks, clips, barley-sugar. Some were wood, some were plastic, but none resembled anything a button should resemble.'

In 1947, Christian Dior introduced the New Look style, a backlash against the relaxed styles of the previous decades. With cinched waists and wide skirts, the style highlighted the epitome of the hourglass feminine form. Overcoats, in swing or tent style to cover these new fashions, became popular, fastening at the neck with one or two oversized buttons. Paris still dominated the couture fashions, but changes had been afoot in 1930s Depression America. During this time, imported couture originals were heavily taxed but their sample *toiles* were not, leading to well designed, ready-to-

While both the zipper and Velcro® caused a blip in the button's use, they did not take over from the well-loved fastener

wear clothing that could be bought off the rack. European designers followed suit by designing not only their couture ranges but also a line of *prêt-à-porter*, collaborating with manufacturers for production. Buttons remained a prominent feature on clothing, with all manner of sizes and materials used accordingly, although not in the quantities seen prior to World War I.

Children's clothing became a new area of design in the ready-made market, and buttons along with them. Where previously all small children wore dresses and older children were dressed as copies of their parents, new clothing styles were practical and allowed for playtime. In the United States, novelty buttons were sold at department and 'five and dime' stores; cute animal buttons dominated the themes, sewn onto attractive cards aimed at children. Hollywood played an influential role on fashion, the buttons influenced by cinema, and later television, characters. Snow White and the Seven Dwarves appeared in button form, as did Mickey Mouse, sparking the birth of buttons made under licence. From the 1930s to 1945, these novelty buttons became known as 'realistics' or 'goofies' and are some of the most weird and wonderful, especially when aimed at the older, adult market.

There were two new inventions that put the button on alert during the twentieth century. The zipper, or 'slide fastener' as it was first patented in 1893, became a commercial success in the 1930s and was used on American bomber jackets during World War II. Elsa Schiaparelli embraced the new technology and some of her designs placed the zipper front and centre, rather than hiding it away.

The development and subsequent general use in the 1950s made a large impact on the recovery of the button industry. Another fastener, known as Velcro®, or hook-and-loop fastener, was patented in 1955 and was commercially available in the late 1950s. Among its first applications was new astronauts' spacesuits. Designers such as Pierre Cardin, Paco Rabanne and André Courrèges, who embraced the Space Age era in their designs, used this fastener in their futuristic garments of the mid-1960s. While both the zipper and Velcro® caused a blip in the button's use, they did not take over from the well-loved fastener. The industry responded with a resurgence of shiny metal buttons,

Buttons that are less ordinary can turn a head, capture an imagination, be an inspiration. Black horn buttons, seared pattern overdyed in green. Large irregular button: carved layered resin, 68mm ⌀; 2000s, German design.

adorning clothes in rows of varying metallic finishes. This not only added to the new Space Age craze, but also made it easier for manufacturers to keep stocks — button colour no longer had to match the garment. All this uniformity led to designers creating buttons with their own logos, helping to identify clothing from their competitors, a practice still in use by clothing brands.

Every manufactured product is designed — somebody decided what to make and how to make it. As mass production of clothing and buttons progressed, it became apparent that manufacturers were disconnected from their end users. The human connection between maker or bespoke manufacturer and customer was lost. After 1945, the increase in plastics use created a new profession of product designer; as big industry began to incorporate button-making, this new profession extended to the button industry and helped re-establish the relationship between the end user and the manufacturer. Collaborations between fashion design companies and large button manufacturers and their product design engineers produce buttons that are satisfactory to both. Smaller designers take advantage of trends created through these collaborations, or seek out smaller companies for a more bespoke product. Or button-making firms create products that they hope will capture the imagination of designers, putting out collections twice yearly based on their own research into forthcoming trends.

Choosing buttons

Customers often tell us that the best part of finishing a project is selecting the buttons, and we take pride in helping with the choice. In my experience in working with customers, many factors come into play when choosing the right button. As with any detail, the wrong choice will stand out glaringly, while the right detail will make the garment complete — it can often be a 'make or break' situation. There are no longer any hard and fast rules, but conventions offer some guidelines from which to start. Sew-through buttons, where the thread can be seen, look more casual than ones with shanks, although a completely different expression is made with a jewelled or ornately tooled sew-through than with a simple tailor's button. Traditionally, light coloured linen dresses or suits with mother of pearl or shell buttons evoke summer days. Woven wool suits with natural horn or corozo buttons ooze quality. Tweed coats and leather knot buttons just seem to go together.

Typically, a garment or fabric swatch is brought into the store and together we discuss the overall look that is to be achieved. There are many different aspects to consider. For items of a solid colour, buttons that blend in make for a more casual or versatile look, able to be worn with a number of outfits as necessary. They can be lifted with a colourful accent in the form of other fashion accessories when required. Or the same garment can be brought to life with a pop of colour, a mischievous shape or some fabulous jewelled or enamel fastening; in the first cases it becomes a fun statement, in the latter a distinguished article of elegant dress. Personally, I am most inclined to choose buttons for myself that stand out and make me feel well dressed, as well as being versatile. If choosing buttons for everyday wear, I am prone to choose interesting shapes as a feature, or ones that have variations of the same tones as the garment. At other times I choose to express myself with buttons that stand out, relate to the personality of the garment, and are a form of jewellery attached to the cloth. I might add, that 80 per cent of our customers think that all buttons should be round, although we do cater well for the other 20 per cent.

With multicoloured items, an interesting element in the choice is how the button may either bring the garment to life or blend in discreetly. Choosing a button in the dominant colour will be discreet. Choosing a button in the colour that is not dominant in the pattern will make that small detail stand out; in this case, I always suggest picking your favourite colour as the standout. There are also those serendipitous moments when a fabric is brought in and we know we have the perfect button to complement it; an embroidered coat with the exact pattern of a rose button that we have in stock, or an abstract pattern that is the same as one of our buttons. Those moments are pure joy.

9

Koumpounophobia

I MIGHT HAVE MADE A TACTICAL ERROR
NOT GOING TO A PHYSICIAN FOR
TWENTY YEARS. IT WAS ONE OF THOSE
PHOBIAS THAT DIDN'T PAY OFF.

—WARREN ZEVON, AMERICAN SINGER-SONGWRITER WHO
DID NOT SUFFER FROM KOUMPOUNOPHOBIA

As a young adult, I came across people with phobias — actual phobias, the debilitating, uncontrollable fear type. To try to better understand their situation, over the following years I did some occasional reading on the subject. This is when I first encountered the term koumpounophobia, the fear of buttons (from the Modern Greek *koumpi*, to button up). I had already started my professional button life in Amsterdam, and over the next three years I wondered about this phobia.

One in 75,000 people are said to have this condition. I didn't meet any of them in the Netherlands, or at least not that I know of, but in the decades since I opened my own business in Australia, I've come into contact with several. Customers would tell me about their friends, family members, colleagues who could never venture

OPPOSITE: The words say it all on these nylon injection-moulded buttons. 38mm Ø; 2010s, France. ABOVE: Anxious, happy and queasy buttons. 15mm Ø; 2010s, France.

into a button store; some couldn't wear buttons on their own clothing (Steve Jobs, a koumpounophobic, comes to mind); some couldn't be in the presence of others wearing buttons; some were alright to come in to the store with others, as long as they didn't touch the buttons themselves; some couldn't even walk past the shopfront, crossing the street if they saw it on approach. One person I spoke to was okay with buttons that were attached to garments, even his own, but if they were loose, on a table or in jars, he couldn't bear it. I would often ask if they knew what the trigger was, or knew how it manifested. The answers are many and varied.

Frustration: As a child, you struggled with buttons, especially those two buttons at the shoulder of a jumper. Your clothes were getting smaller, but your parent still insisted you did up all the buttons. You just wanted to go out and play, but you had to stand still while all the buttons on your clothing were done up, that feeling that someone else has control over you.

Smell: Upon first opening an old tin full of buttons, a particular smell permeates. Some enjoy the smell and the adventure that the contents may contain, while others abhor it.

Feel: Did a grandparent or other, once too often, squeeze you into their bosom until the buttons on their clothing made a physical impression on your cheek? This could also be a response to smell, which was associated with the fastener. Did you find the old buttons in a tin too dirty (a subset of germophobia) or was it just the texture in general that you didn't like?

Look: Does the shape of buttons, most of which are round, disturb you, especially those with sew-through holes and seen en masse (related to the aversion to clustered patterns of circular holes, called trypophobia)?

Trauma: Did a button find its way up your nose, causing alarm and a possible hospital visit? Did you swallow a button? Did someone scream at you as a child, fearing you may choke, 'Don't touch that button!'?

In an article for *The Spectator* entitled 'The tyranny of the koumpounophobics,' Anne Jolis wrote, 'Formal treatments of koumpounophobia tend to focus on childhood traumas that may have precipitated it. In 2002 psychologists at Florida International University chronicled their work with a boy of nine whose antipathy dated back to when he was five, and spilled a large jar of buttons in his classroom.' Perhaps it was the embarrassment, and the anxiety that stemmed from it?

An Australian artist friend of mine told me he has an uneasy relationship with buttons, something I would not have guessed had he not told me. Within the artist community where he lives, the local knitting group asked him to make some buttons for them, possibly not realizing the intensity of the request. As with all things creative, the task of making takes us to a different place; he tells me he enjoyed the process and could possibly become a button convert.

Another friend, in fact a past employee, told us of a former girlfriend who had koumpounophobia. As with all of our employees, they become part of our wider button family; this *buttoneer* disappeared from our lives for five years, and one day turned up again, telling his tale. Not only was she a sufferer, but also thought that we were all mad to be working with buttons, making it hard for him to socialize with us.

Most medical professionals suggest it's a phobia that should be dealt with, as it is hard to participate in a world full of buttons. Steve Jobs made good work of eliminating push buttons from many people's lives, himself adapting to the pull-on comfortable clothing that is everywhere, with zips and Velcro taking care of non-button fastening. Myself, personally, I can't imagine a world without buttons.

Knowing that koumpounophobia exists, and that somehow I had discovered a cluster of sufferers, I definitely did not want to add to their anguish. You can imagine my horror when the film *Coraline* came out! Here I was, trying to nurture future button lovers, not traumatize them, and then this somewhat creepy movie comes out, based on the book by Neil Gaiman about a parallel universe where all the characters have big black buttons for eyes! Several months after its release, when a primary school group came in to the shop to purchase 'big black buttons like Coraline' I was relieved to hear that all the children loved the book and the movie, and were making a group of dolls for their library, all with the tell-tale button eyes.

If you come across any koumpounophobics, be kind. Like all phobias, there is real fear involved. Not all of us realize that the button is a harmless item, a fastener, a thing of beauty.

ABOVE: The movie version of *Coraline* used black classic tailor's buttons as all the characters eyes in the parallel universe. Polyester, 25mm ⌀; France.

OPPPOSITE: 'One Way' plastic button. 25mm ⌀, laser etched; Germany.

Acknowledgments

The information in this book would never have seen the light if not for an important group of people. The people at Exisle Publishing are foremost: Gareth St John Thomas and Nathan James Thomas planted the seed from which to embark, Anouska Jones provided any help I sought, and Karen Gee was my thoughtful editor. The project began inauspiciously, with major repair works to our shop and residence, and then Covid-19 ... The loss of an important resource in the State Library of NSW due to temporary closure, twice, was not helpful. Nor was the loss of travel due to the lockdown of Australia. In spite of these setbacks, those at Exisle Publishing remained committed and patient, something I am most grateful for.

Huge thanks are due to the group of dedicated *buttoneers*, my numerous staff who have kept All Buttons Great and Small pushing buttons for more than three decades. They have been present for important milestones, some joined me in my travels, all taught me much. Besides my immediate family, I owe thanks to Robyn, Leslea, Toby, Carolyn, Anna, Michelle, Terri, Melanie, Jill, Elliat, Sasha, Mikaela, Ro, Anita, Isabel, Wendy, Tim, Christina, Brooke, Melissa, Inga, Bella, Rabia, Tula, Tania, Gaby, Pippa, Maya, Eliya, Nichole and especially Miette, Joe, Lisa, Steph, Cecilija, Velvet, Jane, Hester, and Mandy, who were on hand while I wrote and researched. All are an incredible group of creative people.

Also, to all my dear friends who buoyed my spirits, cooked me dinners on numerous occasions and checked in frequently to offer their support. To Ida, Peter and Tom for sharing their stories, Ford for his enthusiastic button finds, and Christina Gore, Tarn Smith and Femke Roefs for sharing their work. To my dear families near and far flung, a wealth of knowledge, help and memories: mama Olga, siblings Tania and Andrei, daughters Zoya and Kira; to Heather and Marge; and the Prieckaerts clan. To all our lovely customers who asked me questions and enthusiastically listened, sharing their own stories or, even more valuable, donating their precious family button boxes with the knowledge that they would be appreciated.

In remembrance of my late father, my best friend and champion, who taught me to be inquisitive but left us much too early.

To Thea de Boer, who is solely responsible for my life with buttons.

To Oscar, who allowed me to take over the downstairs communal area for the entire time of writing, without complaint, and to Madeleine and Tom who provided a soul-nurturing respite hideaway in which to write.

I would like to acknowledge the traditional owners, the Gadigal people of the Eora Nation, as the continuing custodians of the unceded land that I live and work on. I pay my respect to their Elders — past, present and emerging — and acknowledge the important role all Aboriginal and Torres Strait Islander people continue to hold within Country throughout Australia.

Bibliography

Books

Albert, Lillian Smith and Kent, Kathryn, 1971, *The Complete Button Book*, Doubleday & Company, Inc., Garden City.

Allio, Loïc, 2001, *Boutons*, Éditions du Seuil, Paris.

Bevan, G. Phillips, 1876, *British Manufacturing Industries*, E. Stanford, London.

Bizot, Chantal, de Gary, Marie-Noël and Possémé, Évelyne, 2001, *The Jewels of Jean Schlumberger*, Harry N. Abrams, Inc., New York, translated from French by Bonafante-Warren, Alexandra.

Campbell, Paul D.Q., 1996, *Plastic Component Design*, Industrial Press Inc., South Norwalk, Connecticut.

Chamberlain, Dorothy, 1996, *Button Up Australia*, D. Chamberlain, Umina Beach NSW.

Cusick, Dawn, 1995, *The Button Craft Book*, Sterling Publishing Co., Inc., New York.

Davidov, Corinne and Dawes, Ginny Redington, 1988, *The Bakelite Jewelry Book*, Abbeville Press, New York.

de Buzzacarini, Vittoria and Zotti Minici, Isabella, 1990, *Buttons & Sundries*, Zanfi Editori s.r.l., Modena.

Epstein, Diana and Safro, Milicent, 1991, *Buttons*, Harry N. Abrams, Inc., New York.

Ericson, Lois, 1996, *Opening and Closing*, Eric's Press, Salem.

Farn, Alexander E., 1986, *Pearls, Natural, Cultured and Imitation*, Butterworth, London, Boston.

Frugoni, Chiara, 2003, *Books, Banks, Buttons and Other Inventions from the Middle Ages*, Columbia University Press, New York.

Gorski, Jill, 2009, *Warman's Buttons Field Guide*, Krause Publications Inc., Iola.

Hart, Avril and North, Susan, 1998, *Fashion in Detail: From the 17th and 18th centuries*, Rizzoli (distributed by St Martin's Press), New York.

Houart, Victor, 1977, *Buttons, A Collector's Guide*, Souvenir Press Ltd, London.

Hughes, Elizabeth and Lester, Marion, 1991, *The Big Book of Buttons*, New Leaf Publishers, Sedgwick.

Jargstorf, Sibylle, 1993, *Baubles, Buttons and Beads: The heritage of Bohemia*, Schiffer Publishing Ltd, Atglen.

Jensen, Doreen and Sargent, Polly, 1993, *Robes of Power: Totem poles on cloth*, University of British Columbia Press, Vancouver.

Johnson Gross, Kim, et al., 1996, *Accessories*, Thames and Hudson, London.

Johnston, Lucy, 2005, *Nineteenth-century Fashion in Detail*, V&A Publications, London.

Jonas, Susan and Nissenson, Marilyn, 1991, *Cuff Links*, Harry N. Abrams, Inc., New York.

Katz, Sylvia, 1984, *Classic Plastics: From Bakelite to high tech, with a collector's guide*, Thames and Hudson, London.

Kaufman, Morris, 1963, *The First Century of Plastics: Celluloid and its sequel*, The Plastics Institute, London.

Kohler, Carl, 1928, *A History of Costume*, G. Howard Watt, New York.

Landman, Neil H., Mikkelson, Paula M., Bieler, Rüdiger, and Bronson, Bennet, 2001, *Pearls: A natural history*, Harry N. Abrams, Inc., New York.

Layard, A.H., 1853, *Discoveries Among the Ruins of Ninevah and Babylon*, G.P. Putnam & Co., New York.

Le Couteur, Penny, 2003, *Napoleon's Buttons: How 17 molecules changed history*, Tarcher Perigree, New York.

Luscomb, Sally C., 1999, *The Collector's Encyclopedia of Buttons*, Schiffer Publishing Ltd, Atglen.

Mackenzie, Althea, 2004, *Buttons and Trimmings*, National Trust, London.

Manservisi, Michela and Schianchi, Francesco, 1993, *Under the Sign of Buttons*, Nuova Libra Editrice, Bologna.

Meredith, Alan and Meredith, Gillian, 2010, *Buttons*, Shire Publications Ltd, Oxford.

More, Barbara, 2008, *Collectible Glass Buttons of the 20th Century: A new collector's treasury*, Xlibris, La Vergne.

Morgan, John, 1991, *Conservation of Plastics: An introduction to their history, manufacture, deterioration, identification and care*, Plastics Historical Society and The Conservation Unit, Museum and Galleries Commission, London.

Mossman, S.T.I., 1997, *Early Plastics: Perspectives, 1850–1950*, Leicester University Press, London.

O'Hagan, John, M.A., 1880, *The Song of Roland*, translated into English verse by John O'Hagan, C. Kegan Paul & Co., London.

Osborne, Peggy Ann, 1994, *About Buttons: A collector's guide*, Schiffer Publishing, Atglen.

Osborne, Peggy Ann, 1993, *Button Button: Identification & price guide*, Schiffer Publishing, Atglen.

Pagano, Bina, 2002, *Bottoni*, Frederico Motta Editore S.p.A., Milano.

Peacock, John, 1994, *Costume 1066–1990s*, Thames and Hudson, London.

Peacock, Primrose, 1972, *Buttons for the Collector*, David and Charles Ltd, Pynes Hill.

Peacock, Primrose, 1989, *Discovering Old Buttons*, Shire Publications Ltd, Aylesbury.

Perry, Jane, 2007, *A Collector's Guide to Peasant Silver Buttons*, Lulu, Morrisville.

Rothstein, Natalie, Ginsberg, Madeleine, Hart, Avril and Mendes, Valerie D. Victoria & Albert Museum Department of Textiles and Dress, 1984, *Four Hundred Years of Fashion*, Victoria & Albert Museum in association with William Collins Sons & Co. Ltd, London.

Schiff, Stefan O., 1979, *Buttons: Art in miniature*, Lancaster-Miller Inc., Berkeley.

Schmitt, F., 1923, *Manuel du Fabricant de Boutons et Peignes: Articles en celluloid et en galalith*, J. Baillière, Paris.

Shashoua, Yvonne, 2008, *Conservation of Plastics: Materials science, degradation and preservation*, Butterworth-Heinemann, Oxford.

Sterbenz, Carol Ender, 2011, *Homemade: The heart and science of handcrafts*, Scribner, New York.

Strack, Elisabeth, 2006, *Pearls*, Rühler-Diebener-Verlag GmbH & Co. KG, Stuttgart.

Weber, Christianne, 2002, *Art Deco Schmuck*, Arnoldsche Art Publishers, Stuttgart.

Welch, Charles. F.S.A., 1902, *History of The Worshipful Company of Pewterers of the City of London*, Blades, East & Blades, London.

White, Andrew, 1993, *A History of Whitby*, Phillimore, Chichester.

Wilcox, Claire, 1991, *Modern Fashion in Detail*, Victoria & Albert Museum, London.

Wilkins, John M., 2005, *History of British and Australian Naval Buttons: A collector's guide & catalogue, 1743–2003*, J.M. Wilkins, Melbourne.

Wilzbach, Annette and Wilbach-Wald, Martina, 1990, *Knopf Design*, Deutsher Fachverlag GmbH, Frankfurt am Main.

Worsley, Harriet, 2000, *Decades of Fashion*, Könemann Verlagsgesellschaft mbH, Köln.

Articles

Adams, David. 'What goes into the making of glass?', National Depression Glass Association's News & Views Newsletter, December 2017/January 2018, www.stretchglasssociety.org/the-making-of-glass

'A history of plastics', British Plastics Federation, https://bpf.co.uk/plastipedia/plastics_history/default.aspx

Anzai, Koichi, 'Artisan of the small brings Meiji era button craft back to life', *Asahi Shimbun*, 29 April 2019, www.asahi.com/ajw/articles/13055377

Arnery, Kat, 'A cat turned milk into popular plastic', *Scientific American*, 28 June 2017, www.scientificamerican.com/article/a-cat-turned-milk-into-popular-plastic/

Berger, Raymond, 'Bimini and orplid glass', The Glass Museum On Line, https://theglassmuseum.com/bimini.htm

Bettoni, Barbara, 'Fashion, tradition, and innovation in button manufacturing in early modern Italy', *Technology and Culture*, Baltimore, vol. 55, issue 3, July 2014.

'Bone button manufacturing', Casey & Lowe Archaeology & Heritage, www.caseyandlowe.com.au/bone-button-manufacturing/

Breskin, Charles A., 'Plastics through the years', *Scientific American*, vol. 172, no. 5, May 1945, pp. 269–73.

Brooman, R.A., 'Making articles of gutta-percha by moulding, stamping, or embossing', *United States Patent Office*, May 1848.

By, Paul R., 'Creation by contraption: The 19th-entury machine: Tinker, painter, engraver — art! Art by contraption', *Washington Post*, January 1982.

Chambers, William and Payn, John (ed.), 'How artificial pearls are made', *Chambers's Journal of Popular Literature, Science and Arts*, 32, 1881.

Clark, Marshall and May, Sally K., 'Macassan history and heritage', Australian National University Press Library, https://press-files.anu.edu.au/downloads/press/p241301/html/ch01.xhtml?referer=&page=3

Cohen, Karen L., 'Enamelling history and revolution', Ganoksin, www.ganoksin.com/article/enameling-history-and-revolution/

Collard and Frazer, 'A brief account of the manufacture of gilt buttons, comprising some improvements important to manufacturers. Communicated by Messrs Collard and Frazer, of Birmingham', *Emporium of Arts and Sciences*, vol. 1, no. 3, 1812.

Cordier, Henri, 'La première légation de France en Chine (1847)', *T'oung Pao*, vol. 7 no. 3, 1906, pp. 351–68.

Coutu, Ashley N. et al., 'Mapping the elephants of the 19th century East African ivory trade with a multi-isotope approach', *PLOS ONE*, vol. 11, no. 10, 2016.

Dalton, William, 'A visit to the gutta-percha works', *Eliza Cook's Journal*, no. 45, 1850, p. 291.

De Dekker FAA, Patrick, Reeves, Jessica, Prendergast, Amy, 'She sells sea shells ...', Australian Academy of Science, www.science.org.au/curious/earth-environment/sea-shells

de Vries, Joyce, 'Fashioning the self in early modern Europe: Gender, consumption, and material culture', *Journal of Women's History*, 23.4, 2011, pp. 187, 197, 220.

Dickens, Charles, 'What there is in a button', *Household Words*, no. 107, April 1852.

Dolbashian, Diane, 'Pliny the Elder (Gaius Plinius Secundus), Historia Naturalis, About A.D. 77', Corning Museum of Glass, https://cmog.org/article/pliny-elder-gaius-plinius-secundus-historia-naturalis-about-ad-77

Dorsa, Michael, 'Engine turned fine silver for baisse taille,' *Glass on Metal*, vol. 27, no. 5, December 2008.

El-Bakry, Mamdouh, 'Functional and physiochemical properties of casein and its use in food and non-food industrial applications', *Chemical Physics Research Journal*, 4.3, 2011, pp.125–38.

Gilroy, Clinton G., 'The history of silk, cotton, linen, wool, and other fibrous substances: Including observations on spinning, dyeing and weaving: Also an account of the pastoral life of the ancients, their social state and attainments in the domestic arts: With appendices on Pliny's natural history, on the origin and manufacture of linen and cotton paper, on felting, netting, &c.: Deduced from copious and authentic sources', *The Making of the Modern World*, Harper & Brothers, 1845.

'Gutta Percha Co', Grace's Guide to British Industrial History, https://gracesguide.co.uk/Gutta_Percha_Co

Guichon-Lindholm, Fabienne, 'The power of pearl', *American Spa*, 10.7, 2006, pp. 36, 38, 40.

Helmenstine, Anne Marie, 'Coloured glass chemistry: How does it work?,' ThoughtCo., www.thoughtco.com/the-chemistry-of-colored-glass-602252

'History and future of plastics,' Science History Institute, www.sciencehistory.org/the-history-and-future-of-plastics

'History of Murano Glass', Glass of Venice, www.glassofvenice.com/murano_glass_history.php

'How is plastic made: A simple step-by-step explanation', British Plastics Federation, www.bpf.co.uk/plastipedia/how-is-plastic-made.aspx

Hughes, E., 'On the button', *Country Life*, March 2016. pp. 74–6.

Hunt, Leigh, Fonblanque, Albany and Forster, John, 'Mycenae', *Examiner*, issue 3649, 1878, pp. 113–16.

Ide, Yoshio, 'Traditional handmade buttons gain attention', *Vancouver Sun*, 17 March 2018, www.pressreader.com/canada/vancouver-sun/20180317/282376925108673

'Imitations of tortoiseshell and mother-of-pearl', *The London Reader: Of literature, science, art and general information*, 604, 1878.

'Jet industry in Roman York', An Inventory of the Historical Monuments in City of York, vol. 1, Eburacum, Roman York, British History Online, www.british-history.ac.uk/rchme/york/vol1

Jolis, A., 'The tyranny of the koumpounophobics,' *The Spectator*, November 2014.

Jones, Deborah, 'The basics of bling', *Impressions*, 37.9, 2014, pp. 40, 42, 44, 46.

Kaner, Jake, Ioras, Florin and Ratnasingam, Jega, 'Performance and stability of historic casein formaldehyde', *e-plastory*, no. 2, 2017.

Keller, W.D., Cheng, Hsia, Johns, W.D. and Meng, Chi-Sheng, 'Kaolin from the original Kauling (Gaoling) mine locality, Kiangsi Province, China', *Clays and Clay Minerals*, vol. 28, no. 2, 1980, pp. 97–104.

Knott, Becky, 'Lucie Rie: A secret life of buttons', V&A blog, 24 April 2017, www.vam.ac.uk/blog/news/lucie-rie-a-secret-life-of-buttons

Lewis, Danny, 'Here's why men's and women's clothes button on opposite sides', *Smithsonian Magazine*, 23 November 2015, www.smithsonianmag.com/smart-news/heres-why-mens-and-womens-clothes-button-opposite-sides-1-180957361/

Lindbergh, Jennie, 'Buttoning down archaeology', *Australasian Historical Archaeology*, 17, 1999.

Luik, Heidi and Mirja Ots, 'Bronze Age double buttons in Estonia/Kaksiknoobid Eesti pronksiaegses leiuaineses', *Estonian Journal of Archaeology*, vol. 11, no. 2, Dec. 2007, pp. 122–40.

'Magistrato alle pompe e leggi suntuarie, a Venezia', fioretombolo.net, www.fioretombolo.net/magistratopompe.htm

Matchar, Emily, 'You can now 3D print glass', *Smithsonian Magazine*, 2017, www.smithsonianmag.com/innovation/you-can-now-3d-print-glass-180962951/

Mazzucchelli: www.mazzucchelli1849.it/pages/heritage

Meaney, K, 'Significant events in the history of glass', *Architectural Glass Concepts*, 1, 2007, pp. 6–11.

Nomachi, Motoki, '"East" and "West" as seen in the structure of Serbian: Language contact and its consequences', https://src-h.slav.hokudai.ac.jp/coe21/publish/no28_ses/Chapter1_2.pdf

Pasricha, Anupama and Greeninger, Rachel, '2018 exploration of 3D printing to create zero-waste sustainable fashion notions and jewellery', *Fashion and Textiles 3D Printing*, 2019.

Peterson, Beth, 'The basics of pottery,' The Spruce Crafts, https://www.thesprucecrafts.com/clay-basics-2746314

'Plating on ABS plastics', Sharretts Plating, www.sharrettsplating.com/base-materials/abs-plastics-plating

Prichystalová, R., Stelcl, J. and Vávra, V., 'Glass beads and buttons from the southern suburb of the Breclav-Pohansko stronghold', *Journal of Glass Studies*, vol. 56, 2014, pp. 37–59.

Ralston, Brian E. and Osswald, Tim A., 'The history of tomorrow's materials: Protein-based biopolymers', *Plastics Engineering*, February 2008.

Rawsthorn, Alice, 'Lucie Rie's buttons,' Maharam, www.maharam.com/stories/rawsthorn_lucie-ries-buttons

Rehren, Thilo and Pusch, Edgar, 'Late Bronze Age glass production at Qantir-Piramesses, Egypt', *Science*, vol. 308, June 2005.

'RES/REI — Manufacturing acetate at Mazzucchelli', https://vimeo.com/80471038

Ryan, Luke, 'The mammoth hunters', *Smith Journal*, vol. 27, 2018.

Rydlová, Eva and Kateřina Hrušková, 'Reverse-painted buttons from the Waldes Collection', *Journal of Glass Studies*, vol. 60, 2018, pp. 235–52.

'Secret military compass button', ABC Open South West Victoria, https://vimeo.com/218549979

Shiokawa, N. et al., 'East and West', *Eurasian World*, vol. 1, 2012, pp. 207–23.

Singer, Brian et al., 'Investigation of materials used by Edvard Munch', *Studies in Conservation*, vol. 55, no.4, 2010, pp. 274–92.

Siti Suhaily, S., Abdul Khalil, H.P.S., Wan Nadirah, W.O. and Jawaid, M., 'Bamboo based biocomposites material, design and applications', IntechOpen, www.intechopen.com/books/materials-science-advanced-topics/bamboo-based-biocomposites-material-design-and-applications

Spindler, Amy M., 'From an era in Venice when chic was Illegal', *New York Times*, December 1995.

Sprague, Roderick, 'China or Prosser button identification and dating', *Historical Archaeology*, vol. 36, no. 2, 2002.

Strom, Stephanie, 'Company News: A new button can take a beating,' *New York Times*, 14 July 1993, www.nytimes.com/1993/07/14/business/company-news-a-new-button-can-take-a-beating.html

'The history of a coat button', *Penny Magazine of the Society for the Diffusion of Useful Knowledge*, Charles Knight, London, February 1840, pp. 77–9.

'The material of a thousend [*sic*] uses, the career of the first real plastic', Bakelit Museum, www.bakelitmuseum.de/e/bakges-e.htm

'Trelon Weldon Weil', Alexandre Vassiliev Foundation, https://ns3103723.ip-145-239-9.eu/pawtucket/index.php/Detail/entities/1452

Turner, John Pemberton, 'Resources, products, and industrial history of Birmingham and the Midland Hardware District: A series of reports, collected by the local industries committee of the British Association at Birmingham, in 1865', 1866, pp. 432–51, https://hammond-turner.com/history/the-birmingham-button-trade-part-1/ to part-10

Upton, Chris, 'Buttons that were worth their weight in gold; Fabric-covered buttons and springs to help 18th century gentlemen into their tight leather breeches made the fortune of one of Bromsgrove's most enterprising sons', The Free Library, www.thefreelibrary.com/Archive%3a+Buttons+that+were+worth+their+weight+in+gold%3b+Fabric-covered...-a083678954

'Urea: Molecule of the week archive', *American Chemical Society*, January 2021.

'US Patent and Trademark Office publishes Vergason Technology's patent application for alternating tangent mounted evaporative deposition source mechanism for rapid cycle coating', *Global IP News, Semiconductor Patent News*, 8 November 2019.

Vanriest, Elise, 'La Verrerie Royale de Saint-Germain-En-Laye dans la seconde moitié du XVIe siède,' *Journal of Glass Studies*, vol. 59, 2017, pp. 207–14, 471.

'Venezuelan production of balata', *Journal of the Royal Society of Arts*, vol. 67, no. 3446, 1918, pp. 46–7.

Venturi, Mauro, 'Historical uses of gutta percha,' endonziamauroventuri.it, www.endodonziamauroventuri.it/Guttaperca/Historical%20Uses%20of%20Gutta.pdf

Weber, Markus and Deussing, Guido, 'Acrylic patented 90 years ago (Part 1): Chemical background and pioneering patents', K-online, April 2018, www.k-online.com/en/News/April_2018_Acrylic_patented_90_years_ago_(Part_1)/New_series_Acrylic_patented_90_years_ago

Weber, Markus and Deussing, Guido, 'Acrylic patented 90 years ago (Part 2): Chemical background and pioneering patents', K-online, October 2018, www.k-online.com/en/News/Oktober_2018_Acrylic_patented_90_years_ago/Acrylic_patented_90_years_ago

Weber, Markus and Deussing, Guido, 'Acrylic patented 90 years ago (Part 3): Chemical background and pioneering patents', K-online, November 2018, www.k-online.com/en/News/November_2018_Acrylic_patented_90_years_ago_(Part_3)/Acrylic_patented_90_years_ago

Weller, Anna, 'History of Venetian glass making', Big Bead Little Bead, www.bigbeadlittlebead.com/guides_and_information/history_of_venetian_glass.php

Williams, Llewelyn, 'Lactiferous plants of economic importance v. resources of gutta-percha-palaquium species (*Sapotaceae*)', *Economic Botany*, vol. 18, no. 1, 1964, pp. 5–26.

Wurramarrba, Charlie Galiyawa, 'Macassar story' collected by Stokes, J. in Hercus, L. and Sutton, P. (eds), *This is What Happened*, Australian Institute of Aboriginal and Torres Strait Islander Studies, Canberra, 1986.

General online resources

British History Online: www.british-history.ac.uk/

Encyclopeadia Britannica: www.britannica.com

Hammond Turner Museum: https://hammond-turner.com/history/

Museum of Design in Plastics: www.modip.ac.uk/

Plastics Historical Society: www.plastiquarian.com

The Plastics Collection: https://plastics.syr.edu/

Visual Arts Cork: www.visual-arts-cork.com

Wikipedia: www.wikipedia.org/

World Register of Marine Species (WORMS): www.marinespecies.org

Photographic credits

All images are from the author's own private collection, with the exception of the following:

p. ii author image: Luis Power

p. 8 (top left): Daina Curci

p. 168 (bottom left): Rkaphotography/Dreamstime.com

p. 169 (top right): Derek Tan

Index